Inclusive Marketing

Tina,

Lot's of food for thought

Enjoy Steve
+ distillery

Inclusive Marketing

*Why representation matters
to your customers and your brand*

Jerry Daykin

KoganPage

First published in Great Britain and the United States in 2022 by Kogan Page Limited

2nd Floor, 45 Gee Street	8 W 38th Street, Suite 902	4737/23 Ansari Road
London	New York, NY 10018	Daryaganj
EC1V 3RS	USA	New Delhi 110002
United Kingdom		India
www.koganpage.com		

Kogan Page books are printed on paper from sustainable forests.

ISBNs

Hardback	978 1 3986 0735 4
Paperback	978 1 3986 0731 6
Ebook	978 1 3986 0734 7

British Library Cataloguing-in-Publication Data

A CIP record for this book is available from the British Library.

Library of Congress Control Number

9781398607316

Typeset by Integra Software Services, Pondicherry
Print production managed by Jellyfish
Printed and bound by CPI Group (UK) Ltd, Croydon CR0 4YY

CONTENTS

ABOUT THE AUTHOR

Jerry Daykin is a London-based global marketing leader who has helped champion media and digital at a number of global brands including his current role as VP, Head of Media at premium spirits company Beam Suntory. Previously he led global or regional teams at GSK/Haleon, Diageo and Mondelez. He is passionate about effectiveness, creativity, conscious approaches to media and bringing digital sense to the increasingly confusing world of modern marketing.

Alongside this he is outspoken around the importance of diversity and inclusion in the industry and the power of representation in marketing to positively impact society. He is a World Federation of Advertisers WFA Diversity Ambassador and a voluntary director at the Conscious Advertising Network and Outvertising.

Jerry has been a regular writer on the industry, contributing to *The Guardian, The Drum, Marketing Week* and *Adweek*. He has spoken at many of the industry's leading events including Cannes Lions, DMEXCO, Advertising Week Europe and the Festival of Marketing. He a contributing author to the marketing strategy book *Eat Your Greens*.

He is a big fan of the world's two greatest competitions – the Olympic Games and the Eurovision Song Contest – and has regularly travelled to attend them in person. Jerry grew up in Elton John's home town of Pinner with his parents, brother and sister before attending university in Cambridge. In October 2022 he got married to his long-term partner, Paul, and they now live together in south-east London with their dog Henry.

FOREWORD

BY NICOLA MENDELSOHN, VP OF META

One of my favourite words, which I learned on a trip to South Africa, is the Zulu word *sawubona*. It means 'I see you.' In English we might translate *sawubona* as simply Hello or Goodbye, but as someone once described it, 'more than just politeness, *sawubona* carries the importance of recognizing the worth and dignity of each person. It says, "I see the whole of you – your experiences, your passions, your pain, your strengths and weaknesses, and your future. You are valuable to me."'

As marketers, I'd argue that the single most important thing we can do is to try to *see people*. And it's the single most important message at the heart of this new book. And as we talk about inclusive marketing, as Jerry does so beautifully in these pages, it doesn't matter who you are, where you come from, or what life experiences you've had (for many of us they are wide and varied), the simple crux of the matter is that our goal as good industry professionals (and compassionate human beings) should be to try to see each other for who we are, how we experience the world, and what makes us feel valued and unique.

And then make sure what we see, *gets seen*.

If that's the goal, the reality, unfortunately, is that we're not there yet. As I write this, only 41 per cent of US consumers report feeling represented by the ads they see (Davis, 2021). And the same is felt by consumers the world over. The good news is, there's tremendous appetite among marketers and brands to do better, and because you have this book in your hands, you can be proud that you are one of them!

And just remember, no matter where you are in your inclusive marketing journey – whether taking stock of how inclusive your teams are for the very first time, or leading the way in diversifying your supply chain and sharing your microphone with diverse voices, you can take comfort in the fact we're all still learning, and that there are so many in the marketing community eager to go on this journey with you.

If you're wondering why representation and inclusion are so important, the truth is that all of us like to see our experiences reflected back to us sometimes. It confirms that we have value in the world and, more importantly, that we are the kind of people whose stories are worth telling.

When we never see our experiences or identities played back, it's easier to question whether we belong. And worse, when they're reduced to stereotypes, it makes it even harder for us to shed them. One analysis found that distorted media representations of black men led to negative real-world consequences for them. Couple that with findings that women are 14 times more likely to be shown in revealing clothing, ethnic minorities are 2.9 times more likely than whites to be shown working out, and men are 2.4 times more likely to be depicted as angry and 1.6 times more likely to be shown in an office than women, and we risk serving up stunted caricatures of ourselves that bear little resemblance to the full and nuanced people we really are (Davis, 2021).

I know the consequences of this first hand. I remember being invited to a dinner while I was living in London, and I was seated opposite the chief of staff to the visiting dignitary as well as an ambassador and the successful founder of a business – all men. *Every single one of them* assumed I was there as a plus-one to my husband rather than as a guest in my own right, and no one asked me a question. To them I was invisible. To the point about being seen, they didn't see me at all. At the very end of the meal, the ambassador turned to me and casually asked if I worked or volunteered for a charity. When I told him what I did, his jaw dropped. Now, I'm not saying that marketing can correct all biases, but I'm hopeful that if we do a better job of portraying under-represented groups more fully, we can all look forward to more insightful, inclusive and vibrant conversations around *every* table.

But, as marketers, we have to do our part to make that happen. Given that by some estimates, people see between 6,000–10,000 ads per day, and the large volume of marketing media that people consume, it's imperative that we use our megaphone to correct the record and be a net force for good. And the next generation feels the same. Sixty-eight per cent of Gen Zers expect brands to contribute to society (Facebook, 2019). And 77 per cent say they feel more positive toward a brand when it promotes gender equality on social media. Not only that, but it's been shown that marketing against stereotypes increases brand awareness. So being inclusive isn't just goodwill, it's good business, too.

And we should remember as we do this business that, even though we often speak to vast audiences, marketing, like politics, is fundamentally a grassroots endeavour – building loyalty and excitement one person at a time. And if we do it right, one person becomes two.

As a friend whose child has cerebral palsy said, 'When my son sees an ad with another kid in a wheelchair, not only does he think, "Oh, that might be a product for me," but his mom feels good about it, too.' Not to mention the ripple effects this kind of representation has in helping to close the imagination gap and make progress against things like global benchmarks for inclusion embedded in the United Nations Sustainable Development Goals. Every time we include one more person, whether it's on our teams or in our ads, it becomes a force multiplier for the next.

So how do we become better multipliers ourselves? We can do what my friend Jerry Daykin proposes here: listen, learn and break the marketing journey into small pieces, and figure out how to make each step more accessible and more representative straight from the start. This isn't just a change in tactics, it's a change in attitude. It means building inclusion into your company mandate, hiring diverse teams, soliciting their input from the time a campaign is just a glimmer in the eye, and valuing the long-term benefit of elevating diversity across the whole lifecycle of the marketing journey.

And I think many of the people featured in this book would say the same. I know many of them, and while we all have a passion for this work, what's wonderful is that our starting points for inclusion are as varied as our interests and careers. And I applaud Jerry for practising what he preaches and drawing this roadmap from so many unique voices. There is no one right way forward, but when we put our heads together, we're sure to find the best way.

So, to all of you here committed to making inclusion a part of your mandate: thank you. I hope we cross paths. And *I see you.*

References

Davis, G (2021) Underrepresentation and misrepresentation have no place in advertising today, AdWeek. www.adweek.com/partner-articles/underrepresentation-and-misrepresentation-have-no-place-in-advertising-today-insights-from-the-geena-davis-institutes-ceo/ (archived at https://perma.cc/M4KL-YC4S)

Facebook (2019) Gen Z: Getting to know the 'Me is we' generation. www.facebook.com/business/news/insights/generation-z (archived at https://perma.cc/L25A-JM7S)

ACKNOWLEDGEMENTS

Thank you for caring enough to read this book. My biggest reason for writing it was to try to inspire more inclusive work and to continue this important conversation across our industry. It's hard to believe people will take time out of their busy lives to read it and it means the world to me that you have.

Special thanks to my husband Paul, who has watched me take huge amounts of time out of our busy lives, and our wedding planning, to interview people and write this book. When he found out I had a couple of months of gardening leave between two jobs we both had wonderful visions of idyllic days, long peaceful walks with HenryDog, and a general break from the madness of video calls. He should have known better because, somehow, I managed to find a different project to fill up much of the time instead, and for his eternal patience I am forever indebted. To all my friends and family thank you also for putting up with my endless ramblings on this subject, which I'm sure you realize are only going to increase now.

I directly interviewed almost two dozen people for this book, including some who we ran out of space to print or who preferred to remain anonymous. The wisdom of many other marketers found its way into the book and I thank them all for their contributions and for continually challenging and evolving my own perspectives. I was honoured that Nicola wrote such kind words in the Foreword of the book, and that Camelia did such a fantastic job researching and pulling together the chapter on the business case for diversity. To Will and Belinda who are my other co-conspirators at the World Federation of Advertisers, thank you both just for caring so much.

To all those who volunteer at Outvertising and The Conscious Advertising Network, or who sit on various inclusion forums with me – thanks for letting me soak up your brilliance. It truly takes a village to produce something like this and I'm glad to have been able to give a voice to others throughout it.

Thank you to Stephen, Heather and all the team at Kogan Page. When they approached me to write a book, I was excited that I could finally turn my #DigitalSense ramblings about the pointlessness of organic social media into a 500-page epic. Unfortunately, you'll have to keep waiting for that because they preferred the idea of a book on inclusive marketing, but I have to say it's been a real pleasure writing it.

This book was written with the absolute best of intentions, but diversity and inclusion is a complex topic with differing perspectives and it's easy to get language or terminology wrong. I'm sure we have at various places in this book, so apologies in advance, but I would advise you all to not let this be a barrier to trying to do the right thing.

CONTRIBUTORS

ALI HANAN

ALLY OWEN

ANDREW GEOGHEGAN

ANNA BRENT

ASAD DHUNNA

BELINDA J SMITH

BENAZIR BARLET-BATADA

CAMELIA CRISTACHE-PODGOREAN

CATHERINE BECKER

CHRISTINA MALLON

CHRISTOPHER KENNA

DALE GREEN

EFRAIN AYALA

GABRIELLA HALL

GRÁINNE WAFER

IBRAHIM KAMARA

ISABEL MASSEY

JANE BREARLEY

JESSICA SPENCE

KAREN FRASER

KATE WILLIAMS

LIAM O'DELL

MARK RITSON

MICHAEL BAGGS

PEDRO PINA

SARAH JENKINS

SION WALTON-GUEST

TAMARA ROGERS

ZAID AL-QASSAB

WORLD FEDERATION OF ADVERTISERS DIVERSITY TASK FORCE

PART ONE

Introduction

Representation matters

01

What we mean by inclusion and representation

This is a book about doing better marketing. In many ways it's as simple as that.

Perhaps more so than almost any other industry, it is our job as marketers to really understand consumers. To appreciate their wants, their needs and what makes them tick, and then ultimately to shape products that meet those needs and advertising that helps them realize that.

This isn't your typical marketing textbook. Whilst there is a chapter packed with research, and a helpful framework and checklists to keep you on track, much of the book is dedicated to the personal perspectives of marketers, including my own. These are included as interviews in a deliberately conversational and personal way. There are no definitive right answers in this space, and even at times somewhat opposing opinions amongst experts, which we've tried to capture.

Inclusive marketing is more than just tweaking your casting decisions to show different looking people on screen, but it doesn't necessarily mean 'purpose based' marketing, charity partnerships or big political statements either. It is about understanding the real needs, nuances and cultures of consumers, and avoiding approaches that are focused too heavily on our own biases and assumptions. Inclusion means representing those different perspectives in both our thinking and our output, and in doing so we can have a positive impact on both society and business.

The people we want to buy our products and services are of course hugely varied and diverse. They come from widely different backgrounds and experiences than our own, and each other. They look different, they sound different, they think differently, they act differently. It's all part of what makes humanity so wonderfully unique and interesting, but it is of course a challenge for the marketer who wants to find a way to appeal to them all.

For all our differences there is usually far more that unites us. As detailed as you might get in your marketing thinking about the exact consumer you want to sell to, there are still thousands of very different consumers who will be interested in what you have to offer and hopefully ultimately end up buying from you. I wouldn't want to write a book on inclusion that doesn't start by celebrating the wonderful opportunity that media and marketing has of bringing people together, of creating shared experiences and moments that unite us all.

If you grew up in the UK you probably think of the colour purple as being synonymous with chocolate, because that's the iconic colour that Cadbury has been using on their bars and in their adverts for around 200 years. Whatever your background, there's a good chance that you like chocolate, and as Cadbury are the market leader it is likely that you reasonably enjoy theirs. In fact they even make vegan chocolate these days, if that's what was stopping you before.

Their drumming gorilla advert is by many measures one of the most iconic and famous UK television adverts of all time. If you've never seen it, it may not be immediately clear why a gorilla drumming along to Phil Collins without a square of chocolate in sight is a good way to sell more bars, but one way or another it seemed to work. An awful lot of people love that advert, but unless you happen to be a gorilla you probably don't feel particularly represented by it, although you most likely don't feel excluded by it either. Not every advert ever could, or ever should, be a direct visual showcase for representation and inclusion.

To make our job as marketers possible, especially when working for a big brand that tens of millions of people are one day going to buy, we must simplify and reduce the audiences that we are thinking about. We must look for averages and what unites them, or home in on the sweet spot of who we think our ideal shopper is and hope that others come along for the ride. There's absolutely nothing wrong with this, and indeed one of the greatest tasks as a marketer is coming up with ideas that truly can transcend different audiences. Recognizing the indifference that most consumers have to our brands is one of the greatest creative challenges you can face up to.

That said, we shouldn't be afraid to admit that in reality people are very different, and that any attempt to talk about them in an abstract or averaged way inevitably loses a lot of the nuances and diversity that makes them tick.

A lot of the time that may not be a problem, but there is certainly a positive opportunity for those marketers who are willing to scratch beneath the surface and who do want to understand how different audiences might relate to their products. You can discover entirely different use cases and reasons for buying your product amongst specific groups of people, or simply stand out amongst a field of competitors if you bother to talk to and represent some of the 'minority' communities that typically make up a majority of your audience.

Marketing without inclusion

There is also a darker side to what has traditionally happened in marketing when we look to these averages. Historically we have tended to erase people, to pretend they don't exist, or perhaps worse yet to stereotype them. Think of the frequent portrayals of women as the housewives doing the household chores whilst the husband goes out to work, or the handsome and successful man who stars in many adverts whilst others fade into the background. Inclusion and representation of other aspects of diversity, like those of races, abilities, ages, sexualities, classes or other aspects, has often been non-existent. Or worse yet it comes as a negative stereotype or the butt of a joke.

Work by the Geena Davis Institute (2019) looked at the winning entries into the Cannes Lions Awards, an annual marketing showcase that is considered by many people to be the pinnacle celebration of our creative industry. They found that whilst black people were reasonably present in award winning advertising, they were often stereotyped as being less intelligent or less successful than their white counterparts. Women are still overly sexualized and appear in revealing clothing four times as often as men do. Even amongst this most elevated work they found representation of huge swathes of people to be hugely lacking, across much of the intersectionality mentioned.

People in an advert don't have to look, sound or act like you for that advert to be able to impact you and make you want to buy something. If, however the people in advertising and wider marketing never look like you, never sound like you, or never act like you it can start to feel like those brands really aren't talking to you. If you are black, or gay, or define yourself in some other wonderfully unique way you probably don't expect to see yourself reflected in every piece of media around you, but if you never ever see people who look like you or think like you it starts to make you think you don't belong.

A spectrum of inclusive marketing

Inclusive marketing is about navigating this, about finding ways to make your brand's products or services appeal to as many people as possible, without excluding anyone along the way. It's about discovering entirely new audiences that you simply weren't talking to before and which could be huge growth opportunities for your brand, and wonderfully enough it's about making the world a more inclusive and accepting place along the way.

Sometimes inclusive marketing is very overt and deliberate, straying into territory that might be called 'purposeful'. This is when an advertiser goes out of their way to champion a world view, to deliberately tell a minority focused story, or even to support a specific charity or cause. Sometimes, however, it's equally valid for inclusive marketing to be far subtler, perhaps casual inclusion in casting, location and other aspects that aren't themselves the focus of the advert. Even decisions on which media owners to advertise with or partners to use along the way can enable inclusive marketing. The best inclusive marketing is thinking that permeates the whole marketing process and underpins all the decisions along the way, even if that's not always immediately noticeable in the end result.

There is a watch-out that I've seen in my own work, and certainly in the conversations I've had whilst writing this book, that whilst this casual inclusion can be a positive thing it can also come across as quite a shallow attempt to pander to a trend. Switching out a few casting decisions at the last minute to be seen as 'multicultural' is not true inclusive marketing, which would have begun far earlier in the process. It's not just that we look different to each other, we have different cultures, experiences and expectations, and bringing these to life can be at the heart of some of the most powerful marketing ideas. Many people also see the very act of labelling people as diverse and the signalling out of what makes them different as counter to inclusion, which points to a future state where such labels don't exist at all or matter.

About this book

This book sets out to offer a mixture of inspiration and practical guidance on how to deliver more inclusive, and ultimately just better, marketing. You'll hear perspectives from an intersectional range of marketers, and will be walked through a framework that unpacks the entire creative process step by step and looks for inclusion opportunities within it.

Whilst this notion of inclusive marketing certainly sits within a broader diversity and inclusion (D&I) agenda, that terminology tends to refer more to human resources (HR) initiatives or perhaps charitable projects managed separately from marketing. There is a lot of critical work that needs to be done, and in some cases is being done, to ensure our workplaces are inclusive and welcoming, that we attract employees from broad backgrounds, and that we give everyone a fair chance of success. In practice you cannot separate the two because success in broader D&I absolutely drives and enables better inclusive marketing initiatives.

Whilst we will touch on this at points throughout this book, if you are looking for a deep dive into how to build and develop an inclusive workplace then I am afraid you will have to look elsewhere. Ultimately, I do hope that in 10 years' time our workplaces will naturally be more inclusive and a book like this will have been made redundant by the natural inclusion that will bring, but until then it doesn't hurt to try to move things along a little faster.

Defining inclusive marketing

It's often hard to find consistent definitions of words within the marketing industry, but the Common Language in Marketing Project (2021) has been trying. I'll defer to them for the closest thing we have to a dictionary definition of the term:

> Inclusive marketing (also called inclusion marketing or diversity marketing) refers to marketing strategies, tactics and technologies that have a goal to create a sense of welcoming and belonging, often for members of demographic or societal groups considered underserved, marginalized or legally protected.
>
> Common objectives for inclusive marketing are to communicate that differences among people are respected and valued by the enterprise. These differences can include ethnicity, race, gender, age, religion, sexual orientation, body type, presence of disability, or any other factor.
>
> While individual executions within an inclusive marketing campaign may focus on a specific segment, inclusive marketing campaigns are not narrowly targeted to reach a specific group but are meant for the broader public.
>
> One common tactic of inclusive marketing campaigns is the use of a diverse cast representing various minority groups, but this practice is neither necessary nor, by itself, sufficient for a campaign to be inclusive.

Inclusive marketing is most obviously and overtly seen in advertising, but you can deliver it through product choices and other marketing levers too. Representation is also a critical matter in the wider media environment, in TV shows, music videos, movies and all aspects of culture around us, many of which are themselves funded and guided by our advertising decisions. Whilst we won't try to solve for all of those areas we'll certainly touch on them, and the critical role marketers can have in supporting or challenging content that they may not even directly control.

Navigating this book

The first part of this book will unpack why inclusive marketing is important, and crucially why representation matters to consumers who are at times excluded. There's definitely a business and wider society benefit to this, but it's often best brought to life through the personal perspectives of those who have experienced both inclusion and exclusion in their own lives. You'll see many of those, including my own, laid out throughout this book. It aims to be inclusive not just in topic but also in approach, and is based on interviews with dozens of intersectional people across the marketing industry to build in their inputs, suggestions and experiences.

I worked with some of these other experts, and the wider World Federation of Advertisers (WFA) Diversity Task Force, on a framework for ensuring inclusion and avoiding unconscious bias throughout the creative process. Ultimately that should ensure you deliver inclusive work. That framework forms the structure of the core four sections of this book in which, in a much more practical way, we unpack the various steps you can take to achieve inclusion in your own business. Many marketers and businesses committed to the importance of inclusive marketing still find it hard to deliver it in practice, and by considering key questions and nudges at every stage of the process we believe we can all deliver better results.

My career has seen me work principally at large global advertisers, on brands including Cadbury, Oreo, Guinness, Advil, Suntory and Jim Beam. Most of the people who contributed to the WFA project, or that I have interviewed more widely for this book, will have worked on similarly large global or local brands. It is, however, very much the intention that this book will offer inspiration and practical advice to everyone – whether you work in a huge marketing machine and are involved only at one phase of the project, or you are the entire marketing team yourself and you're just trying to work out where to start.

I've found that many people's fear of getting inclusion wrong can be one of the biggest barriers to starting on this journey, but in all our shared experience we have always found that well-intentioned efforts in this space do deliver, even if some have big lessons and room for improvement. Later in the book we'll cover some of the steps you can take to ensure that your well-meaning inclusion efforts don't accidentally do the opposite.

To whom it may concern

If you're reading this book then I hope that means you also have a passion for this topic. Some of you will be leading experts who probably know more than I do on some of the themes I hope to cover. For others of you this will be an early step as you think about how to approach this in your own work. This is a big conversation that even a deep dive like this can only cover some aspects of, and I encourage you to continue the conversation with the hashtag #RepresentationMatters across social media. I'd love to hear from you all and perhaps your own stories can make it into a future edition.

Some of you will be reading this from a place of exclusion and under-representation yourself, others may not have experienced that but come here as strong allies of those communities, or perhaps you're just here to do better marketing and make more money for your business. The great thing about inclusive marketing is that you can do the latter whilst also doing a good thing for the consumers you serve.

A special welcome to the middle aged, middle class, middle of the road, white men reading this – for the most part I can count myself as one of those too. I know at times we can feel threatened, challenged or just a little awkward about our role in the increasing discourse about inclusion. This book is perhaps for us even more than it is for anyone else, and especially for those who have their doubts as there's no point in just preaching to the choir. Like it or not, we currently live in a society where people like 'us' are more likely to be the ones making decisions and it is absolutely our responsibility to encourage and drive change right through our organizations, hopefully leading to a more equal world for the new generations.

Embracing inclusion and diversity isn't a threat to the jobs we have or the work we currently do – it's a fantastic opportunity to make our working lives and our work output even richer than it ever has been. You still matter and deserve to be represented too, and the great thing is there are plenty of adverts and media moments to go around, although we may have been hogging the limelight a little in the past. I'm thrilled that you're coming on this journey. Whereas the term 'diversity' tends to make us think about people who are different, the heart of inclusion is that everyone should feel welcome and invited.

Inclusion really should mean everyone. All things permitting, everyone gets older and you only need to look around the media landscape to realize that older people are not always best represented. We may well lose our sight, hearing, or other aspects of our mobility along that journey too, but that doesn't mean we'll want to become a grumpy stereotype. There are aspects of diversity which somehow still seem slightly more of a taboo than others too – like social class, mental health and religion, for instance. Inclusion really means for everyone, and inclusive marketing needs to think about all these aspects and more.

Wider perspectives on inclusive marketing

That said, nothing says 'exclusion, entitlement and privilege' quite like a middle class, middle aged white man deciding he should be the one to write the book on diversity and representation in marketing, and with that in mind I will hand the floor back to a range of other authors who have captured what inclusive marketing means to them:

> Inclusive marketing strives to create a visual culture that is more representative. It endeavors to appreciate and understand our various identities, differences and histories while also illuminating places of commonality. Inclusive marketers are willing to cultivate the skillset required to market to specific demographics without relying on stereotypes. Inclusive marketing takes a progressive stand on issues of social justice.
>
> Inclusion is different than diversity. Diversity has become an empty term in most organizations, often denoting little more than the checking of boxes and meeting of quotas. It depends on making one group – say men, or white people – the default and everyone else the other. Conversely, inclusion speaks to the quality of experience, where multiple perspectives are sought out and treated equitably.
>
> Jessica Fish (2016), Facilitator and Consultant

> Inclusive marketing happens any time a business or brand plans and creates communication that relates to people who have been historically underrepresented or stereotypically portrayed, including females, racial and

ethnic minorities, people with disabilities, and multicultural and LGBT+ individuals. In essence, inclusive marketing needs to reflect the diversity of the real world, thereby including people of all backgrounds.

Rob Sanders (2021), Global Technopologist

Inclusive marketing refers to the messaging, people, processes and technologies that enable marginalized or underrepresented groups to fully experience and connect with brands.

Marketing that is truly inclusive considers all facets and layers of a person's identity such as skin tone, gender identity, age, sexual orientation, body type, ethnicity, culture, language, religion/spirituality, physical/mental ability, socio-economic status and mindset. It should also account for intersectionality, which means recognizing that a single person may represent many identities or dimensions and acknowledging the nuances inherent in every individual's personality and preferences.

Roselyn Xavier (2020), Digital Consultant

We define inclusive marketing as marketing that may highlight or solve for an aspect of diversity where exclusion exists. This is something that resonates with all of us – by amplifying a common human value like love, family, safety, opportunity, or enduring stories like the struggle of coming of age or the underdog overcoming all obstacles. Inclusive marketing considers its products, services, or experiences in ways that deeply resonate with people and make them feel seen and accurately understood. This inclusion and thoughtful consideration fuels long term loyalty and growth. This is at the heart of inclusive marketing.

Inclusive marketing is not D&I. However, you do need inclusive culture created by D&I initiatives to drive the flywheel of innovation inside an organization. Innovation is driven by inclusive culture and is expressed as inclusive business strategy and through marketing. The two disciplines of D&I and inclusive marketing go hand in hand – together they can grow business opportunities and optimize people's lives – inside the company and outside in the world – making good on a brand's overall mission.

MJ De Palma (2020), Multicultural Marketer

Ultimately, I believe we're on a journey together, both individually in our industries and together as an industry. We won't all leap to the most purposeful and progressive inclusion overnight, but there is no reason for any marketer to continue total exclusion or, perhaps just as bad, the basic stereotyping that puts so many people in different boxes.

The following simple inclusive marketing journey framework which I helped develop with the WFA shows exactly that journey and how we need to move from a place of exclusion and stereotyping to one of representation and inclusion. Truly inclusive marketing is a blend of positive representation and purposeful inclusion and will ultimately get to the point of authentically representing humanity without needing those labels or silos.

References

Common Language in Marketing Project (2021) Definition of inclusive marketing. https://marketing-dictionary.org/i/inclusive-marketing/ (archived at https://perma.cc/HST6-SGEC)

De Palma, M J (2020) Inclusive marketing: Why it's essential for your brand. Microsoft Advertising Blog. https://about.ads.microsoft.com/en-gb/blog/post/january-2020/inclusive-marketing-why-its-essential-for-your-brand (archived at https://perma.cc/MD5X-3DST)

Fish, J (2016) Make an impact, your guide to inclusive marketing, Forbes. www.forbes.com/sites/womensmedia/2016/06/29/make-an-impact-your-guide-to-inclusive-marketing/?sh=31909eb969fc (archived at https://perma.cc/HY44-4TMR)

Geena Davis Institute (2019) *Bias and Inclusion in Advertising: An analysis of 2019 Cannes Lions work.* https://seejane.org/wp-content/uploads/bias-and-inclusion-in-advertising-cannes-lions.pdf (archived at https://perma.cc/EDJ6-TFB7)

Sanders, R (2021) What is inclusive marketing and why does it matter? Simplilearn. http://simplilearn.com/inclusive-marketing-article#what_is_inclusive_marketing (archived at https://perma.cc/HT7W-XXNU)

Xavier, R (2020) Let's talk about inclusive marketing, Accenture. www.linkedin.com/pulse/why-we-still-lagging-inclusive-marketing-roselyn-xavier (archived at https://perma.cc/FN9H-YWDD)

The inclusive marketing journey

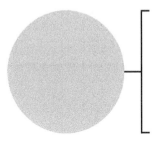

Purposeful inclusion

Truly connecting brand purpose to meaningful action, often with charitable partners and deliberate diversity-focused storytelling

Inclusive marketing

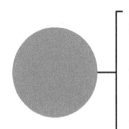

Positive representation

Inclusively reflect different consumers, address different viewpoints, and begin to move beyond silos and labels

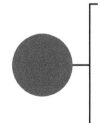

Basic stereotyping

Featuring diverse groups but working with pre-existing biases and stereotypes

Exclusion

No consideration of diversity within marketing or representation of different communities

02

Why representation matters to me and other marketers

Why representation matters to me

For a practical guide to marketing you may be surprised at how personal this chapter is, and indeed how personal the stories are that many marketers share throughout this book. In my experience of this topic there is no better way to bring it to life and to understand the challenges and the opportunities than through real lived experiences. With that in mind I'm not apologetic about devoting time to those stories, but if you'd prefer to get stuck into hard facts and practical advice you may want to skip over this chapter.

Me as a marketer

I'm a marketer who helps global brands make media sense of an increasingly digital world. When I'm not writing books about inclusive marketing I've led local, regional and global media teams for companies including Beam Suntory, GSK, Diageo and Mondelez.

Marketing, media and advertising are fundamental forces of business growth and competitive advantage. I'm passionate about making better marketing through creativity, effectiveness and digital transformation, but also through conscious responsibility and inclusion. I believe in the discipline of marketing science, and that our fundamental job is driving mental availability (front of mind awareness) and physical availability (literal availability to be purchased) to often uninterested consumers.

I appreciate the importance of driving penetration to deliver brand growth, but also the power of creativity to balance the science of marketing with art. I'm a digital evangelist but also a digital realist – new technologies have radically changed how people interact and consume media and we need to capitalize on these opportunities, but without losing sight of the proven basics of marketing.

That's a long way of saying that inclusive marketing and representation matters to me professionally because I know it's good for business. That isn't just a thought experiment, either. I've seen the external research and even carried out my own internally to prove out the value of being more inclusive and thoughtful in our marketing approaches. With nothing but a cold, hard, business hat on I know that inclusive marketing is the right thing to do, and I'm more than happy to stand up in front of C-suite stakeholders, or even shareholders, and show them that.

Representation and inclusion is, however, a deeply individual and personal matter too, and I have many wider reasons for being passionate about and invested in the topic. As marketers and advertisers, we create and fund content that billions of people see every day, giving us billions of opportunities to promote positive inclusion, or to accidentally promote negative stereotypes and division. I don't want to overstate the importance of advertising here, because consumers are more than capable of skipping over, scrunching up, or generally only having a passing interest in the work we produce, but it regardless becomes a background for the society we live in.

We also fund a lot of the media that is produced and have a responsibility to challenge film makers, documentary producers, artists and others on the content and themes of the work we are helping to pay for. When you look at how the internet has developed and programmatic media alongside it, it has created wonderful new opportunities for diverse voices and news gathering, but also for hate speech, misinformation and fraud. As marketing professionals we need to take conscious responsibility for the ecosystems we fund and support.

Chapter 3 unpacks in more detail some of the business and society benefits of inclusive advertising but I wanted to take this moment to talk more personally about why representation matters to me, and cue up some of the experiences of other marketers that have led them to be equally passionate about this space. Once again, if you're not at all interested in my life story and how it's impacted my perspectives, and frankly I don't blame you, then feel free to skip ahead a few pages.

Me as a young gay man

Whilst I recognize that, in many ways, I have lived a very privileged life, I do also have some experience of feeling different to the norm and not represented in the media, advertising and communications that surround me. These days I am a very out and proud gay man, and I had the pleasure of marrying my partner Paul just as this book was being published, but that's a sentence I could never have dreamt of writing when I was a teenager growing up and trying to make sense of who I was.

Being out and open didn't always come so naturally to me, and I was well into my 20s before I was out to anyone in my life who wasn't themselves gay. I don't have the dramatic, or sadly all too often traumatic, coming out story that many LGBT+ people have. I'm still just as close to my parents, family and most of my friends as I was before I chose to come out. I have to think long and hard to come up with a personal experience or a long-term relationship which being gay has obviously had a detrimental effect on, which isn't to say there weren't bumps in the road or impacts you can never truly be aware of.

I've also been reasonably lucky to have experienced relatively limited direct discrimination or harassment because of it, certainly since I was an adult. I am sure the fact that I am ultimately still a tall, big, white man has quite a lot of impact on that, unlike the experiences of some other members of the queer community.

My childhood was, however, very far from the Pride parade that my Instagram Stories sometimes are now. I grew up in an evangelical Christian family who were, and still are, very involved in the church. I attended church every Sunday, like many kids did, but there'd also be a weekend church youth group, a mid-week smaller 'house group' with others my age, church weekends away or even whole weeks at a Christian camp. I was an active and willing participant in all of this, I led a house group for a while and had various voluntary leadership positions in my time. A good number of my friends and the people I hung out with were similarly part of the church community, though at school I tended not to talk about it, to avoid bullying.

Heading to university and being in full control of my life, I still magnet-ized to the church community, and I continued to be a similarly active member there, both at a church in the town and in organizing meetings with new Christian friends in my college. To this day, many of my friends, and certainly those dating back to these times, remain very active Christians – the kind that don't just show up to church on a Sunday morning but who plant new churches, and try to make a real difference in their community.

Section 28, a law that prohibited the promotion of homosexuality in UK schools, was in place for the entirety of my school career. The internet was beginning to exist but was a thing you had to very visibly 'dial up' into on the family computer or go to the library at school to try to access. Progressive as many of the churches I attended were, you can imagine that their limited coverage of LGBT+ rights was not to paint a particularly positive picture. I do feel at pains to add that I have found many progressive churches (and certainly the people who attend them) to be quite welcoming and tolerant, and even at times to live up to the core idea of loving your neighbour that some organized religion seems to lose sight of.

Knowing others like me existed

It seems almost impossible in this digitally connected age, and frankly even would have been for most more worldly kids when I was young, but to an extent I simply did not know that being gay was 'a thing' or that other gay people existed. I understood that 'gay' was a particularly rubbish school yard insult and a thing that you should avoid being called at all costs, although for whatever early reason it already seemed to be a label that was landing on me. I began to understand that I personally found men more attractive than women, though I would confess (apologies to my parents) that some of my early internet searches were open minded on this topic as I began to explore.

Unfortunately, I also came to believe that this 'gay' thing, that I gradually understood myself to be, was wrong and a bad thing to be. That was implied heavily in mainstream culture at the time and it's certainly a topic that the Christian faith remains sometimes oddly fixated on talking about.

With hindsight, LGBT+ representation in media (not least the likes of George Michael and Elton John) was beginning to mature, but in a slightly unspoken way that was too subtle for me to appreciate. Everywhere I looked, I either didn't see people that represented me or heard whispers that there was something wrong with what I felt I was becoming, even though I had no choice or control over it. It was a lonely place to be. Forget not being well marketed to – to a reasonable extent I felt I shouldn't exist at all.

This isn't a 'woe is me' tale. As I have mentioned, I am fully aware that I have grown up amongst great privilege and luxury. I went to a fairly posh, though notably multi-cultural, school, following in my father and brother's footsteps not only there but also when I went on to university in Cambridge. I've always had a social and financial safety net provided by my circum-stances that would be enviable to most people, but that doesn't mean life cannot be tough and hard in its own ways. Even with all that, life can be challenging when you feel isolated, alone and not accepted or represented by the society around you, and I certainly went through periods where I struggled badly with my mental health as a result.

Seeing representation for the first time

An odd glimpse of hope crept into my life as a teenager when my parents had a loft extension and I was moved into a new bedroom, which for some long-forgotten reason was where we had a spare TV setup. Teenage boys can stumble upon some eye-opening late-night television if they go looking for it, and one day I stumbled upon *Queer as Folk*.

This was an iconic Channel 4 series in the UK, which was remade and became a much longer running property in the US. It told the lives of a predominantly gay group of friends in Manchester and focused heavily on Canal Street, the LGBT+ neighbourhood of the city. They had some traumatic and harrowing adventures, but they also had a lot of fun, found acceptance in their own way and yes, most crucially of all, they existed.

Queer as Folk feels like the very first time I became aware that it was possible to be an out, gay man and to live a happy and successful life as part of society. That representation made a huge difference to me personally, and its very existence stirred up public debate and moved wider society forwards. For anyone who's ever seen it, you'll understand that this was a rapid and intense education into gay culture, not only that these people existed, had lives, and went out dancing together, but to a fair extent what they did when they came home together too. It was eye-opening.

The impact of marketers across wider culture

Channel 4 is quite a unique broadcaster in the UK in that it has historically had a 'public service' mandate, and a core part of its DNA is to offer alternative and inclusive programming which the main channels (BBC and ITV) might not otherwise provide. They've done huge service to a wide range of communities over the following decades, including more recently their coverage of the Paralympic Games and their Black to Front day celebrating black talent in front of and behind the camera. *Queer as Folk*'s creator, Russell T Davies, has gone on to other great things too, perhaps most notably rebooting *Dr Who*, and creating *It's a Sin*, a show that gets right to the emotional heart of the 1980s HIV crisis in London.

Despite the service remit, and unlike the BBC, Channel 4 is a fully commercially funded venture and relies on advertisers to fund the programming it produces. It's not enough for consumers to want to see this content, there also need to be advertisers willing to appear alongside it, and I believe one of the most powerful influences advertisers have is to fund progressive programming like this. In some of the conversations I've had, people have challenged whether advertising can ever truly tell cohesive, authentic and inclusive stories that represent some of the more nuanced parts of society in 30 second windows. These are after all stories that sometimes take hours of film or seasons of television to unravel.

Queer as Folk was ahead of its time, and whilst critically well received it certainly attracted a fair amount of shock and backlash. I have long wondered how advertisers reacted to the show and whether their arms needed to be twisted to support it, and indeed Russell spoke about it at a 20th anniversary reunion event for the show. He explained that it wasn't an entirely smooth ride:

> That was a bit of a battle. I think we did lose our sponsors after episode one. It was a family owned beer brand. The daughter of the family was in London and turned on the television and saw all the 'oopsie daisies'. 'Oh mein God!' she telephone her father saying, 'you must take this off, take your sponsorship off the bums and the gays.'
>
> And they did. And that's when the publicity people at Channel 4 got very scared. I was getting phone calls on Saturday night saying, 'Just tell people they've rearranged their European TV schedule.' I did go along with that to an extent because they are our pay masters, so I gave interviews with them saying they've rearranged their schedule. No they didn't, they were homophobic and pulled out!
>
> (BFI, 2020)

It took bold producers to make that show, and just as bold leadership to keep it on air in the face of pressure, including from those people paying their bills, even if they weren't willing to call out why. There will have been thousands of conversations like this with advertisers around the world, and all too often, I am afraid, we have been the ones trying to make things less progressive and inclusive.

There must have been something in the pre-millennium water, because another defining moment of representation in my life happened later that year with the release of Savage Garden's second album, *Affirmation*. The Australian pop duo had topped charts with 'Truly Madly Deeply' and their self-titled debut album had found a place as my brother and I's shared favourite album, with only a little Antipodean competition from Natalie Imbruglia. To this day, I can listen to *Affirmation* and enjoy every song, from high-pace pop numbers to slow ballads, and covering everything from epic declarations of love to sombre discussions of domestic abuse. It was the manifesto-esque title track that most stood out to me and a simple line within it: '*I believe you can't control or choose your sexuality.*'

It's a brilliant song. It covers a wide range of topics, but I was particularly intrigued by the lyrics touching on sexuality and TV evangelists. It was one of the first times, in popular culture or frankly anywhere, that I was told that being gay wasn't my fault, and that there was nothing I could or should be doing about it. It meant a lot to me to hear that, but the power of representation is that it also meant a lot to me that millions of others were hearing it too, even if they might not pay it so much attention.

The band's lead singer Darren Hayes is today out, proud and very open about his sexuality, but at the time was presented very much as a straight man, to appeal to their female fans. Where they sang about love, or when they made a music video, it would always be a woman they were singing to. An interview he gave to Billboard gave me the best insight into what it's like on the other side of this fence, as an artist who wants to be able to represent his true self but is limited by those around him:

Interviewer: Do you think Savage Garden would have had the same success had you come out earlier?

Darren Hayes: No. I remember distinctly the message I got from the top down was that being gay was detrimental to sales. It was never stated, but heavily implied. You could tell it was the topic of many discussions, and I was marketed in a way that appealed to women. It was the period when Ricky Martin had women on his arms at events, and Ellen's career was torn apart by coming out. My entire solo career was filled with songs about men. 'Insatiable' is pretty explicit. My [2004] album *The Tension and the Spark* uses entirely male pronouns. Again, I was out in my music for years.

(Crowley, 2017)

He goes on to talk about his own idols and how a new generation of stars like Adam Lambert have further broken down barriers around acceptance. He does, however, also talk about the very apparent downsides of coming out, of the perception that he was now a 'niche' artist and could no longer be seen as a sexual object. He faced a lot of pressure from senior management to minimize who he was and put on a show that others were expecting.

For me, Darren's story encapsulates a lot of the challenges and opportunities we see in inclusive marketing. He himself was empowered and felt represented by the media and culture which went before him. Whether he realized it or not at the time, he then blazed his own trail of inspiration for others to follow, and in his own solo work he was truly able to be his authentic self. It may never have occurred to you, but it is incredibly rare as a member of the LGBT+ community to ever see casual representation of same sex relationships in music, or really in any media, unless they are a deliberate plot point in themselves.

It also speaks of the challenges many of us will face as we push to make our marketing more inclusive. At times that can be direct questioning or opposition from senior leaders, but more commonly it can be more subtle ways of downplaying or sidelining a project, perhaps finding an allegedly unrelated reason not to proceed. Working in global teams, it's common to get pushback from local markets if they see a script with an LGBT+ or multicultural angle, but of course that feedback is usually very carefully worded to imply that something else is causing the concern. We can even box ourselves in if we start to believe that inclusive marketing should only be shown to the specific communities it is representing, and thus miss the opportunity to amplify it more widely.

Diverse marketing just for diverse people?

Given my relatively conservative upbringing, my first exposure specifically to LGBT+ inclusive marketing came in a somewhat unexpected, place – a gay club. As young adults, I and a few friends started occasionally going out to bars and clubs and became semi-regulars at a gay night club in London called Heaven. This had nothing to do with my personal preferences, it wasn't an early attempt by my friends to try to support me, but it simply happened to be where a really good dance/trance night was hosted.

This was long before I had truly come to terms with being gay myself, and definitely before I was ready to tell anyone. To most intents and purposes, it felt like any other club, and indeed trance music venues have a tendency to be quite male-dominated in any case. Yet I started to notice that there was specific LGBT+ inclusive advertising around the venue – most obviously with brands like Absolut advertising around the bar, but free magazines that were left lying around also had much broader advertisers.

Some of these were niche brands specifically looking to serve this community, but there were also early attempts by mainstream brands to appeal to this audience. You could, for instance, find an advert for an insurance or mortgage company that might show a picture of two men together, or early examples of brands deliberately touting their inclusive credentials.

It was notable, however, that they were doing so in environments where they felt sure LGBT+ individuals would be the only ones seeing them, and where they wouldn't have to worry about what their other customers might think of this support. In my mind, true inclusive marketing begins not just when you are willing to positively talk to a community, but when you're happy and proud for everyone else to know you are doing so.

There were by this stage some examples of brands willing to do that. IKEA is one of the earliest examples I know of an advertiser including clear LGBT+ representation in a TV advert, when back in 1994 they showed a gay couple shopping for a table together over in the US. Here in the UK entertainment had moved even earlier with the soap opera *EastEnders* featuring a gay kiss in 1989, whilst *LA Law* was the first US show to air a lesbian kiss two years later. More nuanced representation has been slower to follow, it was only in 2019 that the drama *Empire* aired the first gay black wedding, and in 2020 Ruby Rose became the first major out superhero in the series *Batwoman*.

Where progressive representation goes, outrage and challenge often follow. All the above moments caused complaints and protests in some form, and a range of responses from subtle downplaying to proud endorsement. In 2008 Heinz pulled a Mayo advert from UK screens because over 200 people complained it featured a gay kiss, though the Advertising Standards Authority commented that 'homosexuality in itself is not a breach of the code' and complaints in the past about adverts showing same-sex kissing had not prompted any punitive action.

Beginning my own career in marketing

My interest in inclusive advertising had been piqued and indeed so had my wider interest in advertising and marketing. I went to university, and soon began my career working for several years at a youth education charity. Many of our communications needed to specifically reach disengaged kids in the local, mostly Bangladeshi, community who had dropped out of education, many of whom didn't feel at all spoken to or represented by the generic messaging the department of education put out. I realized rapidly the importance of truly understanding and listening to your audience, of reflecting them and speaking to them in their own words, and involving them in the process where possible. We went one step further and launched a media and marketing social enterprise that not only created our advertising and started working with other corporate partners, but also gave jobs and opportunities to the kids graduating from our courses.

As a member of the LGBT+ community you don't just come out once, you're basically committing to a lifetime of coming out. Any time you make a new colleague, new friend or have a simple encounter there's a chance you'll have to come out again, in a small way – even a simple friendly question asking what you did for the weekend and you'll have to quickly think about whether to say 'boyfriend' or not. This is the first time I've come out in a book and I'm selfishly hoping it's a fast-track way to avoid a few hundred of these conversations, although these days I am quite comfortable in having them.

That said, today I work in a global team speaking with people from very different cultures and backgrounds and (often unfairly) I sometimes think twice about being so open when I speak with colleagues from more conservative countries. I'm lucky that this has never really been a visible issue for me in my career, but even this sense that you have to continually check yourself and potentially cover up who you are at work can be a drain and is a key reason why we need to continue working on shaping more inclusive and welcoming work environments. I do know many LGBT+ colleagues, especially those who would be seen as 'camper' or to have more nuanced gender identities, who have been told to downplay themselves at work, or who I have seen treated less seriously than their peers.

Coming out in the office

I wasn't open about being gay to my colleagues until a couple of years after I had properly started coming out to my friends. I took the opportunity of a new job at Cadbury and the fresh start of a change in company to be more open about it. I didn't storm into the office waving Pride flags, but, early on, I distinctly remember a lunch with two of my new Cadbury colleagues where I was able to just casually mention having plans to do something with my boyfriend. There was an almost visible sigh of relief, which we have since joked about, that I was making it clear this was something I was happy to be open about, and we didn't need to tiptoe around. It was still a journey, and many years before I became active in internal LGBT+ employee resource groups or would have considered speaking up and talking actively about the topic.

A lot has positively changed around representation and inclusion over the past few years, both more broadly in society and within the marketing industry itself. During that time at Cadbury, I was proud that we started to work with an LGBT+ influencer/chef and whilst there was nothing specifically gay or inclusive about the content, the casual representation meant a lot to me. Since I've left, they've gone much further and even had a gay couple kissing and sharing a Creme Egg in an advert. I have to say that whilst I welcome the inclusive representation, I do find the idea of choosing to share a delicious Creme Egg quite hard to believe!

So why does representation matter to me?

My world view and my personal work experience have inevitably been shaped both by the ways in which I easily fit into and am included by society, and the aspects of who I am that are perhaps a little different and not so easily represented. For me, this is why representation matters. I know the hugely positive impact that seeing representation of my whole self has had on me personally, but I also know of the power for advertising and media to impact and shape society. In recent years there has been some push back on brands seemingly cashing in on inclusivity as a trend, and indeed I do believe brands should back up well-meaning words with thoughtful actions, but it's amazing for me personally to see the wide spectrum of companies that come out publicly in support of Pride each year.

I remember a couple of years back there was backlash from commentators on an 'LGBT' sandwich which the supermarket Marks & Spencer launched – lettuce, guacamole, bacon and tomato. To many it seemed like a cynical way to cash in on Pride and try to make some extra money, but from speaking with the team I know the idea was championed by their internal LGBT+ colleagues who wanted the brand to do something visible. Deliberate acts of inclusion like this, which go beyond casual representation and inclusion, probably should be backed up by meaningful actions such as charitable support, inclusive internal policies, and not just be limited to a certain day or month. That said, if you'd told a young me that one day my parents would be walking into one of the most respected shops on the high street and seeing them proudly supporting gay rights I would have been absolutely over the moon.

To different extents, we all experience what it's like to be labelled, stereotyped and put in a box. Even when we are kids there are huge assumptions put on us about the toys we should or should not play with, some of which echo the careers society has decided are 'suitable' for a binary gender construct. It is true that I enjoyed playing Sylvanian Families and Barbie (well, especially Ken) with my sister, but I also liked building Playmobil fortresses or having Manta Force battles with my brother. Kids are a great example of how naturally creative and inclusive we can be, though all too often adults and the consumer culture around us wants to start imposing limitations on that.

Why representation matters to other marketers

I think I've shared more than enough of my own personal journey and why representation and inclusive marketing has come to mean so much to me, but everyone has their own journey and their own story to tell. There's something unique about all of us, whether it's our gender, our age or something totally different, and we may or may not be comfortable with how society chooses to portray that.

In writing this book, I felt it was important to get advice and best practice from a wide and intersectional range of my marketing peers, but I was also keen to understand why representation mattered so much to each of them. A key theme throughout is that we aren't our own target consumers, and we need to look outside our own bubbles, but whilst that is true individually, collectively we do of course start to represent many of the same perspectives the consumers we are trying to reach will share.

You'll find their profiles, and their own words, dotted throughout all the chapters that follow and whilst there is a business case for inclusion, I really think these personal stories often go a lot further in explaining why it really matters. In all the various training sessions and webinars I've been a part of on the subject, it's always the chance to be truly open with our colleagues about our own personal experiences that seems to cut through. I hope you enjoy reading their words as much as I enjoyed hearing them.

It's impossible to present them all in full, though I wish I could share each of the fantastic conversations I've had. Let me start by summarizing a few that we won't have the space to expand on fully.

Liam O'Dell

Liam O'Dell is an award-winning Deaf and disabled journalist; I've enjoyed and often been positively challenged by following him on Twitter. Liam spoke about how inclusion and representation plays a powerful role both for those who are being represented, and for wider society to see an identity about which they might know very little. It can go a long way towards showing that with the right support individuals can achieve anything, and indeed that there are many more people just like them out there. 'I am always reminded of children and young people who see someone who looks like them in the media and, as a result, feel a lot more confident in themselves.'

There is always the opportunity to educate with representation, and Liam spoke about the need for more of it so that communities aren't stereotyped by a single portrayal or treated as 'one size fits all'. A crucial skill in marketers themselves, this ultimately helps encourage empathy in us all.

I asked Liam about what good representation can look like in marketing and he pointed to a recent Facebook Portal advert which featured two Deaf women signing and a series of adverts from Malteser's chocolates, which also featured Deaf and disabled people. 'It was so natural and casual in its portrayal, the representation was not performative, and I think that's a really important thing to consider when it comes to inclusive advertising.'

'When I see adverts about and/or including Deaf people, a lot of the time it either focuses on older people who are deaf or British Sign Language (BSL) users. There are few adverts highlighting the experiences of Deaf young people, who may communicate using speech or Signed Supported English (where signs are used with English grammar and syntax). Putting Deaf people in front of the camera is one thing, but it's important that the representation makes clear that this is either one individual's lived experience or showcases a range of different Deaf identities to show it isn't one size fits all.

'Unfortunately, if it isn't done right, people can and do assume that Deafness or disability only presents in a certain way, which is problematic. I also think we see little representation of wider disabled people beyond those who have 'noticeable' physical disabilities. I can't think of many adverts featuring autistic people, but then again, because it's a visual medium, I think it's difficult – though not impossible – for adverts to highlight disabilities which non-disabled people have long considered to be "invisible".'

Like many people I spoke to, Liam was keen to emphasize the need to have this inclusion behind the camera as well as in front of it, and that you need those perspectives influencing the direction, the narrative and many of the technical areas. He pointed out some practical steps marketers can take to make their adverts more inclusive and engaging to all audiences, which are now included within the production and post-production sections of this book, but crucially that can start with more adverts doing the basics, such as subtitling.

Anna Brent

As a counterpart to my own experience of growing up as a gay man in the 1980s and 1990s, Anna Brent (Global Head of Brand and DEI at the independent creative agency Across the Pond) shared with me how lacking, or at times dreadful, she felt the representation was for herself as a lesbian around the same time. 'I knew I was gay, and inexplicably had a fair level of confidence and clarity around it early on, but I had absolutely no idea what this would mean for my future, how I could be open about it with others, and what kind of life I would lead. I'm certain that lack of representation was not only bad for me, but equally didn't help the people I feared telling.'

Having a career in TV and advertising, Anna feels even more acutely aware of representation in all forms of media: 'In my TV development days I distinctly recall trying to propose formats for factual/entertainment series that in some way featured LGBT+ life or culture and was blocked at the first hurdle for suggesting what was always described as "far too niche". One executive explicitly told me that the idea of a documentary about drag king culture would just "turn a commissioner off". My partner was working in children's TV on a series about different families in the UK when she suggested some of the families included should be same sex parents. The reaction was the same, and even with the classic rebuff – 'that will never work because parents won't want to have to talk to their children about sex!'

Anna found more freedom and opportunity to really impact decisions in the independent creative agency she has worked at now for the past 10 years. That's finally allowed her to implement more inclusive marketing principles and to explore which values and priorities should affect their work, and indeed the wider community, for the better.

Even with such an inclusive mindset, Anna told me a story about how her son had made her realize the impact that representation has on us all from a very young age: 'When my son started school, he knew the story of how our family came to be pretty well. He has two mums, and we managed to have him (and later his sister) because clever doctors helped us find a sperm donor to help us get pregnant and become parents. Everyone he was in direct contact with was nothing but positive and supportive about this, but one day we found out that he was telling friends at school that his dad had died in a train crash.'

'It was quite a shock to us, and we worried about him. He knows he hasn't ever had a father, but something was making him feel he had to make that up for the sake of his peers. And then of course a painful penny drops – outside of our fairly diverse set of friends, every single image he saw of "family" was the same; one mum, one dad and a couple of kids. From Peppa Pig to *The Incredibles*, from Christmas ads on TV and billboards for supermarkets and cereals. It was always the same reinforcement of just one depiction of family.'

We both agreed that there have been many improvements around the prevalence and authenticity of diverse representation when we compare to our own childhoods, but unfortunately not nearly enough. 'I still have to look for it, and I have to make a point of showing it to my kids to make sure their amazing ever-developing minds understand all the shapes and sizes we come in as individuals and families.' Anna pointed to several adverts that have really stood out to her in recent years, including Bodyform's honest and open 'Womb Stories', Starbucks' authentic trans representation in 'What's Your Name' and the universal, casual inclusion in McCain's 'Here's to Love' series.

Her top advice was to select your creative partners carefully. Don't look for agencies that need to be asked about representation and inclusion, look for the agencies who are already talking about it. 'Being inclusive, authentic and bold isn't just your job as a marketer, this is how you can truly make positive change in society.'

Ibrahim Kamara

GUAP is a magazine and, broader, a youth-led media platform. Working with and nurturing emerging creative talent from diverse communities is a standard part of what they do. Their co-founder and Editor-in-Chief Ibrahim Kamara saw from his own experiences that brands were failing to represent these communities and saw an opportunity to close this gap by bringing those brands and the creative network they are building together.

'Growing up in South London, what I saw around me, all of the different communities, I never really saw them reflected in advertising. It felt like I was living in a different world to the one that was shown to me on the screen.'

When we spoke, he raised Nike's 'Nothing Beats a Londoner' campaign as a standout example where the London he was seeing in the advert authentically represented his own experience of the city and became a more powerful message as a result. 'There were certain nuances within that advert that showed that people from the communities that they were trying to reach were involved in it. There are certain cultural moments that really showed they had young people working on it and it was just very reflective of the audience without trying too hard.'

Working with media owners and diverse creative networks can be a powerful way for marketers looking to get started in this inclusive space to get a head start. By leaning on their insights, their expertise and their creativity, you can rapidly bring in fresh viewpoints to your business that you might not otherwise see represented. A consistent theme in conversations that Ibrahim also touched on was this power of collaboration and getting the right people in the room, 'people who reflect the audiences that you're trying to serve, and ensuring that those people are behind the scenes working on the project as well as getting them in front of the cameras. It's about being open to work with new people to make sure your content is as close to the source as possible.'

As a marketer working in a large organization, it can often feel that it's beyond your influence to be able to drive this change in mindset and approach, but there are always small steps you can take to encourage an inclusive mindset in your team or in the projects you work on. Ibrahim spoke to me about how on nearly every project they've run there's been a key person on the brand team who is the one who has driven it, kicked down the barriers and made it happen. Often that person brings them into new projects or even into new companies as they move around in their own career, which highlights the impact that we can each potentially have in our own areas.

Jane Brearley

One of the spaces where this sort of representation and inclusion matters most is in healthcare communications. We've seen this exceptionally clearly during the Covid pandemic with governments and health organizations having to rapidly develop messaging that cuts through a wide range of audiences and drives behavioural change. In many countries around the world, we have seen vaccination rates and ultimately the impact of the virus vary dramatically between diverse communities. There are socio-economic and community explanations of this, but also a crucial challenge for health professionals to find ways, and means, of communicating critical messaging in ways that different audiences will pay full attention to.

Jane Brearley launched a communications agency at the start of 2020 just as all this was starting to take place, but she did so specifically to build an organization founded on diversity, inclusion and representation. 'In health-care, communications matter – if we are trying to improve health outcomes and tackle health inequities in a multicultural, multi-dimensional society. When you talk to people about health and they can't hear you, nothing changes. If you communicate with clear intent, then everything changes.'

Starting an agency founded on the principles of inclusion is a big step for anyone to take, but Jane stresses that, wherever you work, getting to truly inclusive marketing does mean intentionally creating a diverse team and listening to and learning from the communities you are trying to engage with. In this book we'll unpack the diversity challenges and inclusion oppor-tunities that can exist at every stage of the marketing process, and Jane echoes that this is how we get to better marketing: 'Don't assume anything. Our model is based on representation at every stage of the communications process.'

MARKETER IN FOCUS
Belinda J Smith, founder of The Second Arrow and WFA Diversity Ambassador

I have worked closely with Belinda as my fellow WFA Diversity Ambassador. She led media and marketing at brands including EA Games and AT&T and at the media agency m/SIX before launching her own culture and inclusion consultancy – The Second Arrow. She's been a passionate and outspoken advocate for the need to drive change in the industry and has led the WFA's Global Diversity Census, action plan and work to focus on improving internal inclusion. We talked about the big picture of representation in our industry and how we can all get started by looking at the teams around us.

Q: Why does representation matter to you?

A: I think there are a couple of things. The most obvious is just wanting to make things that represent the world that we live in, and it really seems like it shouldn't be as difficult as it is.

There's also the desire to see yourself reflected in your own work. I have a son and there's an acknowledgement of thinking about the world that he's growing up in – what he is exposed to and how those things are curated. I hope that it will show him a balanced and accurate picture of the world.

More than anything, over the past few years I have been really focused on and obsessed by healthy and balanced teams. This topic of external representation starts internally with a healthy, inclusive and a balanced team, and that just naturally leads to better work. We'd probably label that work as more diverse, but I would personally just label it as more accurate.

The more you can see yourself, the more it is normalizing behaviour, and the more it is normalizing acceptance as part of society. That's really important. What I think about in the context of my son is that it is powerful to acknowledge that our work shapes how people perceive life and reality. To an extent, even how they treat other people – what things they accept, what things seem normal, what things seem good and of course what things seem bad.

I think your own personal story really hits to the heart of that, which is, yes, representation matters. Marketing and wider communications mediums are so much of how we learn to think about the world around us.

Q: Can you think of any really good examples of representation, inclusive marketing or media?

A: My bone to pick with at the moment is ads that try to have one of every type of something in them, rather than truly looking to understand or include any of those communities. I find it more authentic when advertisers just show a Muslim family, or an Indian family, or a black family, or a Jewish family, or a gay family, or whatever community people come in. Understanding those communities and being unafraid to show them authentically, and to make the ad or the message or the creative all about them. It's bringing in inclusion from both a casting and a narrative standpoint, and fully leaning into all the goodness, the culture, and the richness of things.

There is an analogy that I don't love and won't master but I think it makes this point – it's the difference between being invited to attend a party versus someone asking you to dance when you get there. Representation is one thing. Inclusion is separate. I think that, especially in our work, while representation is important it can be shallow.

It's pulling someone from a different community but still wanting to portray them through a white, heteronormative lens, versus pulling someone from a different community and being genuinely interested to see what their natural expression is. It's trying to fit you into my box, into my script and into my understanding, versus looking for something really great and unique.

Q: And where do you think marketers can get started on this journey?

A: I've spent a lot of time over the last few years being really overwhelmed by this topic myself, and I come back to this question of where we should start. Ultimately once again it starts internally, around the table of creators.

The multi-step process you have, starting with the brief, is brilliant as we've never pushed inclusion that far back before, but it starts at the table of the people who are creating the work. That's where you strike the agreement, where you agree why you are doing this work, how to keep each other accountable and how we can have a healthy debate throughout the process.

Even if you have the people, do they feel they can speak up and people will listen to them, and is it a safe space to do so? Do you yourself listen to them and does it change your own business decision making? Do we have the right people around the table so somebody will be able to speak up and say 'This casting seems really unauthentic, and we're probably doing more harm than good'? Having different people at the table doesn't really matter until we're also ready to listen to them.

I think that something we can all do, whether in a big global role or small local team, is start shifting the culture of your team and shifting the discussions that you have about the marketing work you are doing.

Q: Tell us about the WFA Global Diversity Census and what we can learn from that.

A: The census was great because we don't often have global conversations about this topic. That's hard because the topic of diversity and inclusion is very nuanced globally. This was a moment where we invited everyone from the industry, whether you work at a brand, or an agency, or a tech company – wherever you work in marketing. We asked individuals to fill out an industry inclusion survey and tell us about their experiences.

I think the census was great for two reasons. Firstly, it gives us a benchmark of where we are at this moment, globally, as an industry on diversity and inclusion. We didn't see anything that was truly surprising there: we have a problem with age; we have a problem with gender; we have a problem with ethnicity; we have a problem with disability. Ultimately, though, we have this line in the sand and benchmarks that will get repeated and measured year on year.

Secondly, it's starting to bring up some themes that we can talk about. Something that can feel scary in this work is that you don't want to say the wrong thing or make the wrong people upset, and you want to get it just right. You don't want to offend anyone, end up getting 'cancelled', or whatever we all worry about. This really shows us, with data, some powerful themes that we can all talk about.

In APAC we had strong feedback about hiring people of national origin versus global brands which regularly choose to fly in their senior leadership team from their bigger markets – people felt it was a form of ongoing marketing industry colonialism. I would never have had the inside knowledge or the right language to try to talk about that had it not been something that was highlighted by the research.

Another thing that really stood out for me was the delta between the reported experiences from the majority versus ethnic minority populations by country. Even though those minority populations are different in their make-up there seems to be the same gap in experience and inclusion in every country.

So, once again, we have a baseline from where we can speak in an informed and an empowered way. Here are the trends that we know and that are true and present globally, and we can start to measure those over time.

References

BFI (2020) Russell T Davies and the cast of *Queer as Folk* | BFI Q&A, YouTube. www.youtube.com/watch?v=dpIelzM8EzE (archived at https://perma.cc/8L9M-VUMW)

Crowley, P (2017) Savage Garden's Darren Hayes on behind-the-scenes reactions to his coming out, admiring Michael Jackson and Adam Lambert. Billboard. www.billboard.com/culture/pride/savage-garden-darren-hayes-coming-out-reactions-interview-7834056/ (archived at https://perma.cc/L5BA-7B8A)

03

Why representation matters to business and society

CAMELIA CRISTACHE-PODGOREAN

The World Federation of Advertisers has taken global leadership in the space of inclusive marketing and many of their team and members have contributed to or informed this book. This chapter is guest written by Camelia Cristache-Podgorean, their Senior Communications Manager and Global Diversity and Inclusion Lead, who has led much of their work in this space.

It's deliberately designed to curate the wide range of research on this topic and bring it into one place, and is thus densely packed with statistics from a wide range of sources. Every source referenced is itself a wider report with far greater depth of data and insight, if you want to continue your investigations further. We hope this is a chapter you'll come back to when you need data, when you need reassurance, or when you need to present something to a senior leader who is questioning your focus.

Not long ago, diversity was very much still an option that some brands continued to ignore and get by, with no visible repercussions – or so one thought.

Fast-forward to today, and diversity should be a must-have for all businesses, with very clear societal and business cases. Societal because advertising is storytelling, and storytelling can shape culture. The way in which a brand decides to communicate, the stories and characters it decides to show or –

intentionally or unintentionally – does not show in its advertisements, matters for how people see themselves and others in society. In a study by Ipsos (2018) and the Female Quotient, a staggering 76 per cent of respondents agreed that advertising has a lot of power to shape how people perceive each other, and 65 per cent agreed that showing men and women in traditional or old-fashioned roles in advertising influences how young people view the roles of men and women in society.

But diverse and inclusive advertising is not just good for society – it's good for the bottom line, too.

The value of getting representation right

The tangible benefits of embracing a more diverse approach are plentiful, and the evidence is ever-growing: progressive ads are more enjoyable, more relevant, improve credibility and overall have more impact with consumers, boosting brand opinion.

Critically, diversity also increases revenues. Empirical evidence from the ANA (2018) based on the GEM® measurement index in the USA showed that progressive ads drive purchase intent by 42 per cent among women, and they contribute to a 56 per cent increase in brand reputation. Positive return on investment (ROI) tied to high GEM scores also appeared to increase sales by two to five times. GEM is a data-driven methodology to identify gender bias in media. It measures four key characteristics of women in the advertisement: presentation (opinion of how the female character(s) is (are) being presented); respectful (if female character(s) is (are) shown in a respectful manner); appropriate (if female character(s) is (are) presented in an appropriate manner); role model (if female character(s) is (are) viewed as a positive role model).

Similar data from the UN's Unstereotype Alliance (2019) based on their Unstereotype Metric showed that, when benchmarked against other ads, those that were perceived as promoting positive gender portrayals of women performed 2.7 times better on ad likeability, 1.3 times higher on brand opinion and 3.3 times better on purchase consideration. Meanwhile, some 59 per cent of consumers polled by Facebook (2021a) and the Geena Davis Institute on Gender in Media said they are more loyal to brands that stand for diversity and inclusion in advertising, and 59 per cent also said they prefer to buy from brands that stand for diversity and inclusion.

Conversely, advertising that fails to be diverse and inclusive risks negatively impacting a brand, often leaving reputational marks which take time and money to heal. According to a study by Adobe (2019), 34 per cent of Americans said they have boycotted a brand because they did not see themselves or their communities represented in advertising; and this went up to over 50 per cent for certain groups such as LGBT+, African American and Gen Z respondents, who said they have boycotted brands if they didn't feel represented. While less common than in the USA, a substantial proportion of Australians (21 per cent) have boycotted a brand because they felt it did not represent their identity in their advertising, the same study showed. Meanwhile, research by 4As (2020) in the United States showed that consumers are monitoring actions and brand promises and 28 per cent of them would stop buying a brand due to an inappropriate response to movements such as the Black Lives Matter.

In a globalized world of infinite brand choice and endless possibilities, brands must remember there's no such thing as being irreplaceable, and people will vote with their feet if brands ignore them – or, worse, misrepresent them.

Tapping into under-represented groups

The 60+, individuals with different abilities, representatives of the LGBT+ community, people of colour or from different ethnic groups, women – there are a host of groups that the advertising industry has historically ignored or misrepresented. Worse, often these groups are still very much an afterthought for some brands, despite having significant spending power.

A Geena Davis Institute on Gender in Media study (2019) examining the representations of gender, race/ethnicity, LGBT+, disability, age and body size in Cannes Lions ads from 2006 to 2019 revealed that LGBT+ and disabled characters were virtually non-existent (1.8 per cent and 2.2 per cent compared to 10 per cent and 19 per cent of people globally, respectively). Those aged 60+ made up 7 per cent of the characters (versus 19 per cent globally). Even women – who make half of the world's population – were outnumbered on screen one-to-two and stereotyped, while people of colour, despite being well represented (38 per cent), were less likely to be shown as working and 'smart' than their white counterparts. All this across what the marketing industry considers to be its best and most celebrated work.

Alarming as these stats alone will seem, gaps get even bigger in mainstream digital advertising. Facebook (2021a) and Geena Davis research on a selection of 1,000 online ads found certain groups, such as people with disabilities and members of the LGBT+ community, were almost entirely omitted from depictions (1.1 per cent and 0.3 per cent respectively). Women were 14.1 times more likely than men to be shown in revealing clothing, 6.9 times more likely to be verbally objectified and 6.1 times more likely to be shown in a state of partial nudity or to be physically objectified.

These categories of people who are often overlooked or misrepresented, if not altogether erased from advertising, have a huge influence and significant spending power that businesses can no longer ignore.

Women, the purchase decision-makers

Women make a vast number of purchase decisions, particularly when it comes to fast-moving consumer goods. According to EY (2015), women drive between 70–80 per cent of all consumer purchasing, through a combination of their buying power and influence. Silverstein and Sayre (2009) showed that women make the decisions in the purchases of 94 per cent of home furnishings, 92 per cent of vacations, 91 per cent of homes, 60 per cent of cars and 51 per cent of consumer electronics. Their article in the *Harvard Business Review* described women, in aggregate, as a 'growth market bigger than China and India combined – more than twice as big, in fact'. Research by Boston Consulting Group (2020) showed that women are increasing their wealth faster than before – adding $5 trillion to the wealth pool globally every year and outpacing the growth of the wealth market overall.

Yet, while we have seen efforts by many companies to achieve a more gender-equal representation on screen, gender bias continues to be an issue. According to JWT (2016) and their Female Tribes initiative, 85 per cent of women think the advertising world needs to catch up to the real world when it comes to gender roles, and 66 per cent switch off media when it stereotypes women negatively.

A study by Google (2019), again partnering with the Geena Davis Institute, showed that while women-led and gender-balanced videos yielded 30 per cent more views than other views, women were still overwhelmingly portrayed in traditional roles. Looking at advertising sectors individually, they were more often present in healthcare (52 per cent), consumer packaged goods

(55 per cent) and retail (58 per cent) ads, and less so in advertising for cars (28 per cent), business (29 per cent), education and government (33 per cent).

Improving gender representation in advertising is therefore an imperative for businesses if they want to ensure sustainable growth for their brands.

A better representation is shown to have a positive impact on both the short- and long-term relationship with the brand. Data collected by Ipsos (2021) using the GEM methodology across 1,994 ads in ten countries and spanning nine industry categories showed uplifts both in long-term brand relationship scores as well as changes in short-term behaviour when brands showed female characters in a positive way – meaning, according to GEM, when representation is respectful and appropriate. The research showed that ads with positive female representation are linked to higher choice impact scores of +20 per cent, having an impact at the point of purchase. Equally, it revealed that these ads are 35 per cent more likely to score high on the brand relationship index.

The same research showed that when brands portray women positively in their ads, people experience more positive attitudes towards the brand, which they find more relatable, notably on ad ratings such as 'for people like me', 'is informative', 'fits the way I feel about the brand' and 'is believable'.

Ethnic minorities over-index in spending in some categories

Ethnic minorities present businesses with an important opportunity, too. Taking the United States as an example, the buying power for African American, Asian American and Native American consumers was estimated by the Selig Center (2021) at $3 trillion in 2020, up from $458 billion in 1990. The total buying power of the black community in the United States was $1.6 trillion in 2020, higher than the gross domestic product of Mexico, Spain or the Netherlands, and was projected to grow to $1.8 trillion by 2024, outpacing the growth of white buying power. The Asian American market, too, is growing briskly, with a buying power of $1.3 trillion, larger than the annual economic gross domestic product (GDP) of all but 13 countries, while the Hispanic market grew to $1.9 trillion in 2020, an increase of 87 per cent from 2010.

These communities are over-indexing in spending in certain categories. According to Nielsen (2019) research in the USA, African Americans are 20 per cent more likely than the total population to say they will 'pay extra for a product that is consistent with the image I want to convey' and that they shop at high-end stores, while black men are outpacing the total grooming market by 20 per cent.

Yet even though these communities tend to be more open to receiving advertising messages and their buying power continues to be on the rise, companies' investments to advertise to them have not been picking up – on the contrary. Although African Americans are more likely than the total population to agree that advertising provides meaningful information on most platforms, including mobile (42 per cent higher), television (23 per cent higher), radio (21 per cent higher) and the internet (18 per cent higher), advertising spend design to reach black consumers declined by 5 per cent between 2017 and 2018, according to Nielsen (2019).

Similar research in the United Kingdom by Blacklight (2022) shows that 'multi-ethnic' consumers (people from black, Asian, and other ethnic groups) have an annual disposable income of £4.5 billion which is being overlooked by major brands and businesses. These consumers are spending £230 million every month on health and beauty alone, yet nearly four in ten black female shoppers say it is not easy to find the products they need because of a lack of diversity in brands.

An overwhelming proportion of these consumers (93 per cent) think brands have a responsibility to feature diversity and inclusion compared to 74 per cent of those from a white background. For them, diversity in advertising is three times more important (24 per cent) than to white consumers (8 per cent), and they are around twice as likely as white consumers to favour and trust brands that are representative of different communities, have considered ethnic diversity in the creation of their products and services and have diverse staff in their stores and across the business. If a company or brand impressed them in some way, eight in ten (78 per cent) of multi-ethnic consumers would make a point of telling their friends about it, compared to 67 per cent of white consumers, while 59 per cent of black, Asian and multi-ethnic people say they are more likely to purchase products from a brand with an inclusive product range.

Yet the reality is that the way characters of colour are represented in ads continues to disappoint. In a survey commissioned by Facebook (2021b) through Ipsos of 1,200 people in Brazil, the United Kingdom and the United States, a majority (54 per cent) said they do not feel fully culturally represented in online advertising and most (71 per cent) expect brands to promote diversity and inclusion in their online advertising, with Latino and black Americans being 1.8 times more likely to say they see negative stereotypical representation in online ads.

LGBT+ positive advertising outperforms with allies

While screen time for characters of colour has been on the rise in the last few years, the LGBT+ community remains virtually non-existent in advertising, with less than 2 per cent of characters with a discernible sexual orientation in ads being LGBT+ against 10.0 per cent of people globally (Geena Davis Institute, 2019). Moreover, this community is much more likely to be featured in montage ads (43 per cent vs 32 per cent non-LGBT+) and brand-building ads than advertising a product or service (41 per cent less likely) or launching a new product (35 per cent less likely), as seen in Channel 4 (2019).

This data shows there is a great opportunity to further improve representation of the LGBT+ community in more intentional ways that feel less tokenistic and tick-box exercises, and the business case is unequivocal. A study by Hornet (2018) and Nielsen showed that purchase impact from LGBT+ themed ads is 44 per cent higher, and three out of four tested LGBT+ themed ads outperform generic ads in driving brand recall. Furthermore, it showed that 60 per cent of people exposed to LGBT+ themed ads labelled them as progressive and inclusive, and recommendation intent increased by 60 per cent among these.

Not only are progressive brands more positively perceived by the LGBT+ community, but allies said they feel better about brands that include LGBT+ people in ads. Research by GLAAD (2019) and P&G showed that non-LGBT+ people feel that companies that include LGBT+ people in ads are 'leaders in business' (69 per cent), 'committed to offering products to all types of customers' (85 per cent) and 'socially responsible' (75 per cent). The study also showed the impact of positive representation with 48 per cent of respondents who had been exposed to LGBT+ media in the past three months saying they have become more accepting, versus 35 per cent who had not been exposed.

The direct correlation with purchase intent was confirmed by the Center for Talent Innovation (2016), which showed that 71 per cent of LGBT+ respondents and 82 per cent of allies said they were more likely to purchase from a company that supported LGBT+ equality. Seventy-two per cent of allies also said that, all else being equal, they are more likely to accept a job at a company that is supportive of LGBT+ employees than one that is not supportive.

Age and the growth opportunity with the over 50s

People in their 50s and 60s are active, engaged and the top spenders in a host of categories: from household goods and services to new cars, from hotels abroad to eating out. It is estimated by Wunderman Thompson (2018) that the over 50s spend 42 per cent more on retail goods than other age groups, and 66 per cent more than Millennials. Their Women's Index study suggest that women over 50 control most of the purchase decisions in their households (78 per cent), and in more than half of the cases (55 per cent) they are the main breadwinner, too.

The growth opportunity is with the over-50s, yet 67 per cent say advertisers misunderstand them and only care about young people. According to the same research, women over 50 find advertising aimed at them 'patronizing' and 'stereotyped'; as a result, 72 per cent say they pay no heed to advertising. Nine out of ten say they would just like to be treated as a person, not a stereotype.

It is a known and acknowledged fact that the advertising industry has long been grappling with ageism, both in front of and behind the camera.

Despite some relative progress – the Unstereotype Alliance (2021) reports an improvement in the presence of women and men aged 40+ in ads, from about 10 per cent in 2020 to 20 per cent in 2021 – the issue still abounds, and the age bias is often more pronounced when it comes to female representation. For instance, an analysis by Google (2016) revealed that women portrayed in ads are likely to be in their 20s and 30s, while male characters are shown across age groups. Globally, male characters are an average of four years older than female characters in ads. Also, over the five years examined, the average age of female characters stayed relatively consistent, while male characters got older.

Clearly this must change, or brands will miss a golden opportunity.

The differently abled: A community bigger than China

Disability representation is almost entirely omitted on screen, except when it's focused on products that treat disabilities. In 2019 Cannes Lions ads, people with disabilities made up only 2.2 per cent of characters, well below the 19 per cent of people with disabilities globally, while according to 2021 research on US primetime advertising by Nielsen (2021) they were present in just 1 per cent of the ads examined. The same analysis showed that, of all the ad spend on primetime TV ads, just 3 per cent went to ads featuring disabled people or that were inclusive of disability themes in their creative. Of these, pharmaceuticals, healthcare treatments, devices and similar made up nearly 50 per cent of the total dollars spent in disability-inclusive ads, suggesting that advertising fails to portray this community in more nuanced ways that focus more on their unique attributes and personalities than simply on their disabilities.

Living with a disability is a reality for a huge part of the population, and a major opportunity lost for brands to contribute meaningfully to making this community feel more included, while at the same time growing the brand and the business.

Totalling an estimated 1.85 billion people globally, the disabled community is bigger than China and the European Union, and controls $1.9 trillion in annual disposable income (ROD Group, 2020). According to the American Institute for Research (AIR 2018), disability is the third-largest market segment in the United States, and it more than doubles when considering family members, caregivers and others who prioritize goods and services that are inclusive of people with disabilities. Work-age people with disabilities in the United States are worth about $490 billion, closer to the total disposable income of other market segments including African Americans ($501 billion) and Hispanics ($582 billion).

According to Purple (2020), a UK-based organization dedicated to reducing levels of inequality between disabled and non-disabled, businesses in the UK lose approximately £2 billion a month by ignoring the needs of disabled people. In the UK, the spending power of disabled people and their households – known as the Purple Pound – continues to increase and in 2020 was estimated to be worth £274 billion per year to UK business.

The time for change is now

Through the thousands of touch points they have with consumers each day, brands have an immense potential to shape popular culture and define how people see themselves and others in the world. By perpetuating outdated stereotypes or, on the contrary, by purposefully challenging norms and championing positive and progressive representations of people, advertising can have a huge impact in and on today's society.

For our future to be sustainable, brands must use their huge potential to enable, through content, a world where everyone has a voice – irrespective of their ethnicity, colour or race, sexual identity or preference, age, body shape, social background, physical or cognitive ability.

At the same time, doing good will also enable companies to do well and grow their business. As data from this chapter has shown, there is a huge potential gain from addressing different communities in ways which feel genuine and inclusive. At the same time, not doing so will have consequences for the brands' ability to operate long term. Despite all the good intention, research continues to show that we're not progressing fast enough as an industry – scaling diversity, at the end of the day, is not easy business, as all of those who have embarked on this journey will testify. However, we should be optimistic that, by discussing the challenge and the opportunities, we are getting closer to achieving our goal. Hopefully, this chapter will have provided some good arguments for why diverse and inclusive representation is a sine qua non for any brand's growth.

References

4As (2020) Consumers follow brand promises and focus on brand values. www.aaaa.org/consumers-follow-brand-promises-and-focus-on-brand-values/ (archived at https://perma.cc/G75S-HJ4D)

Adobe (2019) Despite 25 years of ad growth, diversity remains a challenge. https://business.adobe.com/blog/the-latest/despite-25-years-of-advertising-growth-diversity-remains-a-challenge (archived at https://perma.cc/GR5T-ZCMB)

AIR (2018) A hidden market: The purchasing power of working-age adults with disabilities. www.air.org/resource/report/hidden-market-purchasing-power-working-age-adults-disabilities (archived at https://perma.cc/S3K4-87TE)

ANA (2018) The gender equality measure, World Federation of Advertisers. https://wfanet.org/knowledge/diversity-and-inclusion/item/2018/12/07/The-Gender-Equality-Measure (archived at https://perma.cc/93YS-JXTZ)

Blacklight (2022) The black pound report 2922. www.backlight.uk/black-pound-report (archived at https://perma.cc/8NLD-6MPS)

Boston Consulting Group (2020) Managing the next decade of women's wealth. www.bcg.com/en-be/publications/2020/managing-next-decade-women-wealth (archived at https://perma.cc/7G4X-M9QU)

Center for Talent Innovation (2016) *Out in the World: Securing LGBT rights in the global marketplace.* www.talentinnovation.org/Research-and-Insights/pop_page.cfm?publication=1510 (archived at https://perma.cc/9KBW-N2FK)

Channel 4 (2019) Mirror on the industry. www.4sales.com/inclusioninsight (archived at https://perma.cc/PQY5-KN9X)

EY (2015) *Women: The next emerging market.* https://assets.ey.com/content/dam/
    ey-sites/ey-com/en_gl/topics/growth/WomenTheNextEmergingMarket.pdf
    (archived at https://perma.cc/Y4JX-PNF3)

Facebook (2021a) Diverse and inclusive representation in online advertising: An
    exploration of the current landscape and people's expectations. https://research.
    facebook.com/publications/diverse-and-inclusive-representation-in-online-
    advertising-an-exploration-of-the-current-landscape-and-peoples-expectations/
    (archived at https://perma.cc/RK5U-VJV3)

Facebook (2021b) The difference diversity makes to online advertising. www.
    facebook.com/business/news/insights/the-difference-diversity-makes-in-online-
    advertising (archived at https://perma.cc/RNM6-RE38)

Geena Davis Institute (2019) Bias and inclusion in advertising. https://seejane.org/
    research-informs-empowers/bias-inclusion-in-advertising/ (archived at https://
    perma.cc/A7JJ-WRMF)

GLAAD (2019) *LGBTQ Inclusion in Advertising and Media.* www.glaad.org/
    inclusion (archived at https://perma.cc/LJ32-DUYE)

Google (2016) Gender representation in film. www.thinkwithgoogle.com/feature/
    diversity-inclusion/ (archived at https://perma.cc/9B8W-L5C6)

Google (2019) What 2.7m YouTube ads reveal about gender bias in marketing.
    www.thinkwithgoogle.com/future-of-marketing/management-and-culture/
    diversity-and-inclusion/gender-representation-media-bias/ (archived at https://
    perma.cc/LL84-8BAT)

Hornet (2018) Brands should be embracing LGBTQ consumers, and this new
    research proves why. https://hornet.com/stories/lgbtq-themed-ads/ (archived at
    https://perma.cc/KRG8-TMCF)

Ipsos (2018) Advertising is out of sync with world's consumers. www.ipsos.com/
    en-us/news-polls/Advertising-out-of-sync-with-consumers (archived at https://
    perma.cc/6Y9P-VVCT)

Ipsos (2021) Women in advertising. www.ipsos.com/en-us/knowledge/media-
    brand-communication/women-advertising (archived at https://perma.cc/
    PQ63-U6LN)

JWT (2016) The Geena Davis Institute on gender in media and J. Walter Thompson
    present revealing findings about women's representation in advertising at
    Cannes Lions. https://seejane.org/gender-in-media-news-release/geena-davis-
    institute-gender-media-j-walter-thompson-present-revealing-findings-womens-
    representation-advertising-cannes-lions/ (archived at https://perma.cc/
    4D8D-49EL)

Nielsen (2019) It's in the bag: Black consumers' path to purchase. www.nielsen.
    com/us/en/insights/report/2019/its-in-the-bag-black-consumer-path-to-purchase/
    (archived at https://perma.cc/HU6G-9LGX)

Nielsen (2021) Visibility of disability: Portrayals of disability in advertising. www.nielsen.com/us/en/insights/article/2021/visibility-of-disability-portrayals-of-disability-in-advertising/ (archived at https://perma.cc/VV6J-RUZ5)

Purple (2020) The Purple Pound. https://wearepurple.org.uk/the-purple-pound-infographic (archived at https://perma.cc/9CXM-H8EW)

ROD Group (2020) Insights, Return on Disability. www.rod-group.com/insights (archived at https://perma.cc/SE94-EG9R)

Selig Center (2021) *Multicultural Economy 2021*, University of Georgia. https://news.uga.edu/selig-multicultural-economy-report-2021/ (archived at https://perma.cc/7RFZ-WR9S)

Silverstein, M J and Sayre, K (2009) The female economy, *Harvard Business Review*. https://hbr.org/2009/09/the-female-economy (archived at https://perma.cc/PES3-R5UE)

Unstereotype Alliance (2019) Empirical evidence based on the Unstereotype Metric. https://wfanet.org/knowledge/diversity-and-inclusion/item/2019/11/19/The-Unstereotype-Metric (archived at https://perma.cc/8FT7-5S33)

Unsterotype Alliance (2021) Unstereotype metric: 2021 key findings. www.unstereotypealliance.org/en/resources/research-and-tools/unstereotype-metric-2021-key-findings (archived at https://perma.cc/8UYH-KNPW)

Wunderman Thompson (2018) Elastic generation: The female edit. www.wundermanthompson.com/insight/elastic-generation-female-edit (archived at https://perma.cc/J34Z-A9CU)

04

A framework to deliver inclusive marketing

We've established some of the personal, societal and business reasons why inclusive marketing (or just better marketing) is worth pursuing, but the challenge then becomes how to effectively deliver it. In theory, our marketing processes have always been geared up to identifying business opportunities, understanding our consumers, and finding ways to communicate with and serve them, so surely, we should be being inclusive already. The reality of course is that more often than not our own unconscious bias, or other business-related practicalities, mean we don't quite get there.

In many cases the barrier is simply that we hadn't stopped to think about an opportunity for inclusion or hadn't had it pointed out to us that something we were doing might be excluding others accidentally. Of course, there are sometimes also active barriers and pushback against diversity and inclusion for a wide range of reasons, but being well prepared and informed throughout the process is also a way to overcome those challenges.

Working globally to shape industry best practice

Marketing is a complex and multi-stage process. At every stage, including but not limited to the communications we create, there are opportunities to better represent. We can all go on a journey from not considering diverse audiences to fairly representing them, or even purposefully driving action for change.

STAGE ONE

Inclusive briefing and strategy

1 Business and brand strategy

2 Strategic insights and data

3 Marketing and creative briefs

STAGE TWO

Inclusive planning

4 Partner and team selection

5 Creative development and product design

6 Consumer testing

STAGE THREE

Inclusive production

7 Production

8 Post-production

9 Localization

STAGE FOUR

Inclusive launches

10 Media and 360 activation

11 Launch and consumer response

12 Measuring success

Across the interviews in this book and through wider best practice that has been developed, there has been a consistent theme of the need for simple nudges, prompts and critical questions that we can ask ourselves, to help us navigate this process in an open and inclusive way.

As a World Federation of Advertising Diversity Ambassador, I co-chair the WFA Diversity Task Force. This is a group of like-minded individuals from across many of the world's top advertisers who have come together to share and develop best practices to help move the industry forward. Active members that have as a result contributed thoughts and guidance to this book include Diageo, Mars, Ikea, Danone, Unilever, P&G, Reckitt, McDonald's, Haleon, Beam Suntory, Ferrero, First Bank Nigeria, L'Oreal, LEGO, Philips, and many more. We also have members from some of the major agency groups and leadership from UN Women and other national marketing associations.

In 2021 this task force developed an open-source guide to potential areas of bias across the creative process. It broke the creative process down into 12 key stages, broadly clustered in four phases, that walk us through step by step. At each stage there are key opportunities and things to watch out for, and a range of specific questions to ask yourself.

This book builds on this framework, fleshes out each of these stages and brings them to life with further advice and experience from across the marketing industry. For each stage we'll try to unpack and explain both the challenges and the opportunities as they present themselves to marketers.

Building inclusion into every step of the marketing process

The figure opposite shows the inclusive marketing framework and potential areas of bias across the creative process.

The framework starts, as the marketing process always should, with the briefing phase. This begins by truly understanding your business and brand challenge, and what your strategy is to grow or develop moving forwards. Good marketers turn at this point to strategic insights and data, to look at what you already know about your business and consumers and what else you need to find out. Ultimately, this turns into a brief, whether that's for a creative and promotional solution, or perhaps a bigger marketing challenge to consider your product, pricing or physical place and sales strategy.

What follows is a phase we think of as planning, when most discussion around what to actually do takes place. Typically that starts with agency and partner selection, though of course it might be about setting up an internal team or task force that is going to help solve it. Then comes the actual ideation and creative development, the opportunity to craft what you think will work as a solution to the task at hand. There may then be some form of pre-testing or sign off that needs to take place, which could be sophisticated research or might just be a leadership meeting where you need to convince some of your peers.

Then it comes to production and making your marketing come to life. We'll explore this largely as if your brief has led you to a creative and communications route, though this could be the point at which you need to start producing or rethinking your product itself, and indeed there are some powerfully inclusive innovations available through design. The advertising production and post-production process is a hectic one, often against a tough timeline, during which a range of temporary partners and experts are often called in. This unfortunately leaves a lot of opportunities for inclusion to be squeezed out. For those working in truly global teams there are then many cases in which a campaign will need to be localized for different markets, and tough decisions to be made on what is appropriate or not for each.

Finally it comes to putting your campaign, product or new initiative live, but you aren't quite done yet. Your media and 360 activation approach is a huge opportunity to either reach and fund diverse voices, or accidentally exclude and defund, or worse yet see your advertising dollars funding hate speech. When you do get your solutions out into the wild it's a great time to celebrate with your colleagues and partners, but it can also be an important point to listen to and respond to consumer feedback. Ultimately, like any marketing activity, you'll want to understand the effectiveness of it and the return on investments you have made, and you'll want to unpack what a difference being inclusive has made to your business. None of this is easy, but we hope this book will nudge and guide you along the steps that start to make it possible.

What inclusive marketing best practice actually looks like

An inevitable question that comes up is 'What does good inclusive marketing look like?' That's a surprisingly tricky question to answer and one that different people will give you different answers to – throughout this book different marketers point to examples of representation and inclusion that have stood out to them personally as best practice. The consistent theme is that inclusive marketing is not just about putting slightly more diverse people in otherwise unchanged communications; it's really a mindset shift that might sometimes be hard to detect from the outside but can really open up new business opportunities and naturally more casual inclusion.

There are examples of inclusive marketing that are very deliberate in their diversity and representation, and these are what people typically think of. Very deliberate casting decisions, storytelling or even issue-based campaigning certainly are examples of inclusive marketing, but there can be a range of subtler approaches built on inclusive thinking and by diverse teams in the background.

A good test of how inclusive your marketing thinking really is would be to look at how well that thinking pulls through to all touch points – it's great to celebrate a disabled person in your main TV ad, but are you also featuring casual representation in your social communications or addressing visual accessibility in your e-commerce assets? Have you considered whether your packaging or retail experience offers any physical barriers to access in itself? Is even your TV advert truly inclusive if you haven't considered subtitles, audio description soundtracks, or how to avoid visual effects that can be triggering to some neural conditions?

If that all sounds a bit too much to consider, don't worry. Inclusive marketing has to start somewhere and the simple answer is that that means with you. At the heart of this approach is a challenge to build and practise our empathy to better listen to, understand and respond to viewpoints other than our own. This book aims to nudge you forward at some points, and you might want to be especially careful that your own bias isn't putting you back in auto pilot.

If this new 'inclusive marketing' process all sounds a bit familiar then you're not wrong – the process is just a good, thorough process that any marketer should go through. Professor Mark Ritson's Mini MBA in Marketing has a strong reputation for teaching marketing essentials, and it walks through somewhat similar stages to the early parts of this framework – market orientation, market research, segmentation, targeting, positioning and ultimately objectives. Such thorough groundwork will set you up for success as you work through this inclusive process, and inclusive thinking can help you get out of your own bubble at each step.

Ritson would be quick to point out that the actual output of such a marketing process is more than just the communications you create, but also the approach you take to your product, your price and your distribution strategy. This book focuses more on the communications side because this is where inclusion is most visible, but you should always consider the opportunities across those other pillars too. It felt only right, however, to interview him and get his deeper perspective on the topic.

MARKETER IN FOCUS
Mark Ritson, Professor of Marketing and business consultant

Professor Mark Ritson is a seasoned business professional who has dedicated his career to trying to improve the standard of marketing, and has not been afraid to call out and challenge things that he finds an unhelpful distraction. He's been critical of some brands' blunt attempts at injecting 'purpose' into their work and sees it as a strategic choice that makes sense in some categories but perhaps not in others. I spoke to him to understand what he thinks makes for good inclusive marketing and how we can find the right balance in the industry, and learnt some unexpected things about his own past studying gay subcultures.

Q: Why does representation and inclusion in marketing matter to you?

A: It matters on a couple of levels. Personally, I'm not politically correct, if I can use that word. I obviously don't want to hurt anyone's feelings, but I don't posture on this topic. I do, however, think it's super-important we take it seriously in marketing and there are a couple of reasons.

First there's a direct reason for me which is that it's just bad business not to represent the consumers that are out there in the marketing that we're building around them. It's just bad business not to reflect those people in an appropriate manner.

It may surprise you to know but I did a lot of work with the gay subcultures of the 1990s and it has had a big effect on me. I did my PhD in qualitative ethnographic research into brand advertising and when I first got to America I had an opportunity to get a research grant. One of my biggest passions was to study how both gay and lesbian subcultures took brand names like Häagen-Dazs and Nike, and turned them into Fagen-Dazs and Dike in the mid 1990s. They sold these brands as T-shirts. I went on four or five different gay Pride marches and essentially photographed the people that created these T-shirts and talked to them about why they were doing it, and why they thought it was popular. They all told me essentially the same story, which was that they were not represented in the mainstream advertising brand narrative and yet we buy their products so screw them, we're going to create our own version.

Back then I wasn't really interested and looking for the gay representation and diversity point, I was just curious as to why they were messing with brand identity, but I stumbled upon gay culture in some very interesting places.

As an aside it was one of the big changing points in my life because in New York Pride I got hit on. Believe it or not, I was quite fit when I was younger, and it was interesting to understand what it was like. I felt quite vulnerable that week because there are these big bears, and they don't mean anything bad by it at all, but I was outnumbered and outsized by seven or eight giant men.

They're only messing around but it's very good for straight, white men who don't know what it's like to feel suddenly surrounded by bigger and more powerful people. It was such an important moment to have the shoe on the other foot and to realize what some people must unfortunately feel and experience in mainstream culture all the time.

One of the results of white male privilege, which I do think exists, is that we just don't appreciate on a Saturday night walking home that, whilst no one is one hundred per cent safe, our vulnerabilities are almost zero compared to other people in the community for various reasons.

It was this gay Pride research that really brought home to me the first point, which is, if you're going to target consumers you have to explicitly represent them, or they get pissed off and they don't want to buy from you.

The second reason, which is almost more important is that the indirect impact of advertising on stereotypes, is incredibly pernicious. Again, when I was doing my PhD, my tutor was a complete Marxist and he made me read all kinds of stuff. Judith Williamson was one of the great early advertising critics of the 1980s; what she pointed out brilliantly was that when an advert shows, say, a woman choosing one cleaning powder over another, consumers have a filter up that says, 'I know this is an ad, I know you're trying to convince me brand A is better than brand B so therefore I will use my perceptual resources to screen that out.' Like a Trojan horse, however, while you're screening out the brands, the representation of the woman doing the cleaning and the complete absence of a man seeps into your perception of sex and gender roles and everything else.

So that's why representation is so important to me – because it's good business sense and because I think advertising has a responsibility for its influence on reinforcing stereotypes.

Q: How do we start to show more inclusion without jumping to new stereotypes?

A: We're probably the only profession that really should be pretty good at this, it's essentially our jobs. You've got to be able to segment the market, and then represent the different shards of that market appropriately.

It's easy, of course, to go wrong. In the classic sense we can just show the stereotypical, traditional, nuclear, straight, white family but it's clearly a mistake to always do that because the world doesn't look like that anymore.

We can also go too far the other way and we can kind of overstate diversity, which is a great intention but at the same time can often stop the audience from identifying with our work. We do have to acknowledge that's another issue – if we kept showing, hypothetically, just gay consumers we might be doing a great job of portraying and legitimizing gay identity which is marvellous, but we may not be doing a great job of inspiring all our other consumers. They aren't homophobic, they just don't see themselves there.

There's another mistake where brands have gone too far, and we've seen it a lot in sentimental Christmas adverts, where there's a big push for a certain kind of family which is made up of every ethnicity and is an amalgam of every possible diversity. I don't think that answers the challenge because no one recognizes that family either.

The answer comes back to good old-fashioned segmentation. You can't represent everyone, but you've got to be nuanced enough to be able to explore. There's nothing better than having a gay couple as one of four or five executions, and we don't even need to make a big deal about that. Casual legitimization of having a gay couple, and all the different strands of the market, and just moving on with the story is the way to do it. You cannot represent everyone every time but if we truly understand our market in each case, we can cover the spectrum appropriately over time.

Q: What role does 'purpose' play in building inclusive brands?

A: There's a big question and it's a strategic question, which is, 'Do I want to position my brand around purpose?' Where I get angry is that in the industry, we seem to either have people who just dismiss purpose completely, or more commonly people that say without purpose your brand will not succeed and will cease to exist in the twenty-first century.

Clearly, both of those points of view are wrong, and so the answer is somewhere in the middle. Brands must make the choice of whether they position themselves to the consumer on a more purposeful impact or not.

Brands can be purpose-driven and not use it as a public positioning, and not having a purpose positioning doesn't mean you are evil.

When I've written about this, I've used the example of the café chain Pret a Manger, who for years have given away sandwiches at the end of the day to homeless shelters, without making a big deal about it. They don't position on that, they don't talk much about it, because it's not that useful to them from a marketing point of view, but they still do the right thing. They've chosen to position on organic and fresh, and not on feeding the homeless, which is legitimate. You can be a positive and inclusive brand without needing to position yourself around a purpose.

Black Lives Matter, for me, was a very important moment for society, but a poor moment for marketing. I thought the idea of every brand blacking out their logo was a bit pathetic – it felt like tokenism, and it allows them to get out of the fact that they're not actually doing anything. I wrote an article about it where I went through all the companies that had blacked out their logos and found more or less zero people of colour at the executive level across the board. If Black Lives Matter then never mind about your logo, hire someone of colour in your senior management team. Many of them were sportswear brands, and I don't understand how they got this far into the twenty-first century with an executive board team that looks like a country club.

Overall, I'm not a huge fan of 'purpose' and a lot of the time it's rubbish, but there are examples such as Dove where it's been brilliantly thought through and applied successfully.

Q: How do marketers ensure they are thinking outside of their bubbles during the marketing process?

A: This is where diversity and inclusion align very nicely with marketing. If you're well trained, you know we begin with market orientation, which tells us that the fundamental starting point for all marketing is realizing you are not the consumer. I train marketers to start by understanding their personal opinion is worthless, and it's actually dangerous to be misled by it. You must get rid of that and then we can turn to research to understand the point of view of the real market in its full diversity.

When you see marketing that way then the answer to your challenge is straightforward, which is that a good, well-trained marketer should drop their own preconceptions and biases as part of the marketing process. They've been trained not to have their own perspective but to allow the data and the market to dictate how they see the world.

Now, that all sounds great, but the reality is that, if you could put a number on it, I would say significantly less than 5 per cent of marketers are properly trained to a level where they not only understand market orientation but can apply it in their approaches. In theory we should be good at this, but in practice our own opinions and perspectives infiltrate our decisions. That's bad from a marketing perspective, and it's also bad from the point of view of diversity where our own biases get in the way.

Q: How important do you think it is that we improve the diversity of our industry itself and how can we achieve that?

A: I think it is slowly starting to happen. Personally the only place where I'm not a beneficiary of the lottery in life is in being very working class. I come from what is currently ranked by a very long way as the worst secondary school in England. Here in the advertising industry, private schools remain massively dominant. I saw the absence of people from my background at senior levels of marketing. When I occasionally met someone in the creative industries from a 'poor' background, who discovered I also was, it was always quite touching and surprising.

Clearly, when you look at marketing departments and advertising agencies, they don't look like the markets we serve, and to some degree we do have to fix that. We still have a fundamental problem with gender diversity, which is one I would highlight. At the ground level of most marketing departments and advertising agencies it's predominantly female, but it's equally clear that when we get to the top women are almost completely absent.

That must be something we focus on. I'm not saying that we should ignore the other elements of inclusivity, but it's just so incredibly obvious in almost every company, and it doesn't seem to be changing very much. Targets are a part of that, but understanding the issues and making real changes is what really needs to happen.

Speaking as a straight, middle-aged, white male, Black Lives Matter pushed me to realize that it wasn't enough just to be generally supportive. I would class myself as someone who has been supportive to women, to the LGBT+ community and to others over the years, but then again who would argue against that? I wasn't actually attempting to do anything practical about it, and it struck me that it's not enough for those of us in that position just to be generally supportive, we have to overtly push a bit more. If you're not part of the solution you're probably part of the problem.

Q: What's your advice to the next generation for how to be a great inclusive marketer in the future?

A: I'm pretty optimistic about the state of youth, in the sense that I think that there is such a difference between the environment when we grew up. That new generation is not perfect, but I think they're very different and I wouldn't worry too much that they would get the inclusion part wrong. I think they come in naturally pre-loaded to be more representative and to think more across the different lines of communities that I think many of us ignored in the past – in that sense younger people come pre-loaded with a much healthier approach to diversity.

In terms of becoming great at marketing, my advice is to hook up with a decent company. I like training in marketing of some kind. I may be in the minority in our discipline, but I truly believe training makes you better. That can happen at university, or it can happen at the company you work at, if you work for a good company. Companies like Unilever or Google are going to put you through that process and you're going to learn on the job.

When you look at a good CMO, they're no smarter or more political than others, but what they've been doing throughout their career is learning from their work – they've almost become their own teacher. When you look at others in their fifties that haven't gone as high, they didn't spend the previous 30 years learning and putting it all together.

That's what I'd always say to our next generation – come and get training, but also then become your own trainer and learn from experience.

PART TWO

Stage one

Inclusive briefing and strategy

STAGE ONE

Inclusive briefing and strategy

1. Business and brand strategy
2. Strategic insights and data
3. Marketing and creative briefs

STAGE TWO

Inclusive planning

4. Partner and team selection
5. Creative development and product design
6. Consumer testing

STAGE THREE

Inclusive production

7. Production
8. Post-production
9. Localization

STAGE FOUR

Inclusive launches

10. Media and 360 activation
11. Launch and consumer response
12. Measuring success

05

Business and brand strategy

Let's start at the very beginning – a very good place to start.

Every piece of marketing starts, one way or another, with a brief. Sometimes that can be a detailed, multi-page document and presentation, sometimes it might be a quick telephone call or a throwaway comment to a colleague. One way or another, you kick off your marketing thinking or creative process and as you do so there are powerful ways to be open minded and inclusive, and easy ways to accidentally cut out representation before you've even started.

Regardless of the inclusive marketing opportunity, the art of a good brief is one that can take a whole career to master. A brief sets up the direction of your project and thinking, it lays out the boundaries that your solutions need to fall between, and ultimately it can inspire those working with you on it.

I've been in far too many forgettable briefing sessions in my time, but also some wonderful, memorable ones that stand out to this day. Briefs where the team has really brought the brand and business challenge to life, when it practically feels like the consumer is in the room with you, and where everyone around you cannot wait to get started on big-picture solutions. Challenge yourself on how you brief. Be visual, be creative, be inspiring, and above all be inclusive.

Yet, good marketing starts ahead of the brief with your business and brand strategy. There's an art to marketing but also a science, and we know that brands grow by expanding their penetration into greater numbers of relatively light purchasing consumers, and that heavier consumers grow in numbers at the same time. We know the people we want to sell to have far bigger things on their minds, and it's thus a marketer's ambition to make sure they're mentally available in their consideration set, and then physically available when they look to make a purchase online or in the real world.

You can play with these building blocks to shape a meaningful and realistic business challenge, but we can also look to the audiences and communities that we might otherwise have forgotten and see where the new business opportunities are.

The best strategies are both backed up and genuinely informed by insights and data. In some businesses you will be lucky enough to have dedicated research teams and budgets to commission your own investigations, in others you'll have to make use of publicly available data points. Yet remember that even data can carry a bias depending on the questions you ask, the people you ask and how you present it. Any attempts to look at average consumers, whilst in many ways practically necessary, can limit our understanding of the rich diversity amongst them.

Sometimes we bring our own stereotypes to the brief, or fail to inspire with our intent or our insight. In this part of the book we'll learn how to try to avoid these mistakes and again we will hear from a range of global marketing leaders about why representation matters and how to elevate all of our work.

Inclusive marketing as a business strategy

We've established that inclusive marketing can just mean 'better marketing', and that as such it can lead to new business and brand opportunities. The question, of course, is whether you can find them in your category. Whilst putting more diverse people in your adverts may make them stand out in some ways, it is not true inclusive marketing thinking unless it is underpinned by real insight, strategy and authenticity.

More progressive and inclusive brands have been shown to perform better, and all brands can positively reflect and engage a broader range of consumers. Despite handfuls of loud objectors, the good news is that a majority of people are broadly quite open-minded and tolerant, and respond positively to inclusive marketing, but this still isn't a business insight in itself.

The real question to start asking ourselves is, what steps are we taking to make sure our brand is accessing all the diverse opportunities for growth? Where are there underserved communities that we could better serve and engage, and in doing so create a competitive advantage?

Any strategy is as much about what you will focus on as what you will not. In marketing we have limited time and limited resources, and so that focus is essential, and naturally we always look for the biggest groups and easiest audiences to achieve that. Inclusive marketing doesn't necessarily change that, and it's unrealistic to suggest that marketing processes should attempt to individually cater for every imaginable subset of people. That said, it is easy to ask ourselves a question about who we are excluding when we define our audience and to look into whether there are potential business opportunities there. It's perfectly reasonable to define a business challenge that talks to a core mass audience but also considers how to appeal and meet the needs of key groups outside of that.

Another key business opportunity is to dig into the changing dynamics of the category that you work in. Perhaps you have a strong understanding of your current consumer, but how are you planning for changing and emerging consumer bases? It's not unreasonable to assume that in most industries your audience will be getting older, but marketing has a historic tendency to exclude or overlook older consumers in favour of younger or more 'glamorous' alternatives. In other cases, there will be subcultures and new demographics redefining how your product is used, or growing in penetration at a far greater rate than your established core audience.

Sometimes, inclusive marketing is about casual representation and simple authentic storytelling, but we know it can also be about deliberate championing of diversity and sustainability. Are there causes and opportunities that are close to the hearts of your consumers, and opportunities to be a champion within that space? The historical existence of dedicated LGBT+ nightlife spaces have, for instance, long since created opportunities for brands willing to really go above and beyond in supporting those communities, and to be recognized for doing so.

The trick is in truly understanding your own brand and the territories it can meaningfully play in. If you've never actively explored diversity and inclusion before it may not be authentic for you to suddenly claim to be a social justice campaigner, but for most brands there are small and purposeful steps that you can take. For example, Cadbury has found ways to support and represent older consumers by encouraging simple conversations over a bar of chocolate, and Arial challenged biased assumptions around who should do household chores with its #ShareTheLoad campaign.

If you're looking to take a bolder step around actively championing inclusion then you need to make sure your business is ready to go on that journey with you. You can be called out as performative if you make grand gestures with your advertising that are not matched by your corporate actions, and even the most successful inclusive campaigns can draw criticism from angry keyboard warriors. You need to get your senior stakeholders sold into the business opportunity and the possibilities it may lead to right from the start – there's no point in exploring wonderfully inclusive marketing concepts if ultimately you know they'll be shot down by the board at the last minute. Save everyone's time and effort, and drive that alignment from the very start.

Exactly how you need to approach those senior stakeholders can vary hugely depending on the nature of your business and the attitudes they currently hold. Many will already be supportive of the agenda but keen to understand what role they can play in driving it, or they may not have realized some of the steps the business needs to take. Others might be more cautious or actively resistant, in which case you'll need to consider how to educate and challenge them. Many organizations have a wider D&I strategy you can point towards and align with, or host wider inclusion events which you could use to land a message around the importance of representation. If no one else is driving this in your business, consider how you can start making the case for change, perhaps using some of the statistics found earlier in this book.

CHECKLIST

Business and brand strategy

Key questions to ask yourself:

1 Who is your audience? Who is excluded? Are they a potential business opportunity?

2 Does your audience reflect the emerging consumer base for the category?

3 Is there a deliberate diversity and sustainability opportunity for your brand?

4 What's the next credible but authentic step forward your brand can take?

5 Is your business willing to stand up for what's right and truly reflect your consumers?

6 Are senior stakeholders bought in?

MARKETER IN FOCUS

Jessica Spence, President of Brands at Beam Suntory

The WFA's internal research has consistently shown that diversity and inclusion is a CMO priority, and rightly so – these senior marketing leaders understand the business opportunity that comes from truly meeting diverse consumer needs. With that in mind, I spoke to Jessica Spence from Beam Suntory, and my boss at the time of writing, to understand her personal journey in this space, and her advice for others as they start this process.

Jessica is a global alcohol industry veteran, having worked for almost two decades in a career spanning SABMiller, Carlsberg and now the premium spirits and whisky company Beam Suntory. During that time, she has worked in Central and Eastern Europe, led a regional business unit across 14 Asian markets and now runs a new global marketing team out of New York.

Q: Why does representation matter to you?

A: It is a little bit of an over-used phrase, but I feel very strongly about the idea that you can't be what you can't see. Oddly, I was born at a time in the UK where a lot of the earliest political leaders I remember seeing were female, and that really shaped what I thought I could do.

When I look back at my childhood, I always believed I could be Prime Minister, but I didn't believe I could be a business leader. Whether I agreed with her politically or not, for the first nearly ten years of my conscious life I had that very strong female Prime Minister figure there. It really hit home to me when I was in my teens, and I was thinking about why I felt certain things are kind of off the table.

As you know, I've been in the alcohol industry now for quite a long time and what really hit me was that there were no female models for me. I have been more than 15 years across beer and now spirits, and I was looking for them inside or outside of my industry, but the dearth of women at the top really made me question whether I could make it myself. I also worried that if there was to be a space for me whether I had to change myself to fit into it, and I would love for people coming up through the industry not to feel that.

I think representation in media, but also representation within companies, is critical because of the level of self-doubt you put on yourself if you don't see that representation. The level of questioning you do, and the negative energy that that sucks, and that you could be putting into just being brilliant. I think it is really detrimental.

I was reflecting on the media and marketing representation I had seen recently and I ended up thinking of something that's not necessarily an advertising story, but I thought was phenomenal. As most people did, I had rather a quiet few months during Covid, and therefore the TV show *Strictly Come Dancing* took over my life (that's the UK edition of *Dancing With The Stars*). I say that without shame, because that season of shows was fantastically interesting.

Two of the couples competing in the final really stood out – in one pairing the celebrity was deaf, and the other was the first same sex couple to have got through to the final. It was really the first time that you'd seen that represented, and it was inspiring watching the show. The commentary was aware of that representation but ultimately still so focused on the quality of the work they were doing. It wasn't tokenistic. They didn't say 'Oh, aren't they doing well!' It was genuine. They did brilliantly, and everyone was in love with the dancing and the art they were creating. It was a real moment, after a rather grim year it was a moment that lifted me and that made me feel a bit of hope.

Q: How does this come together in your mind to be the business case for this kind of inclusion?

A: When you start thinking about inclusion, there are two ways into it. There is a values-led way into it, and there is a very pragmatic business way into it, and I think both are valid and both are important.

The start of it for me comes back to consumer centricity and empathy. I think great brands and great marketers build through empathy at a very deep level. One of the things that has always amazed me is how a lot of marketing doesn't teach you to go deep into who might you be talking to. How might that person be different? We jump very quickly, because it makes our life simple, to the shortcuts and to the stereotypes because it's just easier.

So many times, you look at the brief and think, there's a ton of assumptions in there about who is consuming and, critically, who's buying. I think who's buying often gets completely missed. I remember having been in a new market for about six weeks and they came to me with this great project of 'What do women want?' They were seriously briefing me on 50 per cent of the population, and they thought that was a smart brief. On one level I like the ambition, but what you miss in that is what you find when you start digging down and getting specific about the consumer journey and the shopper journey.

You can break all those preconceptions down. You know they were coming at it from a perspective that women don't like beer and women don't buy beer, but what we showed them was that women are doing a lot of the buying. Whether they're consuming it is a separate question, but in their brief they haven't even gone far enough to think about that mindset. If your bias is making you miss stuff that's that basic, and you're jumping to so many big assumptions, you really need to question whether you're good at marketing full stop. Regardless of the inclusivity angle, you're probably not doing great marketing here because you're not having empathy. You're not having that sense of curiosity.

I think recognizing that the audience you're talking to is much broader than you think it is and is much more varied is so important. Getting to that basic realization that the shopper and the consumer can be completely different people, or the same person in a completely different mind-set. That's a useful trick to break down some of that preconception.

One of the things that I was proud of within our team, which they did without prompting, was a big piece of work on demand spaces. They went away and they unpacked every demand space for a bunch of different audiences. For example, 21- to 25-year-old Hispanic men on the US West Coast versus African American women in the south. They took something as fundamental as 'treat myself' – that's a big space, what people are treating themselves for, what they think of as a reward. What merits that, why do they need it, what kind of pressure are they facing at work? It was stunning analysis, and it really informed our business thinking. It didn't give us a tokenistic piece of diversity work to point out, but it gave us the realization that the campaign that we were going to generate was going to have to be much more multi-dimensional. We ended up with a range of articulations that fitted those motivations. It was the first example I had ever seen of people getting inclusion in right at the beginning.

Q: How do you and your teams manage inclusive marketing thinking across such a diverse and global business?

A: It sounds very simple, but I think the first key step is honing that skill of empathy. I believe empathy is a skill. Yes, there are some people who are perhaps more naturally empathetic than others, but it is something you can train. The training for that level of curiosity, that ability to put yourself in somebody else's shoes and look at it from different perspectives lies at the heart of good brand building, and at the heart of good business.

I think as a business leader you cannot lead an organization unless you really understand how everyone in that organization is feeling about it. I think some organizations see that as soft but you have to be deliberate with empathy. It's critical and it is a hard skill, but it is one that I think needs to be trained and treated as a core functional skill.

You're never going to be able to make sure that somebody in the room has had every experience. Of course it matters, it is good to have a much more multicultural team, but it is never going to be truly representative of every group, or have all the insight into that group, or to be the complete voice of that group. I've had arguments over this with somebody who said global brands wouldn't have made certain mistakes if they'd had an African American or Chinese consumer in the room. You cannot put all that pressure on one person, though, it must be across the group. Every single person in that room must have the empathy and the training to be comfortable thinking about it from different perspectives. How's that going to show up? How's that going to make people feel? You cannot make it one person's responsibility simply because they are from that group.

I think one of the biggest things is how you show up, how you ask questions, and how you express curiosity. I've been working with a diversity coach here at Beam Suntory and one of the most powerful questions is, 'Have you ever had the conversation with your team?' To say, 'What is the one thing I don't know about you that I'm not really leveraging right now for the business?'

It's an interesting question and it opens a different space, and I think as you go through your day-to-day the most basic level up is to open space for everyone. Create space to share different experience and to have it accepted, because it often blows your mind in terms of what you get. You should spend a lot of your time being slightly scared by what people are telling you – that's a very healthy state to be in. It makes our jobs a lot more exciting. I'm a big proponent of nudges and how you constantly weave curiosity, open-mindedness, and acceptance into the start of your team meeting, the start of your briefing process, the start of your agency selection process. Just constantly signalling to the world that I want to learn. I'm not you. I haven't walked in your shoes, but I'd love to know a bit more about it. It should also be fine for people not to share when they don't want to.

I think, particularly in some markets, business becomes very transactional, and opening up the space for people to express becomes even more important. What you then get out of them in terms of creativity and, when you get further into business issues, their willingness to put something forward, their willingness to come to you, because you've signalled you're open may surprise you. Being open to difference is so much better, and you get better results. You get better creativity, better thinking, better challenges, and I really believe it's the combination of those very small things and then big nuts-and-bolt targets and goals.

06

Strategic insights and data

Empathy is a skill that consistently comes up when you ask people what it takes to be a great inclusive marketer. It's a key skill that helps you get outside your own biases and truly into the minds of the consumers. If, however, empathy is an engine, then insights and data are the raw materials and resources you need to fuel it.

How are you ensuring that your strategy is grounded in diverse consumer insight? All too often, our bias can get in the way, and it's impossible for us to truly understand all the nuances of diverse audiences. Data is here to help inform and justify our strategic decisions, and to make sense of very complex consumer and competitive environments. Yet, as mentioned before, data itself is not without bias, and how it is collected and presented can tell radically different stories.

It is important to the marketing process to find ways of simplifying our understanding of our consumers, and to steer our creative development towards a core target audience. It's common in many businesses to create 'pen portraits' of our ideal consumers, perhaps even with specific names and elaborate life stories. In practice they tend to be somewhat cooler, younger and almost certainly more affluent than your real average consumer is likely to be, but there's nothing wrong per se with aspirational thinking.

It is, however, worth stopping to think about the bias that can easily surround the narratives, mood boards and visualizations you choose to use. Are you ultimately always choosing people who look and sound quite a lot like you, that you find it easy to relate to and understand? A key skill of all good marketing is realizing that, more often than not, you are far from being the target customer. Could bringing in some more diverse imagery, or perhaps defining a couple of different target consumers, open wider creative avenues and squeeze more creative and inclusive ideas out of the process?

There is huge variation in your consumers, and so whilst generalizations are helpful, how have you managed to also bring in some more nuanced insights and understanding? If you do find these personas helpful, have you also created space in the brief for capturing some of the more unexpected insights that may have come up in research or focus groups? Have you stumbled upon unusual attitudes towards or use cases for your products that exist amongst certain audiences? It's well worth finding a parking space to keep these alive throughout the ideation that will follow.

Bringing inclusion into brand tracking and research

Do you truly understand how your brand is perceived within representative targets? Brand tracking is tricky and expensive work, and is unlikely to get into much nuanced demographic distinctions unless you really push for it, but consumers of different ages, classes or other backgrounds can have a starkly different understanding or interest in your brands. The modern digital world of targeted media means these aren't just challenges but opportunities; if different communities have different expectations or understandings of you, then think about how your communications could move them forward in different ways too. Outside your own brand, are there cultural tensions and category dynamics that are unique to different audiences, and if you're working across multiple markets how do these show up differently in each?

There's a fundamental challenge here to the market research industry and our colleagues in insights teams around how we eradicate some of the bias that creeps in at the sources of our data. Companies do their best to capture broad demographics in their research, but there are practical realities that affect people's willingness and flexibility to be involved in research projects, which means many groups will be under-represented unless you really push, and perhaps pay, for them to be properly brought in. Research is designed to find common trends, themes and uniting insights that are powerful, but the process is also a rich treasure trove of inclusive marketing stimuli and insights, if you allow it to be.

If you're considering work that tries to talk to or represent specific groups, then look even more carefully at how they are represented in your research and consider working with specialist partners who can truly help you get under their skin. There are fantastic organizations out there that can tap into their networks to form focus groups, do research, or even analyse the trends found in the media titles serving diverse audiences. The best intentions can be negatively interpreted if you don't take the time to understand the real dynamics within communities and especially to understand any stereotyping concerns that may have been issues in the past.

CHECKLIST
Strategic insights and data

Key questions to ask yourself:

1 Is there any bias in research used to gather insight?

2 Does the data capture representative perspectives or just broad generalizations?

3 How are consumer 'pen portraits' or mood boards depicted/visualized?

4 Have you managed to capture nuance and avoid generalization?

5 What are the perceptions of your brand within representative targets?

6 What do you know about the cultural tensions and audience in each active market?

7 Are stereotyping concerns tested with the affected group?

8 Have you engaged experts who can help advise on how specific audiences might positively or negatively interpret your intentions?

MARKETER IN FOCUS
Christopher Kenna, Founder and Global CEO of Brand Advance Group

Christopher Kenna took an unusual route into marketing, having served in the British Army and with the UK Special Forces, before working in media as a TV presenter. He's become an outspoken voice for diversity in the industry, and in particular a champion for the hundreds of diverse media owners that his company works with and represents. They work closely with those media titles to find new ways of bringing the nuanced insights marketers need to start on this inclusive journey.

Q: Why does representation matter to you?

A: I always want to ask, why wouldn't it matter? The obvious personal reason is I'm sat here as a black guy, and then the not so obvious reason is that I'm sat here as a black gay guy. I have two kids, where one is black and one is white, and I've watched the world be different to both of them even though they should be side by side in life.

I looked at the world through the unprivileged nature of some of the things I've just listed and at times the privilege of the exact same things. It's a privilege to work in such a powerful industry as advertising, and we need to make tomorrow better than today because there's so much to get fixed. Brands and advertising have a great responsibility because they can really help to do that.

Q: Can you think of some good examples of representation you've seen recently?

A: I see examples every day, but some of the most powerful inclusive marketing work is done behind the scenes. We worked with GSK and their Centrum brand to help them close an insight gap in countries including the UK, Italy and Saudi Arabia. They asked us to really explore the different communities that live in these countries and tell GSK what these communities really think about the product and healthcare – to find three key cultural insights, three intersectional insights and three media insights that work for these communities around their product. That's not just informing an advert they're making, it's much more widely informing their strategy, their product and their go to market approach.

We also made a film with GSK for their Advil brand in Brazil. It used a famous, MTV Award winning, drag queen called Lia Clark and it's a beautiful film. I love everything about it but especially the process that we went through to make it. Right from the briefing, the team gave us this overarching sense of what they wanted to do, but gave us real freedom to interpret. Freedom to listen to the community, to interpret the brief in an inclusive way and to tell a story that Advil may not have told in that region before. It helped them to authentically engage a community they may not have fully reached before.

There's also the Nike 'Own the Floor' campaign that I think really showcases the nuances of culture. It's showing different body sizes and shapes dancing and making the point that Nike clothes are made for anyone. Any size, anytime, anywhere, any race, any religion, any sexual orientation, it's really good. Cadbury also did a Creme Egg advert with two guys kissing – I know there were a few keyboard warriors on Twitter saying that they disliked it, but my son sent me a Whatsapp message and asked whether I had seen it, because he loved seeing it when it's just like me and my partner Dean.

Q: How can Insights get us towards truly inclusive marketing?

A: It's important to move up the marketing process from where so far there's been a lot of focus – it's not just who's in front of the camera, but who's behind it or even what media are you putting it within.

With insights and analytics, as with those other stages, getting to better marketing requires nuance and you've got to pay attention to who is looking for that insight. There are some fantastic people within agencies and brands who are doing great jobs being analytical with the data they have, but you do need to be engaging with other communities that can really go deeper into those insights. If you're going to get black insights make sure somebody black helped you find the insights – they don't need to work in your company, but you need to engage a company that's going to engage people from that community. The same with Indian, the same with LGBT+ – I think it's quite a challenge to research partners.

There is a wealth of knowledge about every community already out there and it is sat on a string of URLs across the world wide web in diversity media titles. Everything that a community has thought, has said and their key trends is there to be analysed if you know where to look. You can go and work on a piece of research directly with a popular publication from a certain community, like *Gay Times*, *Attitude* or *Diva*. You don't necessarily need intermediaries like Brand Advance and DECA, but we are able to look across, say, 500 publications within that community.

One good point to make is that people from these communities know the names of the publications even if you do not. I'm always an advocate of saying don't make the employees from a community do all the work for you, but there are cleverer ways to engage them. They don't need to fix the problems of your company, but they will love it if you ask them for 10 publications and commit to making an effort to spend with them. Give them a reason to help you out, or pay people to do it. You cannot just go to a black employee and ask how much TV they watch, because that's not how we get insights for other audiences. There's a big knowledge gap, and there's a data and insights gap, but it's possible to close it.

Let's look at this in perspective. When you start delving into the insights for these communities, these are not small communities, they are big. So-called 'minorities' represent 52 per cent of London, or 20 per cent of the whole UK. That is a whole half a world of people that have not really fully been commercialized yet. If you think about how long it's taken us to get to know the mainstream consumers, then you know there is a lot of work to be done.

I don't want to say it's easy, and that you can just wake up and have all these simple insights to drop into a strategy, but the work to reward ratio is unbelievable. I think the key thing is that the more marketers start asking these questions the more solutions and services and partners are going to exist and bring different people into our industry to answer those questions. There's a whole new sector emerging called diversity media, and there are consultancies like mine or the Diversity Standards Collective.

Go out and find the companies that can help you. Marketing has a real problem right now because it's just woken itself up and realized that there's a whole half a world of people that it has been missing. That's great but we're now 20/30/40 years behind on the data it needs to properly reach these people. We've got loads of data about straight white people, often more data than we know what to do with, but do we know anything about the attention of black 25-year-olds that like tech? No one has got the data, because no one has run campaigns to see what works well. No one has put enough creative out to see which works well. No one has bought the media in vast enough sums to understand what is good media and what is bad.

It's all an absolute open book, and the only way to ensure effective marketing is to build insight. Insight into that community. Insight into the media that they are consuming. Insight into campaign effectiveness. It is going to cost a little bit, we're going to have to pay for it, because insight is not free. You're going to need people from that community to help you do it. You cannot just march into a community and ask them a load of random questions when they've not seen you for the last 30 years and don't understand why they're being asked. You need to assemble your own team that can understand that data because then you've got to turn that into actionable insights.

Q: How do marketers get started?

A: I've got a little bit of an acronym because I was in the army for a while and we all love acronyms. It's DMTR: do it, mean it, train it and repeat it.

Do it – just go out there, whatever the fear is that stopped you, the worry of getting it wrong, just go and do it as you'll never know the outcome until you do. Mean what you're doing – engage your team with it, engage other companies, engage the media that you're trying to reach so that they can tell you the dos and don'ts. Once you've done it then train it and teach everybody else to do more of it, because you might be breaking new ground but on a team of 100 the other 99 may not be yet. Then just do it all over again because authenticity comes from repeatedly speaking to that audience like equals – you can't buy it, you can't truly hire it, you can just be it, so repeat it. Do it, mean it, train it and repeat it.

MARKETER IN FOCUS
Karen Fraser MBE, Senior Director at Ipsos

Whilst specialist diversity-focused research companies are clearly a big boost to inclusive marketing, it's also critical to think about how all of your insights and research can be inclusive and open-minded. Karen Fraser has worked in creative agencies, brand agencies, at the Advertising Association, and today works at the research company Ipsos, where she helps brands understand sustainability, consumer trust and reputation.

Q: Why does representation matter to you?

A: There's a personal reason and there's a business reason as well. On a personal level, there isn't anything particularly special about me. I'm from an ordinary background, I was born and raised in Coventry, went to a regular school until I was eleven, and then I got a fee-assisted place to go to a private school. That was something my parents otherwise would not have been able to afford, and that launched me quickly into a world that I didn't previously know.

I saw people who had more and had done more than I ever had. It was quite an experience, and the contrast with what I had known previously was huge. If you go on to study at university, you see the same thing. You see more privilege, more experience and more sophistication than when you're not in that world.

The same was true again when I joined the world of advertising. I did some analysis of stats and the advertising world has three times as many people who have been to public school than in the general population. I was aware of the benefits which that privileged and specialist kind of education can bring you, and I feel that that should be something that's afforded to all. We shouldn't exclude people, we should include everyone, especially when something is as important as education or healthcare.

It applies to business as well. If you want to pay the bills, if you want to do a good campaign, or you want to create a good piece of research – you're doing a disservice to the client or to the audience if you are not embracing everybody. Let's face it, it's just not as interesting if you're not fully representing everyone's views and perspectives within the creative process, and also in the delivery of the campaigns.

Ultimately, it's just a lot more interesting if you're involving everyone. You get a better piece of work, you have more fun while you're doing it, you learn more. By necessity, you keep your mind open to lots of eventualities that you wouldn't otherwise conceive.

Q: How do we use data and insights to look outside of our own marketing bubbles?

A: When we look at the diversity or inclusion profile of the ad industry, we tend to compare it to the national population. It is true, though, that the majority of the largest agencies are in London and the South East, and when you start to compare the profile of our industry versus the privileged population that you tend to find in the South East, it looks fairly representative. When you look at the rest of the UK though, not a hope, not a prayer.

Thinkbox, the UK TV group, have done some great work. They did their Ad Nation and TV Nation reports – they were basically comparing the viewing habits of people who work in the advertising industry to what they call 'normal people', and it was a big contrast. TV certainly isn't dead, normal people still like to watch TV. They tend not to have as long a commute to get home. They watch different things. I'm always up for challenging my own preconceptions, and that was a piece of work that did.

Q: Can you think of a good example of positive inclusion and representation?

A: I was thinking about this over the weekend and quite a few popped up once I started thinking about it. The one that stood out most of all, that made such an impression on me, was when I was a judge on Channel 4's Diversity in Advertising Awards. We had a submission, which subsequently won and was made into an ad – Lloyds Banking Group with their agency Adam and Eve.

They did a whole series of work, which I really still love. One was an ad that you may know, 'He Said Yes' – there was a guy proposing to another guy and I don't recall having seen such an ad in an outdoor environment, and I love how artfully and beautifully that was done. They also did 'Get the Inside Out' where people who had experienced mental health issues would write their issue on yellow Post-It notes and stick them on their forehead. We can't see inside each other's minds but there it was, and they were prompting conversations about and awareness of mental health before any other brand that I can really think of.

Visually it can be hard to represent some aspects of inclusion and you might think you need a 90 second advert to do so, but these were clever ways of doing just that. There's no doubt in my mind that making topics like that the subject of national campaigns, national conversations, helps to release some sort of energy or discussion around those topics and make them more and more commonplace. Ten, fifteen years ago, would anyone have said to their employer that they're having some mental health issues at the moment and they need time to address them? It's still a tough thing for a lot of people to say today, but it's not as hard as it would once have been.

Q: From a research perspective, have you been part of projects trying to bring more inclusion in?

A: I have just joined Ipsos and it's something that I immediately recognize we push to the furthest kind of degree. In terms of how we select people for research, we put an enormous amount of work into the difficult aspects of profiling people and getting the right balance and terminology. It might not be something that people would necessarily see, but it is taken very seriously here.

We believe strongly in making sure that the people that you are interviewing, however that might be, are the people that they say they are and the people that you think they are. We also invest a lot of time and effort into programmes that help to improve the diversity within our own organization, so that we can better reflect the population elsewhere.

Having an inclusive workforce is crucial because you'll then have more options to have different viewpoints, different perspectives represented on any team. Equally, I think spending sufficient time and budget on research is essential. You can't just rush to an online survey because you'll be asking people to confirm your biases or preconceptions.

Discussion with people who are within your target audience, or within an audience with whom you wish to communicate, is essential. Qualitative research has a great role to play here because people have an opportunity to voice their lived experience and give you perspectives that you might not otherwise appreciate if you don't share that particular thing in common with them.

As a large research company, Ipsos can invest in making sure that the people that we speak to are representative. We work so hard to train our people to make sure that they are not introducing biases in work that we do. We genuinely do go the extra mile that's necessary to find people who are appropriate for any particular project.

There are also specialists out there, who work to engage otherwise excluded communities. There are occasions when it might be a good idea to at least consult with them or involve them in something particular that you could miss.

Q: What research have you done which shows marketers the impact that being more inclusive can have?

A: We have tools where clients can test their communications online, one of them called Creative Spark another called Innotest, so you can do that work up front to see whether the messaging is going to resonate with the audiences you intend to speak to. Measurement further down the line is equally important because that's when you're going to know whether things have worked in the way that you wanted, or whether you need to tweak or adapt.

There are people who are more convinced and less convinced in this diversity, equity and inclusion (DEI) space, and I think those who are less convinced would benefit, and their business would benefit, if they look at the research that shows the impact. There have been various pieces of work, but my Women in Advertising and Communications Leadership (WACL) colleague Kate Waters ran a project at ITV that looked at whether there was an uplift or not when diverse groups were represented in ads. In a nutshell, they found that there was, both within those diverse groups of people they were looking to speak with, and more broadly.

Knowing that inclusion is going to do better for the business is really important. As we become more global, and there's a broader range of interests that people can share globally, then it's even more important to understand that there are things that don't necessarily separate people. Just because you might look different or act differently, you can have common interests that are more uniting than the things that apparently differentiate people. Those can work to a brand's advantage.

Inclusivity doesn't need to be forced. It should be as natural as finding difference within the population. I don't think it should be the single sole message, it shouldn't get in the way of entertainment, information or involvement.

Q: How can we ensure that our industry becomes and stays more inclusive? What would be your advice to a young woman joining the industry today?

A: If I were to begin my career again, I would join a network like Bloom or WACL, or one of the number of other ones that exist. I wish I'd joined a network sooner than I did. Not for personal reasons, but just for the ability to support other women, connect with other women. I think resilience within our careers, for men and for women, is crucial. Especially if you're a sensitive person, then the knocks can sometimes hurt and act as a disincentive.

I think that forming an alliance with other women who may come up across the same issues as you just gives more support, and it's remarkable to me how many shared experiences there are. You don't realize when you look at some of the women in organizations and you think to yourself, 'That person's never skipped a beat', but actually when you get to know them personally it's the same for all of us. Those networks are a great way of finding new roles or opportunities – the new girls' networks are as important as the old boys' networks!

Q: What would be your advice for marketers starting out on this journey?

A: I think a great many have embraced greater diversity, haven't they? Big brands, huge corporations, I can't think of many now who haven't begun to develop different ways of talking to diverse groups. From my background I'm going to recommend investing in research – and don't rush it. I've always loved this quote: 'Don't rush to get the wrong answer.' Taking time and absorbing experiences and stories from different types of people is crucial.

07

Marketing and creative briefs

A brief can take many forms, whether a quick conversation, multi-page form, or multi-media presentation. The nature of the project and task you are kicking off will have a big impact on just how much effort it is worth putting into the brief, but as the ultimate steer for everything that follows it's a key step in your process and a chance to double-check that you are heading in an inclusive direction.

By this stage, you've set inclusive goals and explored representative and deep insights, but how are you practically going to bring this into the brief? You must make choices in a brief as to what to include and what not to include, but look around on the cutting-room floor and sense check everything that you're excluding again at this point. Sometimes we bring our own stereotypes to the brief or fail to inspire with our intent or our insight.

Our teams, agencies and other partners respond to what we ask of them, and they cannot be expected to deliver on tasks that we don't make clear. You don't need to just hint at your desire for inclusion and representation, you can specifically call it out in the brief – put in a sentence that just sets it as an expectation or add new sections to your briefing template designed to force the inclusion of and response to some of the specific diverse insights that you have found.

If your research and focus groups have uncovered interesting nuances, anecdotes and stories then bring some of these to the brief. Ensure the visual stimulus is inspiring but also reflects the true diversity of your consumers and not just the specifics of your absolute core consumer. Find ways of passing over more of the raw research and insight you have as an appendix to the brief, but be prepared to give your partners time and resources to work through it if you want them to truly maximize the work.

It's important to be particularly cautious of the target audiences we define and whether those risk falling into stereotypes. There are many descriptions of over-50s audiences making them sound like they've given up on having adventures, when this is a group in the prime of their life and more likely to have the means to make the most of it. Be wary of age and demographic definitions in general, 'Gen Z' and 'Millennials' are vast buckets of people with relatively little in common and it's usually the sign of a lazy brief to see these terms mentioned.

Be careful of stereotyping even within deliberately inclusive briefs

Even deliberately progressive briefs can fall into stereotyping concerns as they try to capture a perspective of a community – for instance, the LGBT+ 'community' is a vibrant group of hundreds of millions of people, many of whom live starkly different lifestyles. It's common for gay men to be portrayed as young, fit and, let's be honest, white men who love going out partying and clubbing every weekend. There are some people who fit that description, but there are far more who do not. Don't be afraid to take your briefs back to some of the people who've fed into your insights and see if they recognize what is reflected on the page. Please consider engaging different perspectives, from within your organization or outside it, to help you with the direction of the brief.

Back to the questions we asked ourselves when we set our business challenge, it's another chance to consider who is excluded from our focus and whether they are a business opportunity. Have you discovered diverse audiences in your process that have unique requirements or where there's an opportunity to communicate differently and create competitive advantage? A modern marketing or communications brief doesn't have to assume the answer is a single, monolithic, creative response when the business need might make the case for something more nuanced.

If you work on a large brand there's probably quite a sophisticated briefing process and system in place. Hopefully your capabilities team has shaped this to allow for some of this nuance, but if you don't think it allows for it then don't be afraid to contact them and ask whether there are opportunities to improve it. There are organizations that specialize in coaching companies on the detailed processes, templates and language that can give you the best possible foundation to encourage inclusive marketing in your work. Your colleagues may tell us off for saying this, but if you don't think the current tools are quite up to the task then you can always add to them yourself until they evolve. Consider adding an extra presentation slide or field in a form designed specifically to call out inclusive marketing opportunities and to ask for responses which champion them.

More established brands are likely also to have done more work around their 'brand universe', their 'brand heart', their brand's emotional benefit or perhaps even the brand's purpose. Even if your product itself doesn't necessarily play into unique and diverse use cases, it is possible that the brand world you have created and the higher-level role you see your brand playing might well lend itself to you taking more progressive approaches to your marketing.

Some key advice, especially as you look to bring your brand's emotional benefit to life in a deliberately inclusive way, is not to over-stretch and to think of the credible voice you can have or the steps you can take. Ask yourselves what the inclusive expressions of your brand's emotional benefit are and don't be afraid to sense check them back with your audience.

I used to work on the Smirnoff vodka brand, which had deliberately focused some of its marketing activity on the LGBT+ nightlife market. Vodka can be a great drink on a night out but it would probably be overstating its role in society to believe a brand can stand up in its own right as a social justice campaigner and win new rights for the community. On the other hand, it was well within reason for the brand to use some of its communications to more casually promote equality (their tag line for several years was 'Labels are for bottles, not for people') and to think about how to meaningfully support the bars and nightlife areas where it was sold. For several years they funded a 'nightlife angels' charity project that saw teams on the streets late at night looking out for the safety of party goers, especially those who had drunk a little bit too much.

CHECKLIST
Marketing and creative briefs

Key questions to ask yourself:

1 Does your brief make it clear that representation is key?

2 Does it bring clear stimulus/inspiration?

3 Is the target/audience definition a stereotype? Could it be more progressive?

4 Who is excluded? Are they a potential business opportunity?

5 Have you considered different perspectives to help you with the direction of the brief?

6 What are the inclusive expressions of your brand's emotional benefit?

MARKETER IN FOCUS
Sarah Jenkins, Managing Director, Saatchi and Saatchi London

Whilst brand side marketers are typically responsible for writing the briefs, it is the agency who has to receive and react to it. Sarah Jenkins is the Managing Director of one of the world's most famous and successful creative agencies and has been working there and at other agencies for more than two decades. She is a strong advocate for inclusive marketing in her business and across the industry. I spoke to Sarah about the marketing process and what it takes to get to a great brief together with a client.

Q: Why does representation matter to you?

A: It genuinely matters for multiple reasons. For a brutal commercial reason, because I run a creative organization and it's as simple as the organizations with the best talent will win. I must make sure that all talent has access, I need to make sure that there is the biggest talent pool to choose from. We also know that diverse thinking shapes better work – that's another important commercial reason, and brilliantly clients are increasingly asking to see our diversity numbers.

So those are all the very rational reasons for increasing internal representation, and all good reasons. And then on an emotional level – I love what I do, and I want the path to be opened for as many people as possible. People who are different for whatever reasons should feel comfortable in our industry.

Q: How have you felt representation and inclusion change within the advertising industry?

A: This is an industry that is growing up quickly. It's amazing how much people are leaning in, how increasingly high inclusion is on the 'to do' lists of leaders, how vocal people are getting and how quick people are to call out the bad behaviours. I think ten years ago people would have let some bad behaviour off as just messing around, but I think there's a proper doubling down now, which is good to see.

We've also seen some brilliant work coming through. I think the 'Fearless Girl' work on Wall Street was amazing. Not just an advert, but an amazing statement – the fact that they took on that incredible raging bull statue to make a statement.

I think so much of what Nike do is extraordinary. Now obviously that is a big organization and they've got glitches and they've got bad things; in no way are they perfect. I think they made a very clear statement about Colin Kaepernick, and they stood by it, and they could have seen some bad commercial consequences, but they stood there.

I love what they've done with oversize mannequins in their stores and throughout their collateral. That is an organization that is growing up and working out its role in the world. So big thumbs up to Nike. So many of their big adverts these days don't preach, they don't feel forced, it's just great casual inclusion. It's them living up to their vision and brand promise that everybody is an athlete, therefore they will talk to and empower everybody.

It would be remiss of me not to talk about the work we've done with BT around 'Hope United'. Over the Summer of 2021 there was some opening up relating to Covid and a summer of football with the delayed Euro 2020 taking place. It felt like an exciting time, but we recognized that BT's and communications' role wasn't simply to be a cheerleader and to help showcase the beautiful game – there was a job to do. BT are in the business of connecting people online to sport but unfortunately that takes you far too quickly into hate speech on social media. It was our job to equip the nation, which we did, and over four million Brits downloaded or read a tutorial that talked about how you could properly help mitigate online hate, and what you can do if you felt uncomfortable about something you've seen or heard.

There are great brands like Nike and BT that I think are truly stepping into their purpose and taking on some new subjects. I think we've also seen lots of other brands and clients doing brilliant things as well, which perhaps don't get the airtime they deserve, but we're seeing change coming.

Q: How do we as clients get to this good work? What does a great brief look like?

A: I think what's great about this book is that it recognizes that it's not just about casting. Yes, that's a contributor, but when we talk about inclusivity and authentic storytelling it starts right upstream. It starts with your business strategy, who you're talking to and how you're going to include them. Understanding that it's a massive source of business, not just for communities that you are necessarily trying to talk to, but as an inclusive business you're going to get more and more people leaning in and wanting to spend money with you.

You need to get as upstream as possible. It's about asking the big questions around where the business opportunity is, and how by talking to different communities we can find greater business growth. A year or two before you're trying to make the work, we should all be thinking differently about sources of growth, then as you move through the various gates and into the briefing stage don't hesitate to put that on there. What might this mean for diverse audiences, and how do we get people involved in the process to think differently? That starts by capturing it somewhere in the brief.

This is not always an easy space to navigate, despite the good intent that we're seeing within the industry. I think it's important to start these conversations as early as possible, so that you are talking about it outside the heat of crazy lead times, or when you're racing into casting decisions. Always start as early as you can in your planning process, or your interview process, or your briefing process – talk about the role inclusion can play to move forward the project or the brief. When you've got that tacit alignment that we are going to do things differently, you can build that into the contract of whoever it is that you are encouraging to get on the diversity journey with you.

I think talented marketers should know that they need to lean in on this, but that means having difficult conversations with their bosses, their line managers and their agencies. It's the right conversation to be having, and in truth if you get constant push-backs and you're a great marketer there are lots of organizations you can join. Don't try to be the change if that change isn't going to come – go and join one of the amazing marketing organizations that do understand it.

Of course, that's not always practical, and if you do want to stay and be the change the organization needs then data is helpful. It's helpful when we look at the composition of our organization, but also looking at the data of the work and the output that you're creating just to see how potentially homogeneous or mono-cultural you are being. It will give you a reference. Then look at what your competitors are doing, or look at brands that you really admire, just to see you've got that benchmark and a reference. However rudimentary, having access to that data is important.

Find the most senior person in your organization who you think is on this journey with you. Find a way to have a coffee with them, get your heads together because change comes from the top. The more you can find a way to have a conversation with someone super-senior then the quicker change will come. Allies are important, so find a tribe of people that you can plug into and be a part of.

Q: How do we make sure our industry is more open and more inclusive?

A: There's an irony in the advertising industry not being able to advertise itself. We've got to make sure that we're doing as much as we can to do the right thing and for me, on a really practical level, we need to spend more time in schools. Really closely working with them. Schools are crying out for support from businesses.

It can just be spending time in schools – you can do that through a templated approach, you can do it virtually, you can do it at scale with very little effort. The more time brands and creative agencies can spend in schools, the more we can power up young people to believe they can do this. We can genuinely make it a meritocracy where, if you're good, creatively smart and sharp, and have a talent, you have the opportunity and you will do brilliantly.

I think the more we can do to make sure that kids understand that there's no barrier like exams, the better. You can come into our industry, and you can do brilliantly, and it's a fun industry to work in. We've been terrible at marketing ourselves, but the joy is we have all the proof points, we don't have to make up the reasons to come in. It's just about making sure we're very systemic with our approach – there's nothing worse than popping into a school and then disappearing again.

At Saatchi and Saatchi we make a seven-year commitment to any school that we work with, so we properly work with the kids, importantly also the teachers, and sometimes even the parents. We can build relationships and really help kids understand what the opportunity is for creativity within the curriculum and within careers, how creativity can do great things in the community. What a joy getting to spend time with a bunch of awesome 15-year-olds with brilliant ideas is, it's definitely not one-way.

Q: What's your advice for keeping inclusion right through the production process?

A: It's most crucially about authentic storytelling versus simply casting people of different backgrounds to tell the story. Once you've got that approved script it's just being clear that you want the best actor or actress, the right person for the role. It's being very clear that you're not going to have any sort of checklist that excludes. There are some amazing casting agents all over the world that you can lean into, that can source some brilliant talents from less conventional backgrounds.

If you're working on a global business, it's about having these conversations a lot earlier with marketers who may feel less comfortable with non-white talent. Sometimes you need to go on a process with people coming from different spaces, and you need the proof that it does work in the market. It's about making sure that the story turns out as authentic as possible, being clear on the direction from the outset to buy yourself time. When you've got a metaphorical gun against your head and you've got to get casting approved, and you want to shoot next week, then there's very little chance you can get people to be brave just in that moment.

PART THREE

Stage two

Inclusive planning

STAGE ONE

Inclusive briefing and strategy

 Business and brand strategy

Strategic insights and data

Marketing and creative briefs

STAGE TWO

Inclusive planning

4 *Partner and team selection*

5 *Creative development and product design*

6 *Consumer testing*

STAGE THREE

Inclusive production

 Production

Post-production

Localization

STAGE FOUR

Inclusive launches

Media and 360 activation

Launch and consumer response

Measuring success

08

Partner and team selection

The planning phase is when you start to turn your plans and your briefs into a reality. It's where the magic really starts to happen. Every stage of the marketing process is important, but this is when your team comes together, where you get to flesh out your ideas, and when you might even get an opportunity to understand what consumers think about your solutions.

For many of us working in the industry, this is the heart of what we do and the opportunity to flesh out our strategies and creative ideas. In many cases, this will be working on a new advert or campaign, but marketing is bigger than advertising and depending on the brief there might be opportunities to evolve your product or how you show up in store.

Price is a powerful, if less creative, tool in the marketing mix and potentially also a barrier that excludes many disadvantaged consumers from buying into your brand. Truly inclusive marketing approaches will consider how all these pieces come together, and whilst that doesn't necessarily mean just making your brand cheaper it can mean exploring different formats, variants, or ways of opening up greater accessibility.

Team inclusion drives better representation

Getting great marketing done means having a great team around the table. We've heard this consistently at every stage of the process, but we've chosen this point to really focus on the importance of the team you partner with to bring your thinking to life. This is a huge topic that moves into the wider HR-related diversity and representation space, and we will only begin to scratch the surface, but it is critical that we start to think about how we do build teams that act in truly inclusive ways.

The creative development process is different in every business, and as much an art as it is a science or process that you can truly lock down in print. That said, there are frameworks and thinking that you can build around your process to ensure you keep inclusive perspectives at the heart of your approach. It's important to consciously avoid stereotypes and shallow portrayals, and to think really hard about the personality and perspective of the characters that are present in your work.

Marketing planners, strategists, media experts and more all have a role to play in a successful planning process, and in big companies working with multiple agencies the best results come from getting those different groups and partners to work successfully together right through the process. The same is true in the smallest teams, where there might only be one or two of you working in an office or on a project but there's still an opportunity to build on each other's perspectives and understanding. If you don't naturally have diversity and inclusive perspectives in that team then think about how you can deliberately bring some in, and remember that the heart of being a marketer is having empathy and understanding perspectives other than your own.

The team that you work with is really the heart of inclusive marketing. Almost everyone that fed into this book has pointed back to the team, to the voices that you have around the table, as being at the heart of every step of the marketing process, so choose wisely. Diverse teams bring new perspectives and make better work, but the reality is our industry is simply not diverse enough.

Sometimes we're choosing an external agency or partner to work with, sometimes you're building out a new internal team of your own, or perhaps sometimes you are the whole team yourself. However many people you can get in the room, you're never going to have every possible perspective represented, and that doesn't have to be the goal.

It is our job as marketers to shape products, campaigns and more for consumers very unlike ourselves, and part of that means getting out of our own bubbles and having empathy for people whose lived experiences might be very different from our own. No one is saying that your own background limits the kinds of marketing you can do or the people you have the right to try and speak to. We do, however, know that having people from different backgrounds, and where possible those communities you are especially trying to speak to, makes it much easier to avoid our own biases and be more genuinely inclusive.

Making the most of a diverse team

To be clear, this also isn't about presenteeism and ticking a box of who you have somewhere in your office or somewhere in the team. An inclusive team is one in which people from different backgrounds and perspectives can actively challenge, contribute, be heard, and be recognized and celebrated for their successes. Just as important as getting people from different backgrounds into our industry and our offices is making sure they are truly included and welcomed when they are here, which takes conscious effort and action from each one of us.

This moves us squarely into the traditional HR territory of diversity and inclusion, and the important steps that many companies are taking to make themselves more open and accessible. The marketing industry has historically not truly reflected the diversity of wider society, and there are now many great initiatives working to try to close that gap. There are some obvious issues facing the industry around class, age, gender – perhaps around every single intersectional aspect of identity. The great thing is that more and more of such dedicated organizations exist and are helping kick down the doors of our industry, and those of us working in it already just need to be prepared to work with them and to welcome those new entrants.

Changing the diversity and inclusion of your own business, let alone a whole industry, may be daunting but there are always small steps we can all take both in our hiring approaches and how we manage and work with our colleagues on a day-to-day basis. Empathy, awareness of other perspectives, and a genuine willingness to be open and challenged being chief amongst them once more. Think about small steps you can take in your own team to give everyone an equal voice. For advice on where to start, look up the WFA's Charter for Change which lists 11 practical opportunities to make an impact.

Supplier diversity

A good place to start is by asking what steps you are taking alongside your suppliers to bring in more diverse talent – is there more that your business could be doing itself, or that you should be asking of and expecting from the partners that you work with? For those reading this who are client-side marketers, there is a big opportunity to challenge and influence the agencies we work with, but of course we also have to be conscious of the need to improve our own inclusion. It's not universally true, but I've often seen that brands put up the highest barriers of entry of any part of our industry, especially requirements for academic qualifications and degrees that are in themselves exclusionary to many talented people.

If you work in a larger company, it's important to consider whether you have an overall procurement and supplier diversity approach. These initiatives set out to monitor and improve the number of suppliers you work with that are minority owned and operated, or which deliberately serve those communities. You can explore this right through your supply chain, and indeed raise the challenge with your direct partners that their own suppliers should be sharing these goals. There are many aspects to a successful supplier diversity approach but inevitably putting in the effort to audit your current situation, so you have a meaningful benchmark to improve on is critical.

In many cases, larger brands will work with larger network agencies whose ownership and makeup are inevitably not as diverse or are simply publicly traded. There are good business reasons for working with such partners, not least that they are often responsible for some of the best and most effective work, but also ways to evolve the model going forwards. Could a minority owned, or focused, partner for instance augment the work of your Agency of Record? Are there opportunities to bring in specialist partners or consultants who bring deep expertise in inclusive thinking, or at key stages in the process (such as bringing in diverse insights)?

The importance of inclusive leaders and directors

At the heart of the creative process are the creative directors who shape our ideas and then ultimately the film directors who bring that work to life. Whilst diversity and inclusion throughout the team is clearly important, it's worth having additional scrutiny on our leaders, and regrettably these are some of the least diverse parts of our business. Once again, it isn't about removing opportunities from established directors, but it is about creating a level playing field where people with different backgrounds and experiences can compete, and there are practical steps you can take, such as ensuring a female director is always one of the bids presented.

It's important that we work together with our agencies on this journey. Being inclusive of everyone includes being inclusive of the fantastic creative partners we already work with, but it does mean giving others a chance to get experience, do great work and be remunerated accordingly. Agencies are service businesses that respond to the demands of their clients, and if more and more clients expect to see better representation and diversity, then naturally they will put more effort and resources into ensuring they achieve that.

As a senior client of Publicis Groupe in the UK, I was delighted to be invited to sit on their diversity and representation board. It was a genuine and open collaboration that both showcased real efforts they were making in this space and was transparent and raw about the challenges we face. We partnered jointly with them on supporting an initiative from the Brixton Finishing School that saw us supporting a training course for potential new entrants to the industry and then jointly offering a placement for one of the students.

These collaborations went well beyond us simply demanding or expecting more diversity in our teams towards exploring how we could unlock that jointly, and indeed in doing so helped build a stronger client/agency relationship as well. As a further example we then went on to collaborate additionally with our media partners at Facebook/Meta and the organization Outvertising to sponsor their awards and encourage better LGBT+ representation in our industry, again looking to take meaningful action where possible.

Put inclusion at the heart of your agency relationships

Make inclusion part of the pitch and selection process, as well as part of the briefing to your established partners. This isn't just about tokenism and diversity statistics, but truly about inclusion and representation.

For a creative agency perhaps the best ultimate judge of this is to look broadly across their overall output to see how much evidence there is of inclusive thinking and, ultimately, positive representation. It's worth asking to understand the steps they are taking not just to support new talent into their business but to truly ensure there are pathways for promotion and towards senior responsibility for those recruits.

We've consistently heard that inclusive marketing is driven by having different voices around the table but let's be explicitly clear that that is only true if those voices are listened to. Nearly all of us will have had experiences in our careers, especially when we were more junior, where we've sat in presentations that we might disagree with but don't feel empowered to speak up and challenge them or have seen other people who try to do that get shot down.

What steps are you taking to make the environment more inclusive? This can be everything from the physical facilities you offer, through to the training and mentoring provided, or the best practices you create around meetings or internal HR processes. Are you thinking about the barriers that might stop someone with a physical or mental disability from being able to thrive in your business? Are you making space for the quieter members of the team to still be able to contribute? Whilst the need to work from home has been forced upon many of us, some of the technologies used to do that can be beneficial and inclusive, allowing people more flexibility in their work commitments, or allowing people to comment through chat where they might not be willing to interrupt the speaker directly.

CHECKLIST
Partner and team selection

Key questions to ask yourself:

1 Do you have a procurement diversity approach and a supply chain of diverse partners?

2 Have you asked partners for evidence of representation across their overall output?

3 Could a minority owned, or focused, partner augment the work of your Agency of Record?

4 Are you working together with your agency on this journey? Is there more you could be doing to support them to become more representative and diverse?

5 Which organizations could you partner with to encourage future diversity within the industry?

MARKETER IN FOCUS
Kate Williams, Head of Diversity and Inclusion at Publicis Groupe

Kate Williams is relatively new to the marketing industry but has been campaigning for fair inclusion and diversity in the workplace for well over a decade. Before taking on a new D&I lead role within the Publicis Groupe of agencies, Kate had been working at the LGBT+ inclusion charity Stonewall where she had directed a range of programmes and partnerships. She speaks here about the changes happening across the industry and the steps we can all take to make it more inclusive.

Q: Why does representation matter to you personally?

A: That's a big question! First up my perspective as a queer woman, that part of my identity has certainly informed my interest in creating a more inclusive world. If I'm honest, though, I think it started even before that, when I was a kid.

I'm from Wales, and a Welsh speaker originally, and I can just remember growing up with this sense of feeling different. I'm from a working-class community, which had quite strong values around looking after one another and making sure everybody's OK. Gradually, though, you become aware of the fact that your identity as a Welsh person isn't always taken that seriously, and that the language you speak is not well understood or well regarded.

I think that taught me something about difference, fairness and injustice, and then as I got older I realized there was something else different about me. I realized that that also would have implications for how I would be able to live my life, and I think that gave me an insight into what it is really like to feel different. To feel like you can't always join in with things. That you need to worry about some things.

You learn to adopt quite negative messages about yourself as well. It's very easy because that's the messaging you get. I think all that complex vortex of a world around me really informed quite a strong sense of social justice. I've carried that through other roles in my career, but I think it crystallized for me around the last decade in wanting to focus on this area professionally.

Q: Can you think of any really great examples of representation and inclusive marketing or media?

A: I think we still have a long way to go, but there are a few that have stood out over the last few years. I think the Starbucks campaign with the charity Mermaids around 'What's Your Name?' was powerful. I thought that was a lovely piece of work with a campaign that was clearly informed by the experiences of the trans community it was trying to reach. There was also an aspect of paying it forward, because if you bought certain items some of that money went to Mermaids in support of young trans people.

Frankly, I also love anything Fenty do. I just want to thank them for making fashion and the world better. One of the things I used to talk about in my previous careers is the way that we think about certain communities and how we think about marginalized people. Often, we don't really understand that we're missing a trick and that there's an absolute business drive to inclusion.

Fenty for me is fantastic, because it is just so unapologetic as well as so energized. They just bring forth different communities. There's such an intersectionality to the way they talk about people that haven't traditionally been marketed to.

Q: How do we make our industry more inclusive to get to more great work like this?

A: Whenever we talk about diversity, equality, and inclusion it feels huge and overwhelming – where do we start? It can feel a bit invidious to begin in any one area, because all these issues are important at the same time.

There are a couple of rules I live by, one of which is the aim to put myself as a diversity specialist out of a job. It's critical that the way we work needs to become a model of empowerment, it can never ultimately be a siloed function in an organization. What you're looking to do is to empower others to look for the opportunities to make their work more inclusive.

The other thing that's important to me is sustainability or legacy. If we are going to be making commitments to people who experience discrimination or marginalization around trying to dismantle that, then we need to keep those promises. That means we must think strategically about the way that we work so that we build capacity in community. Ultimately that becomes a virtuous cycle.

As difficult as it is, one of the things I've had to do in my role is to focus on certain key inclusion pillars, but then try to take an intersectional approach to those. We tend to think about gender equality, or race equity, or LGBT+ inclusion, or disability inclusion, each as separate things. If you investigate those communities each is hugely diverse. It's critical to remember that when you work across something like race equality at the same time you can be working on disability inclusion, LGBT+ inclusion, it could be fighting ageism, and we could be looking at social mobility. It's about always trying to look at the opportunities for us to discover more about the very distinct experiences of different communities under an umbrella.

Inclusion really does mean all of us, it means everybody, and unless we get to a point where everybody realizes the role they must play and the personal responsibility we all have we're not going to succeed. We need to get an understanding that we all must work together and there is space for all of us – we're each diverse in our own way, all seven billion human beings. Of course, we have communities and affinity groups, and there are some life experiences of marginalization that are more profound than others, but what's important is how we find space for all of us to acknowledge our shared humanity.

An inclusive culture for me is a culture where we take joy in the removal of barriers for others without immediately having recourse to worry about ourselves. If we work to be anti-racist, to create an anti-racist society, that elevates all of us. If any of us are left behind or held back we all are. I guess that sounds a bit trite, but it is about giving people the tools and skills to interrogate how it is that you can make a change.

Now that's not to let off governments, organizations and the systems we live in – obviously we need to be working to change those too, but we need to be thinking about the influence each of us has day in, day out.

Q: What practical steps can managers take to make their teams more inclusive?

A: The most important thing is that you must live the values that you espouse. Your behaviour must chime with what you're saying, so don't be disingenuous and don't create dissonance. You need to be the change.

You're only a leader if people are following you, and the best leaders are a support function. It's very easy to interpret leadership as an authoritative function, but good leadership for me is about allowing people to thrive. Trusting people and allowing them to live to their potential. It is about being able to be vulnerable as a leader, to be able to continuously learn and not to be fragile. To be more empathetic, to be able to be challenged and challenge in return in a positive way.

Ultimately it is understanding that it is the behaviours that are important. You need to be open to learning about somebody else's experience – it's OK to not know that something was a problem for someone because it wasn't a problem for you, but once you're aware that it's a problem for them then you have a decision about whether you will do something about it.

You just need empathy; it is the key that unlocks this. In my role I can advocate for change but to effect it takes all of us. However long I pontificate about it, what will drive change in the world is the individual decisions each of us take and how prepared we are to treat one another with respect, care and kindness. That is what denotes inclusion and change.

Q: How do we get the most out of the talent that we do have in our industry?

A: We do have diversity in our industry already, but what we also have are different speed careers for people. It's not necessarily that our pipeline of talent isn't there, although it could always be more diverse, but it's also who manages to make it to the more senior or influential positions.

It's about creating more representative teams, and we do have an imbalance in terms of levels of representation for several different communities in our industry, but it's not about telling people who are here that they are wrong. It's about making other communities realize that they can be invited in, that they should be able to see themselves here. I think we do need to have visibility of role models; we do need to create a culture where people feel able to speak up about their experiences and be advocates.

We'll tell better advertising stories the more diverse our teams are – making these kinds of organizational changes will create better work and better output for all of us.

A big thing to think about is how do we work holistically? Working at an agency, we are a service industry, and we have clients, but there is an opportunity for us to learn together and to figure out new ways of working that are kinder and more empathetic. The last few years of Covid have taught all of us about being more adaptable and I think it would be a shame if we lost some of that and didn't take that forward with us.

One of the real barriers to change is our natural fragility and defensiveness, especially when we hear that we might be in the wrong. The problem there is that we're still centring ourselves in the discussion when really we need to focus on the experiences of others. Being able to move beyond that defensiveness is a powerful tool for change. Inclusion does mean all of us because we all have a role to play in it. There's no passive space where you can just sit and think 'That's not really about me', we're living through a particularly polarizing time and unless you're willing to be part of the solution you might have to realize that unwittingly you're part of the problem.

Educate ourselves, keep learning, understand that we're going to make mistakes because that's what human beings do. We need to be able to learn from those and forgive each other as well.

Call to action: It's time to stop covering up our diversity

Starting a new job or project, meeting a new boss or presenting to a new audience – even for the most confident among us, these are moments that can cause us to question ourselves. If you feel you've got something to cover up, that can be even more the case. It's important to recognize how much of a load that can be on colleagues and what you can do to relieve them of it.

I'm not talking about outrageous secrets. I'm talking about simple personal facts that for many reasons you might feel a societal pressure to 'cover up'. Maybe you're a single parent, you're devoutly religious, you worry about your accent or culture, you have an invisible disability or you're gay – the list goes on. None of these is anything to be ashamed about, but that doesn't mean there isn't a hidden pressure to cover them up – a worry that if you don't conform, you might be excluded or overlooked.

Covering up makes everything that little bit more complicated. I'm a gay man, so for me it means questions about my personal life lead to unexpected micro-decisions every day. When asked what I did at the weekend, do I mention I was there with my boyfriend? When someone asks if I'm married or have kids, do I just laugh and say I only have a dog? Do I use the fact that I'm engaged and say 'fiancé' to swerve the discussion altogether?

I'm lucky enough to have never fully experienced homophobia in my career (although I have certainly seen it), but I still occasionally swerve a moment like this. So I try to do the exact opposite and make a deliberate point of saying it, because I know from my own experience that seeing other 'out' people in the business or deliberate allies has helped make me more comfortable in myself. I'm also a white, middle-class, native-English-speaking, well-educated man, meaning I'm given lots of unfair privilege that to an extent negates my need to cover up. It can be much harder for other people to do the same.

Stonewall (2018) research found that 35 per cent of graduates go back into the closet when they enter the job market, even if they've finally managed to come out in their personal lives. Nearly all of us are covering something up, but chances are this nuance is a fantastic perspective we could be embracing. We're at an important moment in the diversity conversation and understanding 'covering up' is part of unpacking that.

When your colleagues must cover up, they are expending mental and creative energy just to tread water. It can discourage active participation and engagement, and directly leads to well-documented mental-health implications. Ultimately, you're not really benefiting from the diversity of your workforce if you accidentally force them all to think and act the same.

If you personally have an aspect of diversity that you feel the need to cover up, it is not your job to change hostile office environments and it's understandable if you don't think you can try to chip away at those. Sadly, all too often it isn't just in your head. I encourage you to try to bring a little more of your full self to work, or at least to start talking to some colleagues about it, as it can be a huge weight off your shoulders. We all need to create a work culture where it's truly OK to be your true self before we can ask everyone to do so.

If you're in a senior position, I urge you to do so loudly and vocally. When we're back in the office, shout about the fact you are leaving early to pick up your kids, talk about your same-sex partner or share more about your unusual background. Positively role modelling the fact that we're all going through such things sets the mood for everyone else in your team to follow.

Straight, white men wondering how they play a part in the current diversity discussion can join in too – leave the office loudly to go pick up your kids too. Show understanding and compassion for those around you and immediately shut down any back chat you hear or are tempted to join.

Realizing that many of your colleagues will be covering up something is the first step in better understanding and working with them. Leaders need to own this topic, talk about it and even train your people on how to manage it. Look at the systematic processes in your business, identify any that limit diversity and inclusion and ask yourself whether looking for a 'cultural fit' with new hires is just looking for more of the same.

The advertising industry has a long way to go to improve its diversity, full stop. In time, we may get better at hitting diversity targets, but we won't ever be truly inclusive until we learn to stop covering up. There's some diversity sitting under our noses right now that will do more for our businesses and help people go further in their personal careers if we just give everyone a chance to be themselves.

MARKETER IN FOCUS

Ally Owen, Founder of Brixton Finishing School

Today there are many fantastic initiatives globally that aim to broaden the intake and progression of people within the marketing industry. Ally Owen left a successful ad sales career to found the Brixton Finishing School, an organization dedicated to getting talent from broader backgrounds, and especially working class, into the advertising and marketing industry. She reflected on her own experience of working in the industry and why that has inspired her to try to open doors wider for other pioneers to follow.

Q: Why does representation matter to you?

A: I think, for me, it's fairness. My own lived experience is of being somebody who came up through the ranks in the industry. I started as an outsider, I'm an outlier. I'm a single mum, I live on a council estate in Dalston. I have currently got quite a neutral accent, but it wasn't always that way.

I didn't realize how under-represented I was until I started having experiences where it was spelled out to me that I was a pet project for people. One thing that sums it up for me is the accounts you are placed on – you're constantly told you're not the right cultural fit for certain accounts. Luckily for me you get put on big FMCG/CPG brands which is where the money is, rather than the kinds of luxury brands where you are apparently not a fit.

I remember a time when I'd arranged a meeting with a luxury brand which happened to fall within my remit. The fashion manager was coming with me, and it was very posh. There were quite a few of us going to meet them, and then she checked my handbag to see if it was fake before we entered the room. Not anybody else's, just my own. It wasn't fake but the fact is she felt the need to police me even though she was junior to me.

There was somebody else who joined a team I was on, and she'd come from a very different background to me at the same school with members of the Royal Family. She didn't speak to me for a week. I'd been trying to make efforts to speak to her and I was getting nowhere and so I asked a colleague why she didn't speak to me. 'Well she's never met anybody like you before, has she?'

It never occurred to me at that point that I was anything less than equal, and when we talk about affirmation, about being seen or representation, I'd always presumed I was better than people who had to work less hard. It was harder for me to get in the room. I'd always have to be better, and I think that's quite a universal story when it comes to underserved talent. Obviously, I have the immense privilege of not suffering what some people suffer. I am, for example, Caucasian. I can put on a good accent if you need me to, and I was blessed with a university education. Even I am not actually truly representative of most people in the country. Suddenly I realized that's how you see me. It never occurred to me that somebody would see me that way, because I'd always thought I was quite posh compared to my friends and people I went to school with.

Q: Can you think of any great examples of representation that have stood out to you?

A: The worst thing is, I remember the bad ones more than I remember the good ones, and that I think maybe is because I've been conditioned for so long. I suppose if we start with the image of women – when a brand uses a woman of my age and they look like a human, and not a model, that is still so rare. *Sports Illustrated* did a whole issue of normal, beautiful, human women and I just remember feeling this amazing relief when I saw this woman walking down a runway looking like a normal woman. Bear in mind, I grew up in the very toxic diet culture of the 1980s, so for me that's a good example when brands embrace and place their consumer at the centre and celebrate them.

On the flip side, there was a particular shampoo that was apparently designed to alleviate menopausal hair loss with women. Their advert consisted of women in the shower saying this shampoo is really good, and then whispering 'over 40', as if announcing somehow managing to live past your 39th birthday was in itself so shameful one could not utter it at normal volume. You are basically buying into that myth that women have a sell-by date, and you are insulting women. Don't tell anybody your real age, you'll be worthless. It's a product designed to help women with the age they're going through, which is a natural process. You could have elevated and lifted, but instead you went into every trope. Do they ever stop and think why women don't seem to like to mention their age? In part it's because every ad tells us not to.

I remember Sainsbury's the supermarket did a wonderful Christmas advert. It told the lovely story of a black family, and the dad always sang the 'gravy boat' song. I loved it, go look it up, but the amount of trolling they received just for including an authentic family that looked a bit different was unbelievable.

I started here by talking about women because I think that 52 per cent of the population is the absolutely lowest hanging fruit to try to represent. There are all types of women, including women with different abilities, women of different ages and sizes, and more. We haven't even quite managed that yet, let alone when you move into positive affirmations of other groups of people in adverts.

Q: What is the Brixton Finishing School project that you run?

A: Well, it's not a finishing school in the sense you carry books around on your head! It's a diversity and inclusion initiative that links in with communities that are underserved by employers in our industry. That's partnering multicultural, socially mobile, new, diverse talent with exceptional industry training and then placing those people in roles at our partners. It's an end-to-end solution to the talent pipeline issue we see in our industry.

Q: From your experiences, how do we build a more inclusive industry that gets more people through the doors?

A: The problem lies with us. It's in our expectations, which can be exceptionally classist. We do a lot of proprietary research where we look at people's early experiences in the industry – there's a lot of so-called 'micro-aggressions', or frankly just aggressions, a lot of those are race or age based when you are junior, such as commenting on the tone of your language.

To me, professionalism is coming out with the best result for your business. Why have we chosen only one type of voice to be the way to do it and get to that result? I'm not suggesting that we all go around speaking slang all the time, I just think there is a middle ground. It comes back to my own experiences of not being put on certain accounts, or young black talent always being placed on the urban accounts. They may have something amazing to contribute to the luxury car, or to the skiing holiday, but our biases come and get in the way.

Young people from different backgrounds looking at our industry have marked our cards. I think it really hits them when they come through our Brixton Finishing School courses and they first enter spaces as a pioneer, one of the first people to look like them. Your average school child in any major city knows we live in a multicultural society – your school reasonably represents the population, but suddenly in our industry you've gone through this weird filtration device and there's only a couple of people like you.

We're having to push at the back, you have the talent, but we've had to push the door open for you to walk through. In the first few months a lot of our students ask themselves 'What the hell is this?' Suddenly all that stuff you thought had been dealt with by the generation before is real and you're the one as a young pioneer still having to deal with it.

There's a massive bounce rate with this pioneer talent who are not made to feel affirmed and included at all ages. We have better representation than we ever used to have at junior levels, but you look at the top senior tiers and it's not there. If you're an ambitious talent, which probably you are because you've made it through from a pioneer group, and you don't see any chance of getting to the C-suite, then why would you invest your time? Do you want to work somewhere where your physical characteristics, or your mental characteristics, are stacked against you? It's not your problem, it's the company's if they aren't doing anything to deal with it.

One of the things that I've really enjoyed watching and fills me with hope is the number of projects and high-quality programmes that have rolled out over the last couple of years. Pretty much every flavour of community you would like to support in your fruit bowl of diversity is starting to have an organization to support them. The best thing if you are a senior marketer is to realize you don't have to do this on your own – you can reach out to a third party who can help do the heavy lifting for you. Let's face it, you've got a massive brand to run, you've probably got quite hungry shareholders, and this isn't your day job. Luckily for you, other people have made it their day job or at least their passion project, and you can work with them.

Realize also that you cannot ignore it any longer and that you'll quite simply sell more stuff if you get it right.

Reference

Stonewall (2018) Stonewall reveals coming out at work still a problem. www.
stonewall.org.uk/about-us/media-centre/media-statement/stonewall-reveals-coming-out-work-still-problem (archived at https://perma.cc/ECC7-4HTC)

09

Creative development and product design

Throughout this book you've heard that inclusive marketing is about much more than any advert or product you create, it's a broader mindset and approach to marketing as a whole. That said, there's no avoiding the fact that your creative executions and products are the most visible tip of the inclusive marketing iceberg, and the place where people generally look for the best or worst examples of representation.

These fundamental outputs of the marketing process are seen by billions of consumers and inevitably play their small role in shaping societal norms and expectations. When we talk about representation more often than not this is what we start to think about, and so the whole process comes undone if you don't get this part right. This is where you start to shape exactly what story you will tell, how your advert will look, or how this new product or service will work.

This is as close as we'll get to really trying to define what good representation and inclusion looks like – I've consistently heard throughout this process that it is much more than who you put on the screen, but clearly that is a part of it. The question becomes how you will portray those characters, what stories you tell, and who will get to oversee the narrative. Historically, advertising has done a better job of presence and loose representation than it has of true inclusion and equality. There are obvious examples, such as the typical portrayal of women as housewives, and more uncomfortable examples, like the Geena Davis Institute (2019) evidence that black characters in advertising are presented as less intelligent.

Advertising must often condense complex scenes or stories into a handful of seconds, and stereotypes are a natural way of trying to take shortcuts in that process. In many ways, they are inevitable and necessary, and many people have pointed to the fact that advertising will always be limited in its ability to unpack the kinds of nuance longer form content can. That doesn't mean we cannot try, and it certainly doesn't mean we cannot avoid some of the more harmful stereotypes that we might otherwise perpetuate. The key point is to keep diversity top of mind across the creative process and to ensure we're challenging ourselves, or being challenged by others, when we jump to assumptions.

If you've followed the process in this book then inclusive creative development is not about taking your generic ideas and trying to squeeze tick-box diversity into them. By this stage you should be armed with insights, opportunity and thinking that will guide you. Perhaps you've even landed on a specific insight or human experience that comes from somewhere in your audience which could originate a powerful story that everyone will find interesting and relevant.

Some inclusive marketing is very deliberate in how it positively promotes an aspect of diversity and builds a story around celebrating that and championing that, perhaps even leading to charity partnerships and active advocacy. This is one approach, and it certainly has validity, although it moves you more into purpose-based marketing and some of the debates that surround that. If you can find a way to make it relevant both to your consumers and your brand then this can be powerful, but be careful of going too far in this direction if you don't have actions to back it up and it isn't a natural fit with your wider positioning.

Diverse consumers are not, however, charity cases – a person's gender, or age, or class, or race, or sexuality, or disability, or any other label we might try to attach to them doesn't define them, and doesn't mean they are any different to the other consumers you want to sell to. There is a difference, however, between trying, for instance, to target and represent the LGBT+ community in a casual manner, and running a campaign that is deliberately about Pride and inclusion. Both can be brilliant, but when you move into the latter territory you should expect more scrutiny, more questions to be asked about the actions you are taking behind the scenes, and perhaps more cynicism about your intentions.

This can be especially true if you are creating a product or service, where the commercial link to the inclusion initiative is very direct. Are you genuinely meeting a need that this audience has? Have you created something that makes your brand more accessible to them? Are you making a proactive effort to improve their lives, even in a small way? Do you have meaningful internal policies and approaches which support that community within your own business or consumers? If you're going to put a Pride flag on your product, or make a bold statement around gender equality, racism or another aspect of social justice then be prepared to back it up.

I'm not an expert in product design, but I know that solving for accessibility issues or other access challenges can have a much greater benefit on certain communities than ever showing them in an advert will. It's important in any product design process, physical or virtual, to take a step back and look at ways you could adapt the design for greater accessibility. You might solve someone's accessibility needs but there's a good chance you'll make the product better for everyone. At the end of this chapter we interview Christina Mallon who has been a champion of inclusive design across a number of different agencies and companies.

Inclusive marketing is often subtler and nuanced. It can simply be about reflecting the true diversity of your market in ways that draw no attention to that diversity at all. People living very normal lives and doing very normal things who happen to fall outside the most mainstream definition of what is 'normal' in society, not that that definition is ever very helpful. When we talk about a lack of representation in our advertising, it is often this that people are thinking of – not the need for more emotional brand manifestos, but just a day-to-day absence of people who seem to look or act like us in the media around us.

In the simplest terms, representation matters because, as I've heard countless times in the interviews for this book, without it people feel excluded and invalidated. Yet it is not just representation and presence that matters, it matters how those characters are treated and how you avoid them feeling tokenistic or like a 'tick-box' exercise.

The 3Ps framework

The Unstereotype Alliance (UA) is an initiative convened by UN Women in partnership with a number of global brands and creative agencies. It works to improve gender portrayals in advertising, and now increasingly challenges across wider areas of diversity too. They have developed a simple '3Ps' framework which is a good lens through which to evaluate your creative approach.

The 3Ps are presence, perspective and personality. The UA defines presence as being about who is featured in the communication, perspective as who is framing the story and personality as about the depth of the character.

Presence

Presence, or representation, is one of the key themes of this book, and of course it matters. We cannot hope to tell inclusive stories or show diverse perspectives if those voices aren't even present to begin with. It's not everything, but it's where we can start.

Representation starts with who is portrayed in creative work, and of course who the central characters are, because people don't want to only be included in the background. It's important that, overall, your communications feature a representative range of people based on the culture and diversity of your market, even if you have honed in on a specific core audience which only reflects part of that. There are many more aspects of inclusion than those we tend to think of, and it is impossible to write a list that doesn't leave others out, but consider gender, age, race, socio-economic status, sexual orientation, body size, religion and ability.

We'll look in more detail at perspective and personality but it starts here by ensuring the characters feel authentic and recognizable, especially to the communities you are trying to represent. This is made easier if you've done the homework beforehand, and have a diverse team or diverse external perspectives feeding into the project.

Focusing your narrative on under-represented communities can accelerate this, but isn't always required, and be careful about always presenting a community's struggles when there will be many more positive aspects. Check whether the inclusion you are pushing is adding up to be a positive portrayal.

Quotas aren't always helpful or enforceable, but it doesn't hurt to keep an eye on some core numbers. Gender is typically something that you can balance individually in many pieces of work; for broader areas of inclusion you cannot expect to represent everyone every time but tracking your representation over a period of time can highlight whether there are people you are continually missing out.

Perspective

Perspective can be trickier to understand than presence, but this is where well-meaning representation can start to go wrong if brands are not careful.

It's perhaps helpful to think about it in terms of who is directing the action, whose perspective is most central to the narrative, and whether those two are the same thing.

Inevitably, much advertising has historically had an implicitly male perspective – this can show up in voyeuristic camerawork, directly in voice-overs, or just in the ways in which men/women are directed within the piece. If you are having more diverse people present in the work, then think about how you can champion their perspectives. Some of the best inclusive work takes the perspective of one of those characters directly, ensuring that people not only see themselves but also their perspectives represented.

Here you begin to bring in the real human truth. True inclusion isn't so much about people's physical appearances as it is about their culture, their aspirations and their desires. Marketers need to be wary of representing situations and telling stories from their lived experiences and then substituting different characters into the same scene. People live wonderfully different and intriguing lives that are worth showcasing and celebrating, whilst merely recasting a scene does none of that.

As with every stage of this process, this is much easier when there is diversity behind the camera as well. If the script writer, director, casting agent and others bring different perspectives then you are more likely to see an authentic portrayal at the end of the process. Brands don't have to make political statements and campaign, but don't be afraid to challenge outdated perspectives in society about people, communities, relationships, and other norms; you'll be on the right side of history.

Personality

This is ultimately what can really differentiate tokenistic representation from true inclusion – how rounded and developed the characters you portray are. This can be a challenge in advertising, where we are always up against a clock and every second counts, but that just makes some of the smaller decisions (including those of staging, costumes, etc.) even more important.

Stereotypes are often shortcuts in adverts to help us cue the viewer in on a bigger story or joke, but they can be damaging and ultimately derivative. The best characters have three-dimensional personalities, and small actions, gestures, comments or even props bring those to life. Real humans can be funny, caring, strong, thoughtful, respected and more, and are much more than just a generic 'housewife' or 'office worker'.

Writing in the *Unstereotype Marketing Communications Playbook* (Unstereotype, 2020), the team conclude,

It is important that we see people, especially women, owning their own behaviour and taking control of their lives. And that beauty is used to show personality rather than only to suggest physical attraction. We want to portray the whole person in a way that transcends their gender/ethnicity or other intersectional aspect and sensitively incorporates that element. We must not only present people because of their gender/sexuality/race and further the expected or negative stereotypes that go with those aspects.

CHECKLIST
Creative development and product design

Key questions to ask yourself:

1 How are you applying the Unstereotype Alliance's 3Ps?

2 Do the characters come across as empowered, in control of their lives?

3 Have you considered beauty as a dimension of personality rather than just physical appearance and attraction? Is there a stereotypical interpretation of beauty? Tall, thin and fair for women, tall, macho and strong for men?

4 Where could diversity help originate powerful storytelling?

5 How diverse is the creative team and their inputs? Do they understand how different communities like to be represented?

6 How will diversity be reflected in different ad formats/lengths?

7 Have you considered how you can make your products and experiences inclusive, as well as your advertising?

MARKETER IN FOCUS
Andrew Geoghegan, CMO at PZ Cussons

The Unstereotype Alliance developed their framework in partnership with a number of companies, led by Unilever and Diageo. At the latter, Grainne Wafer and Andrew Geoghegan had developed their own internal training around positive gender portrayals that went on to feed into the UA's wider recommendation. Now in his new role as CMO at PZ Cussons, Andrew spoke about the steps you can take to ensure authentic, inclusive and ultimately positive portrayals in marketing.

Q: Why does representation matter to you?

A: I attended a piece of analysis probably about five or six years ago done by the Geena Davis Institute, where they showed data, hard data, on the journey, or rather lack of progress, on representation in advertising through the lens of inclusion in the industry. As somebody who would like to think that they were contributing positively to society through the work they did, I was immediately struck that, despite all the conversation that we'd had, no progress was being made.

I also recognized that the organization I worked for at the time, and advertisers in general, have a responsibility that the collective product that they put out there in communications has a positive and not a negative impact on enabling people to unlock their potential, and be whoever they might want to be.

It left me with a deep sense of responsibility that, perhaps without even realizing it, I was contributing negatively to this and therefore had to act. I also recognized that the fact that there had been no change in a decade meant that we had to work out why that was and what we needed to do differently.

Most of the people you talk to will agree that this is a good thing to do. So why have we made no progress? Why is nothing happening?

There's an intellectual challenge of unpacking how do you do it in practical terms. So that's how I went about thinking about it, and I thought that's what my contribution could be if I could help unlock the practicalities of making more inclusive content – work that did no harm and ideally enabled people to see their potential in the world through advertising and other forms of media.

The enemy is bias. Despite our best intentions we get it wrong, but I would celebrate the mistakes as well as those that get it right. Especially here in the UK with gender stereotyping regulations, we're seeing a lot of examples of inclusion that don't feel authentic to the real society we live in, but we can still learn from that.

Q: What are some good examples of representation in marketing?

A: The work I did back at Diageo with UN Women and the Unstereotype Alliance highlighted some great examples. Snickers has been good at this; in fact I think the work from Mars as a company in general has been really good.

The best examples for me are when it is subtle. I liked the 2021 John Lewis Christmas advert, for instance. I liked the casting of that – especially the alien. It was casual but smart.

We've just completed some new work on Carex, 'Life's a Handful', and with that we absolutely wanted to ensure that you sort of didn't notice it, but that inclusion was intrinsic in the idea. The concept is around the song 'We've got the whole world in our hands' and therefore that should include wide representation, but in an effortless way.

The best work goes beyond representation, it unlocks the character and tells the stories of people that go beyond the labels that we or society might want to put on them. They were only short snippets, but we tried to really bring different personalities and perspectives to life.

I do have a fundamental concern and rejection of the fact that labelling people has become such an important part of this discussion. Even now when we engage with consumers, we hear them choosing to label themselves, but we've got to go beyond the descriptions that codify people's expectations of you based on your gender, your sexuality or your ethnicity.

Great work goes beyond just presence and representation, but I recognize that to get there you may have to first do the numbers exercise of ensuring that across the body of your brand's work you are representing people. You cannot jump into characters if they're missing, or you decide inclusion is just about people's thinking styles.

Q: How do we achieve authentic representation and avoid ticking boxes?

A: The key to it is asking the right questions at every point in the development process and recognize bias throughout. The 12-stage framework you've expanded on in this book and the work I've done alongside Grainne Wafer for the UN are both fundamentally based on that notion. At each step we need to consider what we should be asking ourselves and having frameworks can help prompt and provoke so that you don't fall into the biases, traps and stereotypes that otherwise can creep into all our work.

The other piece is thinking broadly about who's doing the work – the people in your teams, in your agencies, in your suppliers, behind the camera and so on – you need to make sure you're creating a diverse and broad set of people. When you're using tools like research or other ways of learning about your work and impact then you should look to consult with different people.

You don't need to be personally representative of your target consumer to be able to create work that will appeal to them, but you do need to talk to them. I think that's especially true when you are wanting to talk to a specific audience. It's important to have the humility to admit that you don't know everything about their lives and their lived experience. It's just having that sort of wide-eyed humility and curiosity that I think enables the best work to be created.

It starts by people saying they want to see themselves in the work, and often they literally mean people who look like them and sound like them. It sometimes strikes me that as a white male I do of course see people like me superficially across advertising, because the presence and representation of that group is high, but the representation is often full of stereotypes. It goes across the board in all great marketing communications that they have excellent insight, they understand people, they really connect with humanity, and that goes well beyond considerations of presence, which are ultimately only skin deep.

Q: How do we go beyond presence to personality and perspective?

A: Presence is clearly a hygiene factor, but in the Unstereotype Alliance 3Ps framework we show that perspective and personality are the other two ingredients.

Even if you've got the right mix of people present, if your perspective is always still that of a male gaze, or another onlooker, then you are more likely to objectify and not situate your narrative within the perspective of your lead characters, in their world. The point about personalities is that we need to go beyond the surface, so that the narrative that you see is one of the whole person.

A great piece of work that sums this up for me is 'Caring is the Hardest Thing we Do' by the frozen foods brand Aunt Bessie's – it subverts the norm of a mother looking after the family when you discover that she's blind. Now of course her blindness or disability is integral to the story, but her character goes far beyond that, it's about her in the truest sense.

There's an interesting nuance there because you can think of leveraging elements of that person that are 'diverse', for example their disability or their sexuality, but you have to go further. The more you see people who just happen to be deaf, or blind, or something else for no specific reason, the more you normalize it.

Coming back to my point that the best work for me is subtle, I think sometimes when we overly shine a light on difference, we can make it quite inaccessible for people. You might feel that unless you're prepared to stand out and have the courage to fly in the face of society, then this might not be for you.

If you think forward to the world that we want to create, it's one in which those things are no longer relevant, and you don't have to talk about them. It's been over 50 years now since the modern Pride movement started, and if you imagine just 10, 20 or 30 years ago how differently you might have represented gay people in advertising. As the cultural context changes we need to ask ourselves again what is right, how might we do that?

Perhaps 10 years ago it was all about brands putting a rainbow on everything and saying they stand with that community, but that isn't always the right thing to do. Amongst gay men there are a handful of classic stereotypes that get shown and have dominated, but none of those groups are homogeneous. No one would ever look at women as 50 per cent of the population and assume they are all the same, there's always been nuance.

Q: How as a CMO do you lead this across your business?

A: In my business I also lead inclusion and diversity on the executive committee, so it is truly part of my job. The reality in the new job is that there are lot of things to do, and it hasn't always been possible to have it as the top priority, but having it formalized within my role means that people have been coming to me and asking how they can help.

It's easier now than it was five years ago, because people realize that the workplace has a responsibility to do more, and they are prepared to get involved. It's not a minority pursuit anymore, as I think it used to be. For instance, we have a female employee resource group which has an active community of male allies taking part too. You must work out who the people are that are really interested in this in your organization, then use them to gain a bit of momentum, and then start having conversations.

I do think it is useful to set some targets, because I think that holds the tension, but for me it is about creating culture and the environment. That means making people really feel like they can show up as themselves, and that people will be respectful of what their difference brings to the party. As with presence and personality in advertising, culture and inclusion are as important as presence in our teams.

Identify who is the lead and the sponsor within your organization, find the people who are motivated and excited by this agenda, and then just work out two to three things that you will focus on and do really well.

I mentioned the new Carex work. To get to that felt almost effortless, because we flagged it as a consideration to the agency that we used, that we really wanted them to think about it across the project. They took the WFA framework, and the marketing team also took examples of adverts that seemed to be showing diverse families but felt inauthentic, which helped illustrate what we wanted to avoid.

Five years ago, we'd probably have had a debate around whether it will alienate people and how well it would work with our core market, but that has shifted for us.

MARKETER IN FOCUS
Christina Mallon, Head of Inclusive Design at Microsoft

A marketer who has really inspired me in this process is Christina Mallon, who dealt with changes to her own mobility head on and has become an industry-wide champion for the importance of inclusive design and inclusive considerations right across the marketing process. I spoke to her about some examples of the inclusion opportunities that sit outside the obvious communications and advertising routes.

Mallon led the inclusive design and digital accessibility practice at Wunderman Thompson prior to taking on a new position leading inclusive design for Microsoft. Her challenge is always to look beyond the representation in our advertising to think holistically about our products and consumer experiences, and how we can really build accessibility and inclusive thinking into our full marketing approach.

Q: Why does representation matter to you?

A: It's important to me because I'm a part of an under-funded, under-represented community. Both my arms became paralyzed about eleven years ago. I was working in advertising, and I didn't see myself in any of the customer experiences. I really started to encounter ableism in the community, so I tried to understand what the root of that was.

I realized that there aren't enough people with disabilities similar to me represented in adverts, nor in experience design. That led me to set up the inclusive design group at Wunderman Thompson, one of the world's largest advertising agencies, so that we could help brands be more inclusive for people with disabilities like me.

Q: Can you think of any really great examples of representation and inclusive marketing or media that personally impacted you?

A: There's definitely been a few brands, especially in the last two to three years, that have really looked at disability inclusion from end to end. One brand that I particularly love, and I got the chance to work on this project, was Tommy Hilfiger Adaptive. It's a clothing line that has been curated based on the needs of people's different abilities, rethinking why some things are the same way that they have been for hundreds of years.

We started asking ourselves whether this is a good experience for disabled people, since every single person will experience disability in some form at multiple points in their lives. We took a look at the actual product, to see what changes they could make to the fashion line. Only then did we look at how, if they want to reach this consumer with this product, we can ensure that all communications around it are inclusive and accessible. For a disabled person they can actually see themselves in the ad, and they can actually buy the product too.

We helped them look at the full journey of a disabled customer, and looked at their existing touch points with customers, and looked at how to make them inclusive from end to end. Ultimately that's what people want and deserve. It's about levelling up your customer experience to ensure that everyone is included.

When you think in those terms, a lot of innovations have come from inclusive thinking. If we look at the touchscreen, keyboard, the typewriter, email, that was all created to fit a disabled consumer, and now are the preferred ways of working for everyone. When brands really think about that and serve that consumer, a lot of times innovation happens, and that's what every brand needs to be thinking about to really compete in this market.

Q: Rather than just jumping to advertising, how can brands think holistically about inclusive marketing?

A: I always tell brands to first look at the current experience of the products and services and interactions that they have. To make sure you do that journey map with people that have different lived experiences to those who created that experience itself. Subconsciously the creator is always putting their lived experience into the customer experience. We need to ensure that we're collaborating with people who are very different to ourselves, to ensure it's an inclusive environment for everyone who is interacting with the brand.

Then when it comes to new products or experiences and services that are created from the brand, you have to start at the brief stage – ensure that you are putting rules and checkpoints within the brief to guarantee that you're including people with lived experiences that are different from those running the project. That way, you don't have to go and fix these things that you might identify later. You want to try to do that upfront, because it's always cheaper and better to do it before something is created.

It reminds me of Pepsi and their two-litre soda bottle – they realized that the way that it was shaped was very difficult for people to grab, so they did some inclusive design thinking to reshape the bottle. We have also seen some interesting things coming from Olay where they redesigned a cream bottle for people with vision impairments and upper limb impairments. Olay recognized that sometimes stores themselves are not accessible for people with disabilities, so they ensured that they could provide this online and do it at no extra cost. I really like that they looked at the product and then looked at the full experience, and then they also created an advert that saw disabled people who collaborated on the project talking to camera. We saw with this project the value of really working with the community at the beginning. If we are going to make communications that are around accessibility, we need to make sure that the people we feature in the ad have a disability. Thinking like this really helps to ensure authenticity, especially in a market where inclusion is now a big topic for people that have fundamentally been left behind for so long.

Q: How can marketers think about inclusivity in their wider digital experiences?

A: A lot of times, when it comes to the creation of digital experiences, designers believe that accessibility, in terms of making something usable by people with disabilities, won't be beautiful. They believe that accessibility compromises beautiful design, and that's not true. If you go in with that assumption that really hurts accessibility.

Video is such a popular communications tool, but not adding closed captioning is such a mistake. The data we have around consumers' mobile usage shows us that they are not putting their speakers on – your audience is missing out on your story and information when captions aren't added. One of the biggest mistakes that I see is also relying on colour and shapes to tell a story or to give instruction, when 8 per cent of males have some sort of colour blindness.

We need to consider intersectionality when we are collaborating with these communities. Am I just speaking to a broad experience of disability? Or is it just for white men with wheelchairs? Disability ranges across everything from cognitive to physical to motor. We need to ensure that we're covering all those different disabilities and then ensure that we reflect how the wider lived experience of those users differs.

When I worked on skincare we had to check whether we were focusing only on light-skinned black women or showing a different range of skin tones. Then you have the intersectionality of, say, a blind individual from a lower income family that maybe doesn't have access to Wi-Fi all the time. How are we going to provide a digital solution for them for accessibility if they can't access Wi-Fi?

Q: What can positive representation look like in the adverts themselves?

A: In the last few years brands have started to step up and to consider the disabled community, but there is still a long way to go if we want good examples of work. Malteser's did a few great ads around disability that didn't make it something sad – a lot of the times when people with disabilities featured in ads, it's supposed to inspire the viewer, but inspire them to cry. What the work should do is either inspire the viewer to act to make the world better for a disabled person, or it should just include disabled people, like anyone else would be included, and normalize disability. Ultimately it is a normal thing that everyone experiences at multiple points in their lives, either situational, temporary or permanent.

Where it is inspiring the viewer to cry, that can be harmful for the disabled community, because it shows disability only in one light. It shows it as a really bad experience. In my personal case – and yes I'm a person of privilege with a job and income, and a supportive family, which many disabled people do not have – the whole experience as a disabled person is not bad. When you only show it that way it scares people around disability and that's not what we want.

Q: What can we do to make our industry itself more accessible to those from different communities and with different needs?

A: I think there is a desire for the industry to be more inclusive, but are people ready to put in the work? At Wunderman Thompson we put effort in and built relationships that are focused around increasing the visibility of disabled people in the workforce. Unfortunately, I have seen other companies that have said they'd love to have more disabled people at their company, but when they get there, the whole experience for that disabled person is not inclusive and they're not set up for success.

I think that's true for a lot of underfunded communities who are told that they are wanted there but we're not making it inclusive for them, and it's hard to even get in the door. I've heard some horror stories from people about whether they can rise through the ranks, or whether they just feel tokenistic.

One thing that I always try to do when I'm making a decision that affects somebody else is think about how my lived experience might be reflected in my decision. I try to either consult with someone that doesn't have my lived experience or use my experience of working with other underfunded communities to give me empathy.

Q: How can clients get started on this journey, when it can feel a little overwhelming?

A: Initially you can put together a maturity model. Look at your products and your spaces, and see what you need to do for access. Look at the creative and ask whether someone can even engage with it before starting to look at what representation in the ads is. If people can't even access it, that means that they're not going to be able to get the information. They can't even get in the door. Now from there, when the door has been made accessible, then we can ask whether that door looks as beautiful as the other door that's not accessible. If it doesn't, then we want to give that same type of experience – we don't want them to have to go in the back door just because it's wheelchair accessible. And then from there maybe we reinvent the door, or ask, do we even need the door in the first place?

It's going from getting the basics around access, and then going into a place of innovation, which can take time. It can take one year or five years. Often there's not a pot of money that brands have put aside. We do need to focus on this, but the resources are lacking. It's about really putting that maturity model together in that five-year plan and then working with like-minded colleagues within your organization. Perhaps you can ask your manager to let you use 20 per cent of your time, or you can hire someone who can help you achieve these goals, but it's not going to happen overnight.

It's crucial to work with the communities that are not featured in your experience, share with them your goals to become a more inclusive company, and ask them to work with you to get you there. It's like the process that we see in digital design, where people will launch things and just want to get them out there, and then they need feedback to improve on their first step. If you're transparent and fair, people tend to understand and want to help you.

References

Geena Davis Institute (2019) Bias and inclusion in advertising. https://seejane.org/research-informs-empowers/bias-inclusion-in-advertising/ (archived at https://perma.cc/A2NH-K8TL)

Unstereotype (2020) *Unstereotype Marketing Communications Playbook*. www.unstereotypealliance.org/en/resources/research-and-tools/3ps-unstereotype-marketing-communications-playbook (archived at https://perma.cc/CP9U-GRRR)

10

Consumer testing

We don't always get a chance to test our products or campaigns with consumers before they launch, but it can be a key sense check of inclusive marketing if we can find a way of doing so. In some bigger companies this might involve substantial systematic research; in other cases you may be able to find informal ways of gaining perspectives through your network or even simple online surveys.

When done well, consumer testing can help validate your inclusive portrayals, avoid any potentially negative representations and give you valuable steer of any possible aspects to watch out for as you go into the production process. Pre-testing can, however, also validate existing biases and it is important to consider how you ensure the process itself is inclusive in design.

One of the biggest questions relates to the sample of consumers that you are able to involve in any testing approached, and whether this reflects the true make-up of your consumer base and incorporates representative audiences. Broad testing on universal demographics can miss an opportunity to understand diverse perspectives on the work.

It's worth being deliberate around inclusion in your pre-testing – don't just wait to see if topics of stereotyping and bias come up, but ensure they are actively part of the questions you ask. This can help you build in an effective check, which may bring to light considerations your team hadn't thought of. If you are looking to portray a specific community group then it's very helpful to research the work both with members of that affected group, and with other experts who have experience in understanding how those groups are likely to react.

We can also bring bias into the testing process itself in terms of the stimulus we present and the questions we ask, so think carefully about this or work with subject experts. When creating adverts, you may well only have a storyboard and script to show as part of the pre-testing, and many consumers will struggle to fully visualize and understand your concept. Today it's possible to make simple animations or mock-ups to aid as stimulus, or consider including casting notes and any production briefings as part of the presentation – your research subjects won't be able to evaluate decisions that aren't presented to them and may simply give you the benefit of the doubt when things are left vague.

Give colleague communities an opportunity to have an input

Alongside, or instead of, any formal external research it's always worth considering how to leverage your internal colleagues and communities to provide feedback. This can be particularly effective if you have established employee resource groups (ERGs) that represent the interests of various diverse groups. Whilst you cannot expect your colleagues to single-handedly represent vast and nuanced communities, when approached positively they can provide valuable feedback and input.

Work with the group organizers to establish boundaries around the commitments they feel are fair and useful, including agreeing on the cadence and time commitments of any consultation, and being clear on what is in it for them. This might be as simple as the opportunity to positively shape content and see better representation, but be aware that you are most likely asking people to do something outside of their job description and that it can be exhausting to be always asked to be a representative voice.

All these efforts will be undermined if you don't manage to create a safe space where frank and honest critique is welcomed and understood. It's natural not to want to rock the boat, nor to want to criticize the hard work of your colleagues. This can be amplified even further where that feedback can be seen as subjective or is calling on a personal aspect of your culture or identity which you might be self-conscious of. If you're struggling to build that open and honest culture then consider channels for anonymous or less personal constructive feedback, but do ask yourselves what management can do to change this.

Interpreting and understanding testing results

It's important to recognize that pre-testing is both an art and a science. There have been hugely creative and successful adverts that performed poorly in such testing and would never have been made if people didn't have the confidence to look beyond it. That isn't to say that you can ignore such testing if it doesn't suit your narrative, but it does mean it's reasonable to evaluate it and come to clear and justifiable reasons why you might want to ignore certain feedback.

This can be particularly tricky when looking at inclusive portrayals, which can be divisive both within the communities being represented and within wider audiences. If you have reason to believe your approach could be particularly controversial, divisive, or nuanced then it is worth doubling down on the research within the affected group and ensuring you canvas a wide range of opinions to see whether questions being raised are widely held concerns in the community.

CHECKLIST
Consumer testing

Key questions to ask yourself:

1 Does pre-testing include a check of bias or stereotyping?

2 Are stereotyping issues researched amongst the affected group, as well as with experts who understand how those groups are likely to react?

3 What influence could the storyboard have? Does this prompt any areas of concern or opportunity?

4 Have you leveraged input from your own businesses's ERG groups or diversity council?

5 Have you created a safe space for frank and honest critique of the creative and interpretations?

MARKETER IN FOCUS
Asad Dhunna, Founder and CEO at The Unmistakables

Given that our teams themselves are never going to be truly representative of everyone, and that we don't necessarily need them to be, there's an increasing opportunity to work with partners who can help bring some of those perspectives into our business in other ways and help us shape our own cultures in the process. Asad Dhunna had worked in a number of PR agencies before he saw the need and opportunity to open his own consultancy – they specialize in helping brands build inclusive cultures but also 'outsights' which can bring diverse external perspectives and evidence into your business.

Q: Why does representation matter to you?

A: There is a personal side and a professional side. From a professional point of view, as I moved up through the ranks in marketing I started to see fewer people who looked like me at certain tables. By the time I reached the board level, when I looked around there was no one there with the same skin tone or skin colour as me, and there's no one there who's also gay, and then there's also no one there who's Muslim. Then you start going through these things where you ask yourself what it means to be a leader – how do I really lead a business if I don't know if I fit in here and don't know if the work I do belongs here?

At the same time, I had clients asking me how they can better understand different audiences. What do they need to know about the LGBT+ community, or black, or Asian people? Ultimately I just thought that there was something going on there for me that wasn't quite right and that's why I branched off and created The Unmistakables.

All of that was compounded by what was happening in my personal life. I remember as clear as day an example, I think it was probably 2014 and I was in Westfield Shopping Centre in Stratford. I just stopped and looked around at all of the adverts, at H&M, and Zara, and every other brand. I looked up and I couldn't see anyone there who looks like me. I started to feel like I didn't belong here, but I was born and brought up in this country so how do you square that with the feeling of not being seen when you walk around?

The two things came together and made me think I've got to do something about it because I can't let another generation go through that same sort of feeling of not belonging. Being in the world that I was in with my agency life I knew how and why some of those decisions were getting made, so I thought if I can influence some of that change then I really need to.

My eye is more tuned to advertising because of who I am and what I do, but I think the everyday person, even if they might not be conscious of it, would still feel it. I'd like to think it's getting better now, and certainly the pendulum is swinging. That said, I also used to live in Peckham, South London, and I remember cycling to work in the City and it just felt like I was in two entirely different places. I struggled to square these two things because it was just a half an hour cycle, it was just four miles, but such a big difference in culture.

Q: Can you think of any really great examples of representation and inclusive marketing or media that had a personal impact?

A: There are two things that come to mind. There was a Rowse Honey advert that re-imagined the 'Three Bears' nursery story. They did an activation where they had three gay 'bears' living in a house, trying different porridge, and I thought it was absolutely brilliant. It was really clever because they had tapped into something genuinely within gay culture, they've understood the concept of bears, they've leant into it, they riffed with it, and it was just really funny.

At the time I was the Communications Director for Pride in London and I loved the advert so much that I found the agency that did it and then found the planner, Jamie Inman. He led the strategic insight. Jamie, as it happens, is a straight man. He told me how they made space to really understand the community and what was going on in culture, and how the client really loved and respected that process.

If I think of where I've seen the best representation recently then it's on *Strictly Come Dancing* (the UK version of *Dancing with the Stars*) and seeing how effortless that was in including disability with Rose, AJ in terms of representing black women, and Johannes and John, a gay couple together in the final. I think we cannot underestimate how important that is for people to see.

It got me thinking about how you squeeze something that needs nuance and depth into a 60 or 90 second advert. When you look at where culture is going you look at shows, films, TV, that's where you're seeing real depth and the next level of positive representation.

Q: How do marketers get the right balance of voices inputting in their work and thinking?

A: There are a couple of ways of approaching this. I think it starts with listening to colleagues who are themselves, for instance, LGBT, who maybe have different ethnicity, who might be disabled, or whatever their identity might be. You've got to have a culture where people feel like it's safe to do that and safe to talk about their experiences. It must not be extractive, so it starts with setting up the cultural conditions for that within a business – otherwise the risk is that you bluntly go and ask the person in the corner, who's already feeling that they don't belong here, to give you the insight to try to help you win an award.

There's some risk in there. There are companies that rely overly heavily on their ERGs, or who make their team members tokenistic and expect them, for instance as a black person, to know everything about the black community. It's a lot of pressure to put on someone, and even more importantly it might not be why they are there. They're just there to do the job you are paying them to do.

You've got to create that balance, so one of the things we've done is build up a network of people who we call 'culture makers'. They could be activists, journalists, artists – people who are all on the frontline of accelerating inclusion in what they do. We bring their voices into marketing planning sessions with clients. Those are people that are being paid to be there, paid to talk about what it is like to be from a certain background, and what it is like to be on the frontline of activism for, say, trans communities. You get to hear those voices and you just get a different perspective. That doesn't mean you take everything that they say as gospel and run with it, but they can expand your thinking. Ultimately, I think that's what good marketing should be about – finding sources for creativity, finding new sparks, and then building that into an idea.

I guess those are two ways, setting up your own structure in the right way so that it's not extractive, and then looking at the networks your partners or other companies might have. There are companies that do exactly this, and bring in under-represented voices in an equitable manner to help guide and spark creative thoughts.

Q: Marketers are sometimes afraid to shape and launch progressive work. How can we help them with that?

A: I think you've touched on something around fear and that people are living in a culture of fear. I think fear is then a block to innovation and creativity.

We did some research in our diversity and confusion research report and we found that people are not sure about what language to use at work. What to do around a certain cultural event or worrying will they get 'cancelled'. All of these are pretty big things that you might be grappling with in your spare room or at home by yourself. You cannot deflate that worry or talk it out on your own.

We need to create space to say that if people are offended, or if we start testing and we're seeing it's going in a certain direction, then you will address that or change that. Quite often, mistakes happen unnecessarily because any possible offence comes from things that haven't been considered or looked at in a different way.

Or you can say that you're going to prepare yourselves for what we know could happen, and how then do we take a strong position around that and lean into it? That's where marketers can work more closely with reputation and communications leads to look at things they are testing and what they see coming, but knowing that this will be a way to spark a conversation or start an important debate.

I think marketers do face a bit of a bind now. There's a squeeze on resources, and with so many things going on a lot of it is a race to the bottom line in the execution. What that means is that people are rushing or reverting to old processes, but those processes need to be interrogated, need to be blown up and re-thought. There's something critical about having a shared language and some shared planning tools. That's something we've worked on with a couple of agencies and their clients.

If you've got lots of time and you're creating a long spot that will have a number of different executions you can really get into some deep inclusive planning, but if you've just got some almost throw-away content how does that show up? Have you made space to talk about it or are we just rushing into decisions? That's when you might cut corners and decide just to change the face of the person that you're going to show, or just put a Pride flag on the image. In pausing for just one quick second and looking at your shared language you can avoid this. Looking ahead to the end of the year and across all the campaigns you will have run, we encourage our clients to consider what they'll want to look back and say they have achieved in totality. A lot of the work we're doing is just helping our clients and agencies find space to talk about this.

Hopefully over the next five or ten years our industry will become genuinely more inclusive and diverse, and perhaps we'll have to have fewer of these conversations about inclusive marketing because it will be happening naturally. Until that point, I think that if you're not there yet, you can get there faster with some help.

PART FOUR

Stage three

Inclusive production

STAGE ONE

Inclusive briefing and strategy

1. Business and brand strategy
2. Strategic insights and data
3. Marketing and creative briefs

STAGE TWO

Inclusive planning

4. Partner and team selection
5. Creative development and product design
6. Consumer testing

STAGE THREE

Inclusive production

7. **Production**
8. **Post-production**
9. **Localization**

STAGE FOUR

Inclusive launches

10. Media and 360 activation
11. Launch and consumer response
12. Measuring success

11

Production

It's taken many steps to get there but you've finally reached the point of making your ideas a reality. Whether it's a physical manufacturing process, or (in most cases) a content creation and production process, you'll now be producing the most visible outputs of your inclusive marketing efforts. Many people jump to this stage by making minor tweaks to the casting or creative team at this point, but we know it's important to come much more prepared and with inclusive thinking built right into the project.

Production is an entire process within the process, and often relies on different teams and partners who might have had limited exposure to your previous discussion. They are most likely working under considerable time pressure and potentially across multiple different clients at the same time. Once again, the teams we typically work with are likely to lack broad representation and will bring their own valid but specific life experiences and biases into play.

This can create something of a perfect storm in terms of squeezing out your inclusive efforts at the last moment, but as with every stage in the process there is also a positive opportunity to explore. It is important to deliberately keep diversity top of mind throughout the process and not to leave that to chance – as with the earlier briefing, don't be afraid to deliberately call out to new partners that this is something to be prioritized and considered.

Casting isn't everything, but it is important

Whilst not the magic bullet it is sometimes seen as, casting is clearly a key stage in the process with a big impact on how inclusive your work will appear to be. It's critical to have an inclusive casting brief, which leaves room to explore different directions and limits assumptions to those that are critical to the work. If you're bringing the experiences of a specific community to life then clearly the brief will want to focus in on that, but if the brief is much broader don't jump to excluding diverse communities from it.

Timing is a key consideration here, and after a long creative process it's common for the actual production to be run against very tight deadlines. Putting ourselves under that pressure forces us to take shortcuts like jumping to using familiar actors and faces, which may not give casting agents the space to explore broader and more inclusive options. It's also worth deliberately sense checking whether there is an opportunity for an under-represented group to casually play a greater role in that piece, without needing to change the overall flow of the narrative.

There are some fundamental decisions you'll make that surround the actors themselves which can create unwanted subtext, stereotypes or simply undermine your authenticity. If you are casting a more diverse group then challenge the other creative teams, such as wardrobe and styling, on whether their decisions reflect this, or if they are erasing some of the uniqueness of different cultures.

Production locations are a good concern to raise, both in terms of how inclusive the on-set environment is, and also how authentically they reflect the nuances of your cast in their décor and sensibility. If we are trying to attract and include broader acting talent in our productions then, as with our own workspace, we need to ensure we're shaping inclusive environments where people don't feel discriminated against, and where practicalities such as access requirements and facilities are considered. It may not always be necessary, but you should be prepared to evaluate the need for quiet spaces, prayer rooms, gender neutral toilets, accessibility ramps, and any other factors that could physically limit the inclusion on set.

The visible staging, wardrobe choices and props you end up using can in themselves reinforce stereotypes or build new positive associations. Be careful of falling into simple traps such as always presenting the man as getting ready for work whilst the woman stays home, or countless other stereotypes. Whilst there are many ways in which people dress and style themselves the same, regardless of their culture, there are of course distinctive differences that we shouldn't look to erase. If you have cast a black family but everything about where they live, how they dress, how they style their hair, and what decoration they have in their home is the same as if you'd cast a white family then it's worth double-checking that you're truly allowing them to be their authentic selves. It's possible you are, but also possible you're missing the kinds of human details that will make your work more effective.

At the top of any creative production is the director, whose job is ultimately to bring their interpretation of your vision to life and rally the team around that. There is currently an indisputable lack of diversity in these senior creative positions, and also in the teams they work with. There is of course no reason why a director cannot pull together an authentic portrayal of a life very unlike their own – in fact that is arguably their entire job description – but they'll need to continually sense check and ideally have a range of inputs around them to achieve it.

We also need to continue pushing to increase the inclusion we see in the teams themselves, and especially in leadership positions. This involves getting a broader cross-section of the population to want to join the industry, but also ensuring they have a fair and equal chance to succeed when they do. There are steps all marketers can take to try to help with this, especially at the point of team selection and bid tendering – until we naturally see more diversity in the pool of talent it can be helpful to have targets and processes to give female and other under-represented directors a fair shot at tenders.

This can mean more than just 'levelling' the playing field and giving them a chance to pitch and compete. Where we've historically given people less opportunity or experience, we may need to consider mentoring, apprenticeships and other ways to allow them to build up the same portfolios and experience as others have been able to.

CHECKLIST
Production

Key questions to ask yourself:

1 What is the casting brief? Have you allowed enough time for an inclusive casting process? Could an under-represented group play a greater role?

2 Have you considered whether props or wardrobe choices reinforce stereotypes?

3 What is the diversity of the full production crew?

4 Is the shoot an open, inclusive and unbiased environment, with safe spaces and accessible facilities (e.g. wheelchair access or gender-neutral bathrooms)?

5 Will there be a triple-bid tender including female/other under-represented directors?

MARKETER IN FOCUS

Efrain Ayala, Global Diversity and Inclusion Director at Reckitt

Reckitt is one of the companies that has been loudly championing the need to create inclusive production environments if we are truly going to create inclusive work. It is also a rare example of a business with a role dedicated to D&I within marketing, a job Efrain took having previously led substantial transformation in its broader digital capabilities. He shared some of the key considerations that we should all have around inclusive production.

Q: Why does representation matter to you?

A: As a person who has intersectional identities that are often pushed into the margins, I grew up being put in that marginalized space either through my queerness, or through just the class that my family was in. We're a Puerto Rican family that was in the suburbs of Chicago and we didn't fit in with the white upper-middle-class population. We were this working-class Hispanic family that ate weird foods and had too many vowels in their names.

I've lived a life where I've experienced being 'othered' first hand, and while being a white, CIS-gendered, suburban person puts me in a square of privilege, it certainly was something that I did experience from time to time. Being able to take my professional career and do something about that for others in the ways that I can is really important to me.

It has felt like paying homage to my younger self and all of the queer little Puerto Ricans out there, in fact all of the queer kids – being able to harness that experience in a positive way through the work that I do now.

Q: Tell me how you came to have a dedicated role leading D&I in marketing.

A: I come from the creative agency world, an Ogilvy and Mather alum, but I moved seven years ago to work client-side at Reckitt. I started in a digital role, and I was leading the digital transformation of our hygiene business, but then a new opportunity came up to take on a dedicated diversity and inclusion role. It was a nice combination of what I am passionate about but also my ability to create change and create new behaviours within our marketing culture.

We agreed at the highest levels that D&I needs to be treated just like digital – a capability future marketers need to have. I was asked to come in and combine my previous experience in creating those new processes and changes, but also the passion I have for doing good with the power of our iconic brands.

Q: Can you think of any examples where representation has really stood out to you?

A: To answer that I will go on a journey. I'm going to flash back to the first time that I remember seeing a queer person on the TV, because it is still fresh in my mind, it has been burnt into my memory. It was Walter Mercado, who was a Puerto Rican personality on the Spanish language news in the United States, and he read the horoscopes daily to viewers. He was a very flamboyant, opulent character and I remember the first time seeing him on the TV as a young queer, closeted, Puerto Rican boy. 'Whoa – who's that and why does he have everyone's attention?'

He was different but he still commanded this attention and respect. If you don't know Walter Mercado, he was extremely loved by the Latin American community. I remember being so fascinated because any time before that, any sort of queer character was shown as being the butt of the joke, or perhaps 'trauma porn'. People were looking and laughing at their experiences. But this is the first time where I saw a queer person command respect and attention.

He was on the news giving those horoscopes every day and so that was the first moment I remember seeing someone who felt like me in front of me. It's so powerful to me that I still get excited and goose bumps thinking about it, because I really felt for the first time that people like me existed out in the world. A man who wants to wear make-up, fabulous capes, and jewels – yes, I can see myself there.

Thinking more recently, the things that stick out to me today are the things that are not meant to stick out, if that makes any sense. I tend to find myself really pleased and feeling positive when I'm in a brand space where I'm not expecting to see people like me, or different people who aren't typically the norm.

It's the Nike product page, for example. Recently I was on their website and scrolling through the pages and just seeing so much body diversity was powerful for me. You might think it's only a product page, but what it unlocked for me is that it's in these hidden moments where representation really matters. It's not just in those big splashy moments that we tend to see and celebrate, there are all these unspoken moments that can be just as powerful.

Q: I know you've been focusing a lot on how to improve the production stage in the marketing process. Can you share a bit of that?

A: Most times when a marketer hears diversity and inclusion, they tend to immediately think about casting choices and who they are putting in front of the camera. If they're being slightly more nuanced and sophisticated, they start to look at how they can be relevant to their lived experience. For us it's about that but also creating a sense of belonging and inclusion behind the camera and on the set is often overlooked.

It's just as important for me that our marketers and production partners have the same shared values. If we are going to bring a bunch of talent on camera, off camera, or in any way part of the process to help tell stories featuring historically excluded communities, or even just our business-as-usual product coms, I want to make sure everyone feels welcome in those spaces. Everyone should feel safe in those production spaces, and they should have an opportunity to provide feedback so we can continue to improve and provide these environments.

We talk about inclusion of our people a lot from an internal HR perspective, but if we really want to tell stories and connect with people that sense of belonging is also required in the production space. That's really going to enable teams to bring the best out of everyone, from the on-screen talent to the behind-the-screen talent. When everyone feels that they can contribute in their own unique way and bring their full selves to those spaces, the output is going to be so much more impactful, authentic and meaningful.

When you think about the production phase, of course think about what's happening on camera, but also think about how you choreograph those people and how you are going to style them. Who's going to be styling them, understanding their needs and making sure that talent is being protected?

One thing we've found in the work that we're doing to understand and explore this complex space is that models and actors are treated very differently. Actors typically belong to an association or a guild where there are standards, parameters and benchmarks that need to be met in terms of how they're paid, how they're treated and their working conditions. Models don't have any of that, so there's an inequity there.

Sometimes when you're working with a fragmented production system, such as if you are using a lot of influencers, then the standards can be completely missing. We've seen stories emerge from the industry, outside of Reckitt work, where influencers are using their children to produce content in a way that the Screen Actors Guild would deem inappropriate. As brands we are the producers of these pieces of content, and we should care just as much for the on- and off-screen talent as we care about the communities we want our brands to be advocating for.

There are simple steps we can all take – ensuring the spaces we use are accessible for people with physical or invisible disabilities, for instance. Also considering the need for prayer rooms for people of different faiths. It's really thinking about this space, and then how do we make sure that we're enabling everyone who we may invite into it to feel welcome and bring their best self and their best work to the process?

The production process itself can come under a lot of time pressure, which is exactly why the work should be done upfront and everyone should be clear on what is to be expected. You need to think about how to write a bias-free casting brief ahead of time, so when the inevitable crunch happens there's a framework for people to use.

Q: Working in a global role, how do you think diversity and inclusion can be approached and localized?

A: It is something that is dynamic and challenging, but the way that we like to think about it is a 'glocal' approach. At a global level we try to take a particular point of view where each of our brands must distinctly define which communities can actually benefit from the use of their product. That approach enables us to have a positive impact on society, but also stay connected back to the business strategy. In doing that it helps the local teams understand what kinds of communities exist in their markets, which are added into the broader global commitment that's being made at the brand level. That collaboration between the global and local teams means that we can synthesize what a D&I strategy at a global level means from a growth opportunity but allow the local teams to translate that into meaningful work that's going to connect with the people in their markets.

Depending on your role, you may not feel that you have a huge amount of influence directly on the marketing outcomes, or perhaps you are just so busy with competing priorities that you don't know how to fit this in. There are small ways we can all make a difference – start with practising equal share of voice in your meetings. That is something you can do two seconds after you have read this. Simple actions that invite more diverse voices to participate in the process will create more collaborative teams, dialogues and outcomes.

12

Post-production

This is a part of the process that many of us give relatively little thought to, but your best intentions can still be left on the cutting room floor and there are specific technical steps you can take to ensure greater inclusivity.

Even if you are now racing to a tight campaign launch deadline it's important to step back and ensure your final edits are delivering on your original inclusive vision. Post-production can change the final impression and impact of your work both positively and negatively, especially in terms of what you choose to highlight and what you decide can be cut out.

It's at this point you'll really face tricky decisions around what you can include on screen, especially if you're having to create cut-down versions of longer adverts, even down to edits for digital channels, which might just be seconds long. It's not uncommon to see longer form videos that broadly represent society cut down into shorter edits that suddenly only show a very specific or average portrayal – whilst you may well not be able to always show everybody, challenge yourself on what is driving your decisions around who makes the cut.

If you're turning your key campaign creative into a suite of assets, then really push yourself to maintain the spirit of diversity within those. If you're running a campaign across multiple out-of-home advertising sites, then consider showing different cast members on each. Don't forget any of your touch points such as your website or your commerce content where inclusion can continue to play a key role.

It helps, of course, if there is diversity in the post-production team, but as ever consider leaning on the other perspectives and research you may have collated. If your pre-testing flagged any potential aspects to watch out for, or essential aspects to be included to feel authentic then this should be part of the brief to the team to help avoid them falling into a trap.

There's absolutely no reason why inclusion can only feature in longer form content, though of course it is easier to show more rounded representation in such contexts. Truly inclusive brands bring that inclusive mindset through to their websites, their catalogues, their stores and even their most fleeting social media posts, but this requires deliberate effort and consideration.

Post-production is where you'll be applying any visual or audio effects and these bring with them opportunities both for inclusion and exclusion. In researching this book, I spoke to a number of neurodiverse people who pointed out that some of the visual effects, camera techniques or fast editing that adverts employ can be uncomfortable for them to watch. I also heard from hard of hearing and visually impaired people that advertisers are rarely taking the necessary steps to be truly inclusive to them, and that attempts to portray them on screen sometimes felt disingenuous whilst this remains the case.

Building accessibility into our marketing

There is a challenge to advertisers to ensure we are making use of accessibility features like subtitles where they are available, and even to consider building them into the original video where they are not. Such accessibility brings wider benefits to advertisers, for instance helping them communicate to consumers who are seeing their adverts in naturally 'sound off' environments such as their mobile phones.

There are other emerging accessibility features, such as audio description soundtracks, which need advertisers to advocate for them and take advantage of when they do launch. Companies like P&G have been pushing for the introduction of these features on the media owner side, but advertisers need to follow through with making the content that takes advantage of them.

For those willing to embrace this inclusion there are both creative challenges and opportunities. You may be concerned that putting subtitles, sign language or other visual clues into your creative will lessen the creative vision, but there are ways to build the two together, such as developing subtle branding around them. Audio description soundtracks require a new piece of sound production but also sufficient gaps in any dialogue to allow for the description to take place; this is a new skill that forward-thinking directors and scriptwriters will need to consider.

Whether it's for audio description or a more standard voiceover, this is another area where stereotypes can sometimes creep in. Diverse casting should play a role amongst voice talent too, and there is often powerful distinctiveness that comes from exploring the colloquial nuances of accents.

As you go into your final approvals and sign-offs, it's the last opportunity you'll have to check for bias, look back over your process to date, and see if you've managed to bring your inclusive brief, insights and identified opportunities to life. Don't take this for chance, build a deliberate sense check into your approval process where you ask yourselves these questions one last time.

CHECKLIST
Post-production

Key questions to ask yourself:

1 Is there diversity in the post-production team?

2 What is the casting for any voiceovers? Are you avoiding stereotypes?

3 Have you considered colloquial nuances of accents?

4 Are there opportunities to make assets more accessible (e.g. closed captions, audio descriptions)?

5 Have you ensured the approval processes account for bias?

6 Have you double-checked that the final edit delivers on your diversity ambition (in all cut-downs)?

MARKETER IN FOCUS
Michael Baggs, Strategy Director at Social Element

Autism and other forms of neurodiversity are an area of inclusion that many marketers struggle with, not least because so-called 'invisible' disabilities are difficult to practically represent. Beyond just including their narratives in our marketing, there are, however, a range of practical steps marketers can take to make their work more accessible, and in doing so probably make it more impactful for everyone. Michael Baggs is a seasoned marketing strategist who has also spoken out regularly about the challenges of being autistic in our industry and the opportunities that come from listening to people who think and see the world a bit differently.

Q: Why does representation matter to you?

A: I think from personal experience neuro-divergent people don't show up well in the industry, and in fact until the past couple of years haven't really started showing up in the media at all. I think the honest reality of it is that one in eight people, so about 15 per cent of the population, are in some way neurodiverse but because those stories are missing it's quite a lonely space to be in for a lot of people.

That's particularly tough for people who have social issues, so I think simply by including those voices, including those stories, it just adds an awful lot to a massive number of people.

Q: Can you think of examples where you have started to see positive representation?

A: I think TV has begun to be a really great space for this, with real world casting and acting. It's still relatively fresh, but there have been some wonderful examples – there was a programme called *Everything's Gonna be Okay* which I think has recently finished but the comedian director Josh Thomas is autistic, and he was also one of the leads in that. At the start of it Kayla Cromer, one of the lead actresses, also self-identified as autistic so that's the first time we've had a television show about autistic people, with autistic actors and an autistic director. It has helped break a lot of the stereotypes about dyslexic people always being brilliant at maths. There's a harmful trope for autistic people to show up in media as white, male and robotic, and they're not – it's a full spectrum of people.

It's fantastic to see those walls come down because people are allowed to represent themselves and I think that's also true if you look at other aspects of diversity, for example how non-white people have shown up historically in television and film and how they are now, now that they are writing and directing their own shows. It's a world of difference, and I think that is starting to happen around neurodiversity, and as a result people can truly see themselves. The first place to really break through is animation and that's because lots of neurodiverse people are creative – I think 20 per cent of people that work in the creative industry are either autistic or neurodiverse.

Recently Pixar had two shorts back-to-back called *Loop* and *Float*. *Float* was directed by Bobby Rubio, who has an autistic son, and the short is essentially the story of him and his son which he brought to life. That's an important thing that James Victore, the brilliant creative mind, has often said – if you're not telling your story and not being honest about yourself, it won't mean anything to anyone. That's a key element here not just within neurodiversity but for everyone within a diverse landscape.

Loop was a first across the creative industries in that they had a non-verbal autistic character played by a non-verbal autistic voice actress. Thinking about marketing and media, that's just not something I imagine many people would have considered, but I think this kind of representation is so vital that I cried when I saw it. It's the first time I've seen a non-verbal autistic person ever outside of a documentary.

Q: How can marketers get better at approaching and representing neurodiversity?

A: I think education is really the first step. It's the important piece. Until there's training and understanding it's not going to open space for people. Universal Music Group (2020) has published *Creative Differences*, which is a brilliant handbook that basically has a walk through for neurotypical people about how to work with, how to hire and how to nurture this talent.

It's not just a case of how you get people through the door, it's how you manage neurodiverse people, how you accept that some people want to go in careers that are different paths to what you think they should have. It's helping people be their best selves and by doing that they create great work. It's about how you make people feel included, able to be themselves, and able to bring their unique perspectives. How do you enable people to bring their unique worldview into the office? From a marketing perspective I think it comes down to neurodiverse people representing themselves – if you have neurodiverse people on your staff, their voices and their stories come through.

It's probably not, however, just a case of saying 'How do we make this commercial look like it's got neurodiversity in it?' Someone recently said to me that autism is very 'buzzy' at the moment and that set off an alarm bell. Whilst it's great to see more representation, it means people are going to start trying to force themselves to do more autistic commercials, but across media there've been a lot of representations in the not-too-distant past that have been quite awkward. That said, there are many wonderful examples of creatives who are divergent and have brought that to the screen, whether explicitly or implicitly.

Q: What practical steps around accessibility can marketers take?

A: Accessibility in websites and content isn't something people always consider. Kat Holmes, the SVP of Design at Salesforce, said in her wonderful

Mismatch (2018) that whilst approximately 15 per cent of people are disabled, the reality is that we all start disabled and likely end disabled in some way.

The number one ability that deteriorates when we age is eyesight, so we should be planning a lot of our visuals to consider that or looking at how to boost audio so that you can still reach those audiences. We need to balance our marketers' intention to make our images and graphics and marketing very buzzy, with the notion of accessibility and being clearly legible and understood.

Captions in videos is a key one, and really thinking about how you can best display those. There are lots of people who are neurodivergent or dyslexic who have issues with flickering and moving backgrounds. Bright colours and high contrast don't always work well either, especially for those who are colour blind.

It's also easy to forget that the primary way we consume content today is on mobile phones. Screen size and brightness vary, and everything is shrunk, so if you have moving text or beautiful fonts that shift around on a small screen it gets very confusing for some people. If your content isn't appealing to look at and easy to take in, all sorts of people will skip past it. If you have too many fonts, too many different sizes and capitals, it can get very difficult for people with dyslexia to read, but you know it will also be harder for everyone else as well.

My personal sensory needs are fairly standard, but I have some aspects that are a bit different, and I can get confused by too much visual stuff happening at once. If I'm in the confined London Underground on an escalator it's fine and there's no issue at all, but if I'm at an airport or shopping mall where there are four or five escalators, and you can see between them, I become like a cat on a roof. It's awkward, and I start to have no idea what's going on. That happens to me sometimes with videos as well.

In cinema, with new technology, people now film in higher frame rates for more fidelity and they think it's great because they can remove frames and it still plays normally – for instance if they want to play it back at a lower speed. What happens, however, is that when you reduce the frame rate there are some people that it really affects. In *Deathly Hallows* there's a chase scene that is shown in the first person, and because it was filmed in a different frame rate, to me it just looked wrong and it made me feel sick.

Frame rates and visual effects are practical things that people involved in production and post-production need to be aware of. It can be the same with panning shots filmed in a high frame rate and slowed down; for people with the same issues as me it's just horrible to watch and I don't think many people realize that.

Q: How does this come to life in social media marketing?

A: I think it frequently gets forgotten. A comparison for me is when a brief comes through the door and the client is asking to activate against gaming audiences. Typically, the strategists and creatives who work on it aren't people with a gaming background, so instead they try to hammer something together from Google and maybe a few white papers. The reality is if they spoke to people who were gamers, they'd have had a completely different perspective. If they went and spoke to Twitch they'd know the games these people are playing, where the community is, the hashtags they're using and how to get involved in the conversation. You need to have the data and the understanding.

Hopefully it's less of a shock now to learn that the blind community is heavily involved on platforms like Instagram, but when people start realizing that, they also need to ensure their copy can be read, and that they include alternative descriptions of their images.

There's a concept called 'camel back copy', which is when you use multi-word hashtags, and you need to capitalize each word so it's easier for screen reader software to interpret. That's a small practical thing but it's starting to come into standard practice, and it makes it easier for everyone to read. If you don't have anyone with that background or knowledge then perhaps no one is going to suggest it and you're going to miss out on these simple steps.

Q: How can marketers really get started at being more inclusive of neurodiverse people?

A: For me it comes back to the phrase 'nothing about us without us'. To understand where these communities are, you need to take a lead from them. If you're looking to recruit more diverse staff, then ask yourself how the actual advert shows up and think about the spaces and communities where you might reach different audiences.

If you're going to look at using neurodiverse people, then have them represent themselves. Have them involved in how you write and design, as part of the people doing the research.

References

Holmes, K (2018) *Mismatch: How inclusion shapes design*, The MIT Press

Universal Music Group (2020) *Creative Differences*. https://umusic.co.uk/creative-differences (archived at https://perma.cc/7TKK-V5V5)

13

Localization

Localization is a specific concern for global businesses that may not directly impact you if you work only in one country, but regardless of the scale of your business it's impossible to ignore that the nature of diversity and inclusion varies hugely around the globe.

If our role as marketers is to understand and reflect the society around us, then it's no surprise that we need to adapt our thinking when faced with different consumers. There are many consistent themes and similarities globally, and of course many differences and nuances too. Occasionally there are legal considerations for inclusion and representation (most notably relating to local LGBT+ laws) but whilst all areas of diversity exist globally their expression and priority may justifiably vary.

It is understandable that racial considerations are one of the most common challenges, given the very real demographic makeup of countries and communities around the globe. That said, it is always important to unpack where local market push-back reflects a genuine desire to be reflective and representative, versus where they are objecting to valid progressive portrayals.

You will need to consider local nuances and ensure that both global and local impacts of your decisions are being considered. As with any marketing, you can find unique insights, opportunities, objectives and needs in different markets, and when you are considering nuanced portrayals of minority groups you must be careful about local stereotypes and pitfalls.

Consider local cultural nuances that could make your content inappropriate, and find ways to have different perspectives (including any you are trying to represent) feed into that discussion. I have seen great examples of markets choosing to run an international creative locally specifically because it then becomes a distinct and representative copy, but I have also seen fair justifications for why a global creative might not be appropriate. If your casting is very typically Western, for instance, how will that play out amongst more Eastern audiences? It's possible it will make perfect sense in the context of your story, or it may come across that you haven't tried to speak to and represent them locally at all.

It's quite common for global companies to film multiple versions of an advert using different casts during the same production shoot, and if this fairly helps you reflect local diversity it can be a sensible approach. Remember, however, that it is more than just the presence of the cast that reflects their diversity – their setting, their clothing, their accessories, their social interactions and other aspects can vary between cultures and a truly inclusive production brief needs to consider this.

You should also ask yourself tough questions around whether you are changing the casting to truly reflect local diversity and be more representative, or in fact to achieve the opposite. I have seen many local teams hesitant to take progressive global creatives, for instance those featuring LGBT+ or black representation. Their feedback may not bluntly call this out, and there are often different reasons given as to why this execution just cannot work, but it's important to have an honest conversation and read between the lines. This can happen just as easily in markets that are sometimes considered progressive, such as the UK or the Nordic countries, as it can in countries which you might assume would be more cautious.

Where you do encounter challenge or resistance that you are not sure is fair then the best way to solve it is to look for data or evidence to make a balanced decision. This might be as simple as using publicly available demographic data but could mean commissioning some dedicated research or focus groups to evaluate the concern. This can be particularly helpful if you are localizing an older creative where changes to the global or local context might have made it less appropriate, and fresh eyes can help you avoid possible miscommunications. Throughout the Covid pandemic, for instance, marketers had to make rapid decisions about whether their existing adverts, many of which showed people effectively breaking local Covid regulations, were appropriate to continue running or not.

CHECKLIST
Localization

Key questions to ask yourself:

1 Are there any local cultural nuances that could make your content inappropriate?

2 For the adaptation of existing asset, does the casting truly reflect local diversity?

3 If replacing diverse casting, are you changing it to be more representative, or the opposite?

4 What data can you access to support a more progressive agenda?

5 If you are using an older copy, is the content still appropriate?

6 Has the global or local context changed?

MARKETER IN FOCUS
Tamara Rogers, CMO at Haleon (formerly GSK Consumer Healthcare)

Localization speaks in detail to a broader challenge that global businesses face, which is how you bring all your colleagues and markets along on this same journey with you. No one understands this challenge better than a global CMO, and so I turned to my former boss Tamara Rogers to get her perspective. Tamara had led global categories at Unilever before becoming GSK Consumer Healthcare's EMEA President and then global CMO.

Q: Why does representation matter to you?

A: There are lots of reasons why this matters, some of them closer to home and some of them not, but both equally important. The close to home part is to do with gender – I am a woman and I want gender equality. At the same time, a core value for me is to be part of a meritocracy – so I want to be where I am based on my abilities, on my own merit.

Since we're on the topic, though, I am a woman. I identify with being female and I came up through the ranks during times when being a woman at work was, and in many places it still is, in the minority. There were assumed roles and actions which we would probably now call micro-aggressions and I think I just took them in my stride. I'm the daughter of a working mother, I have quite a lot of self-confidence, my father always treated my mother as an equal, and the same with myself and my sister. They believed we could do whatever we wanted, and so we did too. The micro-aggressions didn't feel that bad in the moment, but I think that's important to recognize, as times change and what was accepted then just isn't acceptable today – there has been progress.

When I think back, I did some playful things, where I would just take on some stereotypes – say if I was in a room with a load of men and I was the only woman I might say to one of them 'Do you want to be mum and pour the tea?' I know it gave them a millisecond pause for thought. I think my love of sport helped me too. I'm a massive fan of Chelsea Football Club, and back then just being able to talk about things like sport caught the guys off guard, but I guess it also put them into a place of familiarity and me on an equal footing in a subtle way.

I took a lot of it in my stride, but I know plenty of women who have faced tougher situations and found things way more difficult. Personally, I just always felt like I was an equal and in turn my natural reaction is that I think of others as equals, and expect them to, also. My real passion comes from working with people, and if I'm not getting to the real person I know it, you can sense it, they're sort of hesitating.

If people can really be themselves, you can get to the real stuff that matters and you lose the fake, the front. I think you get to real conversations much faster, and you therefore deal with real issues. I love getting people to be themselves and seeing what people can do. We know that diversity drives performance, so it starts and ends with us.

Q: Can you think of any examples where representation has really stood out to you?

A: Absolutely, including from a few folks I had the privilege of working with. Simon Clift, who was the CMO at Unilever, was a real inspiration for me. He was open about being gay and he was obviously very comfortable in being open, which was great as it set the tone for us all.

I remember a dinner, I think it was an awards ceremony, and I stepped in to get folks organized, and started suggesting to people where they should sit. I was going, 'Boy, girl, boy, girl' and Simon said to me, 'Oh Tamara, you are so old fashioned!' which made me laugh. He said it very affectionately, but he was doing something important, and I learnt something that day, which was pointing out an unconscious bias, or old-fashioned traditional view I had.

Simon came into the CMO role on the back of being an incredible marketer, and in my opinion he did some of the best campaigns at that time. He loved to encourage a maverick, and in doing so he got the real person out. I remember him asking provocative, searching questions of me to disarm me – for example did I think I was doing a good job as a mother by going for a big job, a promotion? Sounds terrible, but he was supportive of my progression and was pushing me to fight, to feel my hunger, my passion for what I do. I had to drop all the baggage of trying to be a 'suited important woman', and it was just fantastic. I grew up with people like that around me in the industry.

A piece of his work came straight to mind when you asked for examples, from when he was working on Impulse (a fragranced body spray for women). He created one of my favourite adverts which is called 'Chance Encounter' and worth looking up on YouTube. It was set in Old Compton Street in Soho, well known for being an LGBT+ area of London. The Impulse brand promise back then was that men can't help acting on impulse, and there was a simple formula to the ads – man notices woman as she comes past, because he captures her scent, he then grabs flowers and chases after her to give her the flowers.

Simon flipped this narrative to guy bumps into girl and sends the groceries she was carrying, flying. They both bend down together to pick up all the pieces and there is this moment and connection between them as he breathes in her scent. But, then they stand up together and she notices his boyfriend watching and they both laugh, shrug, and go their separate ways.

I think it was the first time that a gay guy was featured in mainstream advertising in the UK, and it made Impulse really cool overnight with its teenage audience. Obviously for youth culture this was not such a great shock, but it made the brand fresh and contemporary. Of course, not everybody loved it and sadly the company had all kinds of complaints, but were ready. The team handled the negativity, broke new ground, really challenged what was normal and drove change.

Continuing that theme, the GB team here at Haleon (formerly GSK Consumer Healthcare) created a partnership with *Gay Times*. We were specifically wanting to make sure we better connected with the LGBT+ community but also wanted to make sure we created distinctive content. We took a casual approach to our existing Sensodyne Moments and Faces campaign which shows people reacting to teeth sensitivity with a wince when they eat or drink hot and cold foods. It was just wonderfully diverse with a fantastic, distinctive cast representing a range of the community.

There's one more I'd like to talk about, which is less about casual representation, but really making sure that you reflect your consumer base and, instead of being stereotypical, being quite provocative. This one relates to the sort of racism, discrimination and inequality that's experienced by black people. It was done by Beats, who I think had tons of authority to do this super-powerful and provoking piece.

It launched, I think, in November 2020, just a few months after George Floyd was murdered by a police officer in the USA and we saw anti-racism demonstrations in many countries around the world. It was called 'You Love Me' and I won't get the words completely right but it's something like 'You love me. You love me not. You love black culture, but do you love me?' and it ends by saying 'Do you love me? What a world that would be.'

It was beautiful, painful and really thought-provoking. That film really demands us all to imagine a better world, because this is the world that loves black athletes, musicians, black culture and music is revered – but does society really love black people and treat them fairly? It gave me goose pimples. I thought it gave pause for thought. A fantastic piece of work. Advertising dollars supporting cultural change.

Q: What do you think is the business value and the commercial bottom line of inclusive marketing?

A: I think there've been so many very authoritative pieces written on this. The data and the business case is proven already, but there is one finding that proves a north star, which is that companies that have greater diversity have a greater chance of financially outperforming others.

It really shouldn't be a surprise, should it? One way or another most of us are in the business of serving others – in marketing we sell stuff and if we really need to understand what consumers want, what matters to them, it's critical how we engage and talk to people. When that audience is diverse, you just are not going to know how to deliver unless you have diversity in your business.

In marketing there's nothing like a good workshop and diverse thinking and points of view unlock creativity. You're always going to think what you think, but as soon as somebody chucks in something a little bit different that's the catalyst for everyone thinking differently. On so many fronts, it makes a huge amount of difference.

Our marketing jobs are not easy any more. Brands used to just be able to tell people things – you'd tell people how to do their laundry, for example, and would tell people what they need. Now we live in this world of access and transparency, and people really know when they're being marketed to. They're savvy, they can sniff it out, they can cut the cord, they can swipe you left and then you're done.

We launched our marketing mission to 'build brands with humanity', which is all about digging deeper, understanding and caring enough to want to make a difference. In healthcare you want to be looked after, but there's also the need for some straight talk. Sometimes if you're doing something that isn't making you feel good, someone must tell you to stop doing that. Caring means caring enough to say the tough thing.

Every one of our brands is re-examining its purpose. Our brands are super-functional, they have to address real issues. In healthcare we do things such as make you feel better when you've got cold and flu, but we want to go beyond that. For example, our Theraflu brand purpose is fighting for a flu safe world.

So yes, there is a massive business case for diversity and understanding on how best to engage.

Q: How do you drive this change across an organization of 1,000 marketers?

A: It isn't easy, but I think if we just leave folks doing things as they've always done them, you're never going to get a change. You do have to make an intervention. The work that we did with you and the WFA, and I know you build on that in this book, has been helpful and a big part of what we've done.

We've put in place our own internal training. We have e-learning and central resources. I think it is about being mindful at every single step of the end-to-end process, from insights and planning, through content creation and media, and then into market delivery. We've partnered with procurement to help us do even more to make sure that we're working all the way through, end to end, to the suppliers and partners we're working with through the process. And we are setting targets too.

Everything from briefing, planning, production through to go live has opportunities. It's not just about giving teams instructions, its also immersing them and building awareness, helping them be aware of any unconscious bias they may have, what they could do differently. With consciousness you don't need to be directive, but to start with you have to take a more formal approach.

Q: How can global marketers approach inclusion when diversity varies so much from market to market?

A: I honestly think the job of global marketers has become really complex. Even for local teams it's more complex to embrace multiple audiences that reflect the diversity we serve, but it is critical.

It is massively different in terms of what you can do and say in some Eastern European markets, versus in Saudi, versus America. I think the UK's probably one of the most advanced. We've got this massive breadth of markets that we must think about, but we must start somewhere in all those places, because in all those places there is a journey to travel, wherever the start point is.

Our global teams are now thinking with much more breadth, for example recently we created over five hundred assets for a campaign. We must create with relevance. We know we must. We can't just assume one size fits all and make one ad that goes everywhere. We are also having to think about how we continue to drive our production costs down, so that we can re-invest and get our amount of content up.

How can we work in partnership with markets to make sure that we are hearing what's needed? Looking at how we create – some creation by global where assets are needed in multiple markets, some created locally where only that market needs it. Getting the non-working and production budget split right between a global team and a local team is key, so that we can be as global as possible and consistent but have that lovely local touch as much as possible.

For Sensodyne, for example, eating occasions are a brilliant way to bring to life sensitivity challenges and be locally culturally relevant. From that first sip of iced soda when you're about to break Ramadan fast, to that chilled pint at a barbecue or tail-gating at a sports event, these can vary hugely. We've had to create way more content that tells different stories and is socially relevant, but at the same time when you do that you can also then think about how to push the needle on inclusion and diversity.

How am I portraying in media what real life is like, not some weird 'ad land' version of life? We push ourselves to look at situations and consider what we could do differently, such as do a role-reverse of a stereotype. Of course, it happens in real life, but advertisers can be a bit fearful about portraying it, for instance in Colombia showing a local business owner being a woman and not being a guy. There are always little tweaks you can make, which the audience see as normal. It's sometimes our own internal teams who want to be safe and not offend, whereas I think having a point of view gets you noticed in our world.

Q: How do you support or encourage teams to make those bolder decisions?

A: So much of this is about having each other's back. To get the diversity out in a team, people must feel psychologically safe, comfortable to be themselves. Everywhere from the top all the way down we have to make it clear that we care about this and we want to see it, live it. We also have business resource groups who can look at what we are proposing and give us feedback to build confidence in moving ahead.

One of the reasons I think people feel uncomfortable to act is worrying about getting it wrong. Whether they're going to get the language right when they talk about issues such as race. Can I say black? Can I not say black? How do I talk about the LGBT+ community? Again it's about education and bringing in those communities to perhaps say it doesn't matter if you said it that way, but it'd be better if you did it this way and then you get it right in the future.

It's about building the confidence from within and then there's always research. You can do really quick testing now, just building the confidence in taking actions.

PART FIVE

Stage four

Inclusive launches

STAGE ONE

Inclusive briefing and strategy

1 *Business and brand strategy*

2 *Strategic insights and data*

3 *Marketing and creative briefs*

STAGE TWO

Inclusive planning

4 *Partner and team selection*

5 *Creative development and product design*

6 *Consumer testing*

STAGE THREE

Inclusive production

7 *Production*

8 *Post-production*

9 *Localization*

STAGE FOUR

Inclusive launches

10 **Media and 360 activation**

11 **Launch and consumer response**

12 **Measuring success**

14

Media and 360 activation

When the time finally comes to launch your marketing initiative you'll be in a good place if you've followed the advice of previous chapters, but put the champagne on ice just a little bit longer and you'll see the opportunities to deliver inclusion and representation continue right through into how you get your work out there.

There are clear diversity, equality and inclusion opportunities for advertisers to consider within their media choices. These include working with minority owned and operated media vendors, helping to fund narratives and people that are breaking new ground, and empowering community inclusion and diversity. It's also important to take steps to prevent the funding of hate speech and misinformation, without blocking positive voices that represent diverse communities.

Launch is also the first chance you'll have to truly understand how consumers react to your work, and if your marketing is deliberately provocative or inclusive you can often expect plenty of noise. That noise is usually a good thing – it shows we're doing our job as marketers to get noticed and also often shows that we're upsetting exactly the people who need to be upset. But this is also a key time to listen out and learn from what you do hear. Negative and hateful commentary can be loud and hard to ignore, but in every single case I've seen it is substantially drowned out in sentiment by those that love and appreciate the work, or don't think it's a talking point at all. Pay close attention to the voices of communities you have tried to represent and learn positively from, or be challenged fairly by, their feedback.

A new campaign or initiative is a great time to celebrate internally, too. Many businesses these days have sophisticated ERGs where voluntary colleagues come together to celebrate their own identities. I've seen great responses from these groups and wider businesses when you launch work that is truly inclusive and representative of them. A great benefit of inclusive marketing is the colleague engagement and external corporate brand-building it can support, so don't miss out on the opportunity to make the most of it.

Some of the most critical questions then come as you wrap things up and look to measure the impact and effectiveness of your work. Was it worth doing again? Did the inclusive elements help make it perform better? There aren't easy answers here, as it is never easy to measure the true impact of a marketing campaign, let alone one with potentially such nuance. Regardless, across this section we'll look to provide clear and practical advice on how you can really launch your campaign with pride, and ensure inclusivity stays core to it right to the finish line.

Driving inclusion with your paid media budgets

We tend to think of diversity as a challenge for our creative or HR teams, but media also plays a critical role. The way a campaign is planned and bought can have a notable impact on reach and engagement across different audience groups. Making the right decisions can both help brands create more effective campaigns, and critically ensure they play their part in funding a richer and more diverse media ecosystem. There is a delicate balance between ensuring we block hate speech and increase the funding of positive representative voices, and whilst the solutions can get technical, they all start with advertisers asking some of these simple questions in their brief.

Just as important as the messages we put out, is where they show up. Advertisers' media planning buying choices can play a significant role in supporting diversity and inclusion in the mainstream media landscape and conversely they can also have, often unintentionally, a negative impact too.

Delivering scale against wide ranging, diverse consumer bases is rarely a challenge in itself (thanks to mainstream media) but there are substantial opportunities to build more nuanced relevance and fund a richer media ecosystem. Decisions that advertisers take can heavily impact the platforms, publications or editorial that get funded, which in turn plays a key role in shaping the overall media landscape.

Media is in itself a process, and often one running concurrently to your wider marketing and creative processes. Good marketing doesn't just think about media at the end of the process as a way of launching an advert or communicating to an audience, it considers the implications of media decisions right throughout that journey. The following sections review four key considerations that span the media process, from your upfront thinking and planning, through to the details of your execution.

Inclusive audience planning

Insights are a crucial early stage and ongoing input into the marketing process. Having rich consumer insights feed into a brief sets you up for more relevant and impactful marketing activity getting the right messages to the right audiences in the right places. We need to ensure audiences are diverse and inclusive at the planning stage.

When it comes to media planning, a diverse and nuanced understanding of your audience is critical, especially where targeting decisions could specifically exclude different groups, or lead to generalizations rather than capturing representative perspectives. Truly understanding your audiences and ensuring they are diverse at the planning stage sets you up for success in your approach.

Just as with a wider marketing or creative brief, it's critical to ensure that representation is clear. This helps remind and focus your team and any partners you work with, and keeps these questions front of mind during the process. Don't be afraid to specifically call it out.

Any brief or marketing approach must at some point define an audience, and inevitably that means some others are excluded and not focused on in our marketing thinking. In many ways, there is nothing wrong with that, and we do after all have to focus to be able to do our jobs, but it's always worth checking who is being left out and whether it is right to do so. In media, and in highly targeted digital channels, your initial prioritization can turn into active exclusion, where you might be almost invisible to people outside of your core, even if they are key growth opportunities.

Even in how you present and boil down the insights and brief you have, you should be careful about getting caught up in stereotypes that limit your considerations. It's easy to give our core consumers a friendly name and simple life story but 'pen portraits' like this can hide a lot of the true diversity behind the people buying from us.

Supporting diverse voices

Striving to be more representative means actively supporting inclusive content and diverse voices. That could mean actively targeting diverse coverage or editorial in mainstream media, or identifying specific diverse publications or individual influencers to advertise with.

There is a huge opportunity to make deliberate media decisions and build partnerships that better help you reach and resource different communities. As more businesses adopt supplier diversity programmes, media can be a highly impactful opportunity to fund businesses that are diversely owned and operated, or heavily championing minority talent and voices.

Forging deeper partnerships with minority owned or focused media owners can help brands communicate more effectively and find more meaningful ways to increase relevance to different audiences. In exchange, it enables diverse creators to have a louder voice of their own. There are often rich opportunities to not just run existing adverts, but also to collaborate on new content, develop new insights, or find innovative ways to engage a particular audience.

As media owner content is often funded by the advertising that supports it, advertisers' money can have a considerable impact on what does or doesn't get funded. Many of the more progressive and inclusive TV shows in recent years have only been made possible by the support of advertisers around them.

There's also an opportunity to look beyond more traditional media owners and into the individual influencer and creator space. By working with people who are themselves representative members of their own communities you can accelerate your own journey to have an authentic voice, positively reach that audience with relevant content, and be sure that your advertising is helping amplify and support those voices.

Balancing brand safety

Strong brand safety protections protect brands from appearing alongside hate speech, misinformation and other harmful content, and in doing so remove some of the incentives for creating it. In the modern world of digital media buying, there are often automated settings and key word lists that are integrated into your bidding approach, and typically you are not making individual judgements on much of the content you appear alongside.

It's critical to balance managing brand suitability and safety whilst still enabling inclusion. Whilst most brands have measures in place today, it's important to recognize that this is an ever-evolving situation. It's become increasingly clear that there can be unintended side effects of brand safety approaches if they are applied over-zealously. Whilst such settings are designed to protect vulnerable communities, they can also begin to defund or silence positive diverse voices too.

The media platform Vice (2018) found that terms as broad as 'gay', 'lesbian', 'Asian' or 'Muslim' were being used more commonly than words like 'rape', 'death', 'heroin' and 'gun' in advertising keyword blocklists. Research by the tech platform CHEQ (2019) found that 73 per cent of neutral or positive LGBT+ related articles were being blocked by some brand safety approaches. If such articles are blocked from being effectively monetized, then it can become increasingly challenging for mainstream media editors to commission them, and it can entirely stop the funding of dedicated titles and voices.

Brands can reduce this risk by ensuring their keyword blocklists are not prejudicial or discriminatory in nature, ensuring a diverse group has input, as well as working with verification technology partners to minimize the overall potentially negative impact of brand safety controls on diverse audiences and media. As a side note, the terms 'black list' and 'white list' in this sense are potentially discriminatory in their own right, so consider using terms such as 'block list' and 'inclusion list'.

Many media agencies, including notably Group M, have created lists of 'do not block' words which they advise clients against ever including on their brand safety keyword lists. These also appear too broadly in positive or neutral mainstream media coverage. Beyond defunding diversity, use of these words could heavily defund the overall news media landscape. Consider sense checking with your own media agency or buying team to better understand what words you might be blocking.

Measuring success

Diverse media titles and audiences tend to be smaller and harder to track. They may even be totally excluded from some of the industry monitoring tools you might use. Demonstrating the true value these media choices bring is key to making it a business imperative, and that means finding ways to measure fairly, where necessary investing in new research.

Diverse environments, or the data approaches used to find harder to reach audiences, often carry a cost premium, but the same can be said of many high-quality media destinations. We must be careful to move beyond chasing the cheapest CPMs to truly understanding, through measurement, the value of context, relevance and attention.

Reaching audiences in spaces where they pay most attention, and in doing so supporting the voices they most enjoy, can be worth the premium.

Whilst every company will choose to measure success differently, it's worth investing in dedicated research such as brand lift or sales studies to capture the value that a more diverse media mix is having on your bottom line. Without this, you can't hope to make the right business decisions.

CHECKLIST
Media and 360 activation

Key questions to ask yourself:

1   Are your media plans safe from funding inflammatory content, hate speech or disinformation?

2   Are there any channels that would be inappropriate to be present on?

3   Could your marketing mix, data usage or brand safety settings exclude certain groups?

4   Have you considered actively including or partnering with diversity focused media partners or influencers? Could you even create new content together?

5   Are there unexpected touch points relevant to new groups?

MARKETER IN FOCUS
Isabel Massey, Global Media Director at Diageo

Diageo has been one of the companies leading best practice in the responsible media space, and their global media lead Isabel Massey helped co-write this chapter of the book. She is on the leadership team of the Global Alliance for Responsible Media (GARM) and co-chairs the WFA's Media Forum. This section also benefited from wider input from the GARM community, which includes many large advertisers and media companies including Twitter, Facebook and Google.

Q: Why does representation matter to you?

A: For me it does link to my day job, because imagine a mainstream media landscape where you don't see yourself represented? Or, perhaps worse, you just see a stereotypical depiction of yourself in TV programmes, in news editorial or in advertising. Well, sadly, many people today don't have to imagine this, it's what they experience day to day, and it affects so many people.

I've personally experienced this and I'm sure you have too. I've experienced it as a female leader and as a family going through fertility treatment. Why it matters to me is that because of my day job as Global Media Director I can do something about it.

Representation boils down for me to a very straightforward ask, which is that what we are seeing in media should be a true reflection of today's society. That's thinking about diversity in its broadest sense possible, including ethnicity, gender, age, sexuality, ability, social class, education, experience, ways of thinking and many more. If we don't sort it out, we won't progress as a society, so that's why it matters to me personally.

Q: Can you think of any really great examples of inclusive marketing or media that had a personal impact on you?

A: When I think about the media landscape in general, the one that stands out for me and probably had the most impact in my life is *Queer as Folk*, which those of you in the UK may remember was a programme on Channel 4 going back many years ago now. It's referenced in the introduction to this book. I think it was the first time, as someone who was very young at the time, I had seen what an LGBT+ lifestyle could look like, and as someone watching it I remember feeling like I was being inspired and educated as an ally all at the same time.

It was just so different and unique, and quite frankly it shouldn't be different and unique, that should just be part and parcel of what the media landscape looks like. Sometimes when I think about that show, I question, has the video landscape really moved on that much since then? Sadly the answer is no, in many ways I don't think it has, so that for me is what I'd like to see – I'd like to see more of those shows and more of the media coverage that is really reflective of society and represents people in different ways, because everyone is different.

Q: Can you talk about media and audience planning and some of the work you've done in that space?

A: It starts with audience planning, because when it comes to media planning a nuanced understanding of an audience is critical. Especially when targeting decisions could specifically exclude audience groups or potentially lead to generalizations rather than capture those representative perspectives. We've worked on some particular questions that you should ask yourself at the moment of planning. They're very simple questions but ones that are supposed to be quite piercing and really make you think about the answer. For instance, does your brief make it clear that that representation is key? Who is your audience, but more importantly who is excluded, and is it right that they're excluded? When you look at your target audience and how they are visualized, is the definition a stereotype or generalization?

An example of audience planning close to my heart is the approach that we took with Guinness. It's a brand that hopefully you know is synonymous with sport, especially rugby, but we became acutely aware that media visibility around women's sport is very low. Globally just 6 per cent of sports coverage is dedicated to female athletes and teams, which is just outstandingly low.

So as Guinness it was vital that we stepped into that space and supported female rugby and the players to get them the visibility that they very much deserve. We did that both through our sponsorship and advertising, but also through actions that ensure that they drive visibility. For example, we made sure the players' social media accounts were verified and made sure they had good Wikipedia write ups as a start, and we will continue to support them.

Q: How have you managed to measure and prove the effectiveness of your diversity and representation in media work?

A: This is always a challenge. Diverse media titles and audiences tend to be naturally smaller, or harder to track. That means they sometimes don't make it onto plants in the first place, and if they do then demonstrating the true value of these media choices can be trickier. It's worth investing time and money in dedicated research – that might be a brand lift study or an approach to measuring the sales impact that it's having on your business.

At Diageo, when we set out on our journey to intentionally buy more media that was representative of today's societies, we put in place a learning agenda. We used econometric models to understand the true business impact of buying the media in this different way. To be honest, when we first looked at the results, we saw a low return on investment. It was a surprise to us in some ways, but not others, because it was the first time that we've tried this activity. We could have very easily concluded that this approach does not pay out and therefore stopped our efforts in this space, but we fundamentally believed that this was the right thing to do and that doing the right thing can also be the right thing for business.

We needed to figure out how to make it work, and so over time with close monitoring we were able to significantly improve the results through optimization. Today these are some of our best-performing media channels.

Q: How can people get started with bringing more diversity into their media thinking?

A: Hopefully we've shown that the magic really is in the detail and so you've got to get into the weeds of media planning and buying and ask yourself some simple but tough questions as to whether you could be doing more. Whether, for instance, the brand safety approaches you're taking and keywords you're using are inadvertently blocking diverse voices.

My second tip would be to be restless for change. The mainstream media landscape is not fully representative of our wonderful, diverse society and that's not good enough. Challenge and support media owners to get progressive content off the ground – I think it's with our collective efforts that we can drive this change.

MARKETER IN FOCUS
Catherine Becker, Freeda Media

Inclusion-focused media owners are a powerful way of tapping into diverse audiences, not only in terms of directly reaching them but also in terms of the insights and creativity you can bring in by working with their teams. Titles exist that talk to every imaginable community, however small, but Freeda Media was set up to talk to half of the population to offer a more positive representation of women and their achievements. I spoke to Catherine Becker to understand the opportunity for brands.

Q: Why does representation matter to you?

A: It's a hugely important topic for me. I'm very passionate about equality and making sure that lots of different representations are heard. When you get to such a stage in your career and the industry has been good to you, you also really want to give back – to be able to inspire the next generation of talent, and make sure it does come from diverse backgrounds.

Not everyone's fortunate enough to find it easy to get into our industry. It's important that we have that diverse range of role models, and it's our responsibility that we are representing them in the media. It's important to me that we give back and that we have inspiring stories.

Q: Can you think of any examples where you've seen great representation?

A: I was thinking about this and whether, when I was growing up, there was much representation in the marketing and TV ads, whether there were examples of strong women running businesses that I could really aspire to. There were obviously a lot fewer than there are now, which is great progress, so we've come from a place where there really wasn't much representation, but there's still a long way to go.

When you get to diverse groups, there are definite pockets that don't feel represented. The more we can influence that and develop talent so that they can then inspire the next generation, the better.

When you even look at how women have been presented in the media, and that's not a minority at all, but they were often in the kitchen doing the cooking whilst the man was out working. A lot of my female friends now are the primary breadwinner and that's not necessarily represented well in media. The more we can do on that the better, and it is improving.

That was really the foundation of Freeda Media, we wanted to show those really diverse talents doing really well. We had this great example, we were working with Jimmy Choo, and we were trying to find a really good inspiring story and role model. We found within their own organization a lady called Sandra Choi, who was the Creative Director. Especially in creative businesses, women only represent something like 11 per cent of the cohort.

She'd had an amazing life, but it was more about telling her personal story, how she was into punk and what had inspired her. It was just so inspiring for young Gen:Z and Millennial women to see that there was a really successful woman in that business that they could look up to. Across our social media there's a lot of interaction and you get to see all the comments saying how inspiring it is to see a woman at the top of their profession.

Q: Tell us a bit more about Freeda Media. What does your team stand for?

A: It was born out of a couple of things. One is that there wasn't, especially for women, much positive representation in media. Beyond that, we see that social media is such a cruel space with so much negativity and nasty language, and we wanted to create a safe space where we really celebrated all shapes and sizes – all diversity, including ethnicity, but also neurodiversity. We wanted not just to be accepting of everyone for who they are, but actually celebrating that they've all managed to achieve remarkable things.

If you look at body diversity, it's OK to feel you look awful one day and fantastic the next, but that's not something that's ever really spoken about or acknowledged. We had an amazing story of a Down Syndrome lady who was just incredibly positive and upbeat. She actually became a model, and to be able to show positive examples of that in a safe space is really our mission. For brands that similarly find it hard to communicate to that Gen Z female audience, we help them understand through a combination of data plus creativity how we can communicate in a really engaging way.

There are a lot of social media sites and media businesses, but there are not many that are really in that kind and inclusive space, trying to make social media a nicer, safer space. Diversity communications can tend to focus on the difficulties and the struggles that people face, but people are just people and these are wonderful and unique people achieving great things.

Q: What's your advice to marketers wanting to move more into this inclusive space?

A: It's interesting when we talk to and advise brands, that our team is not the traditional sort of agency of marketers. A lot of our team are young, opinionated and they will push back and they will say 'no' to brands. 'No' you cannot say that because this audience will go onto your annual report and have a look at that. If you're not diverse or you're not driving the sustainability initiative you're talking about, they will call you out. We'll advise on that, which is key to getting that genuine engagement.

Our whole platform is a combination of data and creativity, so we look at every element, whether it's the tone of voice, or the visuals, or the content – we look at what works and what doesn't in terms of the audience you are trying to reach.

I got feedback from across some of the team on the key learning we've seen, and the first piece was really 'Don't assume.' You need to ask people, especially if you're getting into a sensitive topic, and especially if you're talking about a certain cohort of the community. Ask them directly about themselves, find out what motivates and inspires them. Don't assume that just because you're featuring them that is inspiring; work to get that tone right first. Ask them how they overcame adversity, again rather than assuming it yourself.

The really key thing is surrounding yourself with different voices and cultures. We have master classes and workshops where we either watch videos or listen to a different viewpoint so we can really understand and ask questions. Be curious, really read around the subject and generally educate yourself all the time. Create that space for your team to do that.

Q: What's your advice for brands trying to work with media owners to fast track their own inclusion approaches?

A: Be open to the community, be open to listening to the experts you're working with. We're quite unique in the sense that our community is effectively our editor, which is amazing. They are guiding both what we are doing editorially and what we do with our client partners.

We do a lot of these little polls, where perhaps our clients have got questions – they're thinking about approaching a topic in a certain way but they're not sure. We do a lot of fun quick questions and you can really get a sense from the community, before you publish, what they're going to like and what they're not.

I'd encourage brands to do focus groups with all sorts of intersectional people, find the people that are engaging with that social content the whole time and understand what their latest thinking is.

A big responsibility marketers have is that they have big budgets to spend. Perhaps the majority of that spend will go on those big high-reach media owners, the Facebooks or Amazons of this world, but I think it's really important to look beyond that if you are saying diversity matters to you. Obviously your customer base is very diverse, and you have to reach them authentically. You're not just going to get them to engage through those generic platforms so go with some specialists.

That helps you in terms of getting that depth and breadth of coverage, but also you're then supporting those media owners which are in turn supporting those communities, giving them voices. The dividend that pays is when your audience recognizes you're making an investment in a channel they really care about, and conversely you're avoiding some of the negativities with the bigger channels.

To be able to put even a small percentage towards them is ethical, it's inspirational and even from a profitability point of view it pays. That money means a lot to those smaller channels because it enabled them to support the voice of those communities that they're representing.

Q: How can brands start to measure this and understand the value it brings to their business?

A: Well Freeda and digital media are very measurable. To begin with, we get reach figures and we can guarantee millions of people will see your content every month, so you know that you're getting value.

We've actually got a full funnel of offerings. We tend to be at the top of the funnel, which is awareness and reach, but also importantly the engagement. We measure that engagement as a primary measure, and in many cases we're two or three times better than a lot of the traditional media owners. We use that data not just to see who clicks but to really understand what's going on, to keep people paying attention until the end, or see how they interact in a positive way.

Social commerce is getting much bigger and so we're increasingly able to offer direct links through to websites and client owned social channels and through to direct sales. We've found it to be very measurable and haven't seen that as an issue. In fact, we've got a number of partners that have started small but keep on increasing that and support us now all year.

It's a real privilege to work for a company with a real mission, a purpose led organization. We really want to create stories about amazing people that are properly changing the world. Brands that also want to do that, and are genuinely into that, are our favourite brief. If you have really strong values that align with our own, and you want to engage with that community in a really positive way, then we know that it works. The best content works from a value based, rather than a product or a service based brief, but we find ways to work to that and deliver real value for our partners on any brief.

References

CHEQ (2019) *How Keyword Blacklists are Killing Reach and Monetization.* https://info.cheq.ai/hubfs/Research/Brand_Safety_Blocklist_Report.pdf (archived at https://perma.cc/ABS7-V6XR)

Vice (2018) Vice slams brand safety keyword blacklists after alarming probe. www.campaignlive.co.uk/article/vice-slams-brand-safety-keyword-blacklists-alarming-probe/1495610 (archived at https://perma.cc/V2F9-TFUT)

15

Launch and consumer response

There's nothing more exciting than when a product or campaign you've been working on for months, or even years, finally launches. It's often rightly a time for celebration, but it isn't quite the end of our process as even the launch itself and the immediate follow up can be opportunities for positive inclusion, or unfortunately still exclusion.

A good starting point is how you launch internally – some companies send an email round the team, some throw a party and give out products, others bring the advert to life in their lobby. I've always felt that internal launches are important engagement and 'thank you' moments that are worth investing in, but this is particularly true if you've been leaning on your ERGs or other colleagues throughout the process. Speak to the leaders and individuals who have helped inform your process and ask them what they think would be an appropriate celebration of your inclusive work. If you've ended up deliberately representing a minority group you might want to use this as a positive time to showcase that internally.

Be prepared for feedback, good or bad

It is important that your launch plans have broadly considered the potential impact amongst diverse groups, and indeed you should be prepared for both positive and negative responses from consumers and colleagues. It's unfortunately true that most progressive and inclusive work does receive some degree of pushback, but typically from a very small if vocal minority who oppose diversity for various reasons.

What can be more challenging is if you receive critical feedback from the groups you have been trying to positively feature and represent, and it is important to listen to and try to understand these challenges. Regardless of how inclusive it is, your marketing will never please everybody, so it's important to try to unpack what is individual preference or opinion and where you might have made genuine errors you should learn from and improve on.

Either way, it's important to have a monitoring plan in place so that you can quickly identify the kinds of conversations that are being generated, both to positively look for opportunities and to protect yourselves and anyone involved in the work in the case of any negativity. Ensure you have briefed any social media teams or community managers, and consider putting some specific social listening in place around the launch or adding some new relevant keywords to your existing approach. The first step of any campaign response is of course understanding how it is being received, and once again it can be helpful to have different perspectives in the room to help you sift through and evaluate that feedback.

You should also have a plan for how you are going to respond. Some reactions will always take you completely by surprise when there is something in your work or in a culture that you hadn't expected, but for the most part you can predict a good amount of what will happen. It's fair to say that if your work cuts through there will be people who hate it and criticize it and people who love it and want to praise it, or perhaps are even inspired to share their own stories.

How you should best respond will no doubt depend on how conversational and responsive your brand normally is on social channels, but prepare for extreme circumstances in which you might need to be more vocal than usual. In any case, if you've chosen to positively support and represent a community then it is your responsibility to stand by your work and that community. Some of the absolutely worst missteps I've seen in the representation space are from brands who have stepped back from or apologized for perfectly reasonable inclusion when they have received criticism from traditionalists. Ensure you have internal alignment and buy in at a senior level that you will stand by your work, or else you have bigger issues to solve internally first.

Any negative comments about our work can be hard to receive and this is often amplified when they are hateful and extreme in nature. In my own experience I have found these negative comments whilst challenging to be far outweighed by the positive discourse, and even more substantially outweighed by the silent majority who will have no issue with your work. It's important to put any 'backlash' in perspective as quite often the scale is nominal and making any drastic changes on the back of it will be disproportionate.

It's a popular tactic of trolls or hateful communities to try to draw more negativity on work they disapprove of by re-sharing it across their networks and setting it up to be a target for bots. You may find you are receiving negative comments and even complaints from people who have never actually even seen the advert but have simply been encouraged by someone else to object for whatever reason. In the UK I've seen this lead to complaints and investigations by the Advertising Standards Authority, but to their credit they have always been quick to dismiss such prejudiced cases.

Before you become too worried it's worth saying that we are talking about worst case scenarios here. Much casually inclusive work will receive no inflammatory response at all and even a lot of positive progression receives only positive or neutral commentary. It is however wise to have discussed potentially negative implications and have plans, including signed off responses, in place before you go live just in case.

Amplifying the success of your campaign

At the other end of the scale are the positive opportunities that can come from amplifying or building on a campaign as the response to it occurs. Modern marketing is inevitably more than just creating an advert and leaving it, and there can be great ways of extending campaigns by amplifying and engaging with a positive response. There have even been brands who have been able to make a positive thing out of a negative response, like the Mondelez brand Honey Maid which printed out every negative comment it got to a commercial on scrolls and arranged them into a positive message spelling out love instead.

As hinted at previously, the most important voices to listen to in many cases are of those communities you have tried to feature and represent. Whilst we sometimes label large groups of people together (such as in the LGBT+ community) the reality is these are millions of individuals with different perspectives and considerations. Even with plenty of due diligence there may be some in that community who see your work in a different light or don't appreciate what you are trying to achieve. In most cases you'll find far more who are excited to see inclusion and representation, and who will respond hugely positively to the work.

Inclusive marketing means always being open to challenge and opportunity and listening to these communities as best you can to inform future work. If they do have any issues it can be helpful to positively engage them and show the due diligence you have put in and the positive intentions you have. One common criticism of brands is that you are just jumping on an inclusion band wagon for commercial benefit (such as 'rainbow washing' when brands put rainbows on their logos for Pride). This is less likely to be the case for casual representation and inclusion and more of a risk for campaigns that have a deliberately pointed message or campaigning platform, and it's a healthy reminder that if you want to take a stronger position you should be backing up your words and communications with tangible actions.

CHECKLIST
Launch and consumer response

Key questions to ask yourself:

1 What is the monitoring/response plan for any feedback on representation? Are your social media teams briefed?

2 Are you prepared for how to respond to any hateful comments you receive?

3 Are you ready to respond if the communities you are trying to positively represent raise questions?

4 Have you prepared responses to best/worst possible outcomes?

5 What are your internal launch plans? Have you engaged your ERGs?

MARKETER IN FOCUS
Pedro Pina, VP, Head of YouTube EMEA

YouTube is the video hosting platform where most adverts end up, and when your campaign launches it can be one of the first places you'll see a consumer reaction to it. Pedro Pina has been a role model and inspiration to me personally in my career, as a highly successful and visible person within the industry who has both been open about being a gay man and an active advocate for inclusion right across the LGBT+ community. He's worked client side, agency side, and in recent years media owner and partner side as he's led many of Google's global advertising accounts and then taken on a total lead role across the EMEA YouTube business.

Q: Why does representation matter to you?

A: For me, it starts from personal experience. I'm a gay man, and when I was a child I remember that I felt different. When I looked around, I would not see anybody with a life that I would relate to. I remember when I was 12 or 13, thinking 'It looks like either I'm going to be a hairdresser or I have to be Elton John, in order to be minimally acceptable, and there's nothing else in between.'

There's nothing wrong with being a hairdresser, of course. I admire them. But these were the two options that were visibly available. So I really had to navigate this on my own. At school I was bullied all the time and there was no one I could talk to about that. I had to grow into myself pretty much on my own. No mentors, no points of reference, nothing.

Like everybody else in this space you eventually come to terms with it and you decide to come out. At that point I realized it was my duty to be visible. Visibility matters to everyone else younger than you, or the same age, or even older – the opportunity to look and see that you can have a decent life, and an OK career, and be gay and out.

Visibility speaks to representation, so representation to me is being able to see yourself in culture and around you in society. It's about your difference being normalized, accepted and embraced.

Q: Can you think of positive examples of representation?

A: I was a huge fan of the TV show *Sex in the City* a long time ago, and with its comeback *And Just Like That...*, although it's kind of clumsy, you can see they are attempting to address some of the original issues of representation and inclusiveness they've been critiqued for. I find it super-endearing and I welcome that because finally this big entertainment brand is trying to get it right. Sometimes they are not doing it perfectly, but kudos to them because they're trying.

I recently watched a play called *A Normal Heart*, which is a tragic story around the 1980s AIDS crisis. The actors that were on stage were really a cross-section of representation from race through to disability and it was phenomenal to see that effort. Notably their race or disability were not included as part of their characters, but they were just casually present and included. I was also recently at the Royal Opera House, and, again, half of the cast were people of colour. Quite frankly, five years ago you would not have seen that. Interestingly, at the opera, not only were the people on stage more diverse, but the audience was a cross-section too. You can see this change happening and the impact it's having.

You can really see this shift where any expression of arts or pop culture is starting to go the extra mile to make sure that representation is there. Some are doing it well, and sometimes it feels like they just did a box-ticking exercise, but even that is OK because everyone is starting on this journey to get it right and making an effort. I love seeing it.

Q: What kind of opportunity does a platform like YouTube provide for breaking down barriers and inspiring inclusion?

A: Specifically for LGBT+ and we also see this for the black community and other under-represented groups, people are able to find their community online on YouTube. You have no idea of the amount of content we have on 'how to come out', which is, as you know, still a significant moment in someone's life, though hopefully in the future less so.

YouTube is about knowledge and access to that knowledge. Not only can you learn how to fry an egg, you can also find out how to tell your parents or how to tell your friends that you are gay. What is Pride? What is the flag of Pride? Why does it have so many colours? Where can I find bars around me or how can I find friends? Is it OK for me to feel like this? You can see the way the community starts to find protection and acceptance.

One of the things that I find fascinating is that the biggest concentrations of traffic and content around these themes are in countries where it's hard to be in the LGBT+ community. That goes to prove that we are playing a role in supporting the community in environments where it is incredibly hard. In countries like Poland and Hungary, let alone many countries in Asia and Africa. Those are countries where our community is vibrant and where people come to find rescue and safety.

In that sense YouTube's mission comes through in ways that are tremendously important and that makes me incredibly proud.

Q: How can brands support diverse content when their own brand safety protections sometimes start to block it?

A: We see this all the time and it's disheartening, to be honest. My challenge back to the brands is to do a proper soul-searching exercise – look at yourself in the mirror and put your consumer in front of you. Really listen to your consumer. If your consumer is listening to this certain type of music, and this is where the audience you want finds community, why would you block your own presence from being part of that community?

We will never go back and ask Hip Hop to be 'appropriate' with their language; that's completely inappropriate. The alternative is to make brands comfortable with the real world. I think, as marketers, we live in this bubble and a lot of boardrooms are bubbles too, where we say 'our brands will never be connected to curse words'. We must ask ourselves whether we live in the real world, because that is not how your children speak. Brands themselves must come to terms with that, if they really want to be visible amongst these communities.

Q: How can brands best manage the feedback and comments more inclusive work might receive on a social platform like YouTube?

A: From a YouTube perspective, we try to protect creators from any very negative comments. We give creators tools that enable them to filter the comments being sent to them and only publish what they feel is appropriate for their channel. We use machine learning to help with this filter, so they can hold back 'potentially objectionable comments'. Brands can do the same.

We don't tolerate hate speech or harassment on the platform. We try as much as possible to remove that from YouTube before anybody sees it and to do that we rely on machine learning.

Regarding brands, the best advice I've ever heard in this space comes from Aline Santos at Unilever, and her approach is simply to say, 'I don't care.' They don't want those sorts of consumers and they know they are on the right side of history. You know that you are going to get more consumers because you're doing this and if you must lose some then so be it. If these are the hateful comments they make then I don't want those consumers to consume my brand. Now that is incredibly brave and incredibly honest, but in a world of transparency and scrutiny this is exactly the right thing to do.

My advice for brands is to be brave and believe that it's better for you to gain the consumers you want, than those you don't want.

Q: What has your experience of exec sponsor of the Pride at Google ERG taught you?

A: We've done a lot of work engaging with and continuing to work with our ERGs. I'm not only the sponsor for the Pride chapter within Google, I also sit on the D&I council for the whole company. One thing we do is we connect those ERGs with what we do, with our products.

We have created a product council and if we are going to launch a product it allows us to listen to feedback from the voices of representation. You can make sure there's a filter you have to go through before you launch any new product or feature. We have an initiative where even our presentation decks, when they are important, go through a filter with the ERGs to look at, for instance, the images we're using to illustrate our points.

For example, I recently learned that more than 10 per cent of people are colour blind, and typically people have work dashboards with green, yellow and red colours for their activity. People who are colour blind may struggle to see those dashboards, so there are a lot of people quietly in the room looking at the situation and not knowing whether the screen indicates that they achieved their objective or not. As a result, we decided that we needed a new colour scheme for our presentations.

To be inclusive in all our internal video meetings, we have closed captioning that is AI-enabled, so that people can follow the conversation. We recently moved so that all our internal VC systems will include the pronouns in front of your name, which was not automatically done before. That came through collaboration with the trans community inside Google, ensuring there were trans people in the room with an engineer discussing how best to do it, where to do it, how to communicate that we're doing it, and how for instance to manage it when someone is transitioning.

As much as possible we try to integrate what we do with the ERGs so they can provide perspective.

Q: How can smaller or newer companies build up to this?

A: The first thing I'll say is that it must come from the top, from the CEO or the person managing the team. Sometimes more junior people really put in a lot of the effort to make this change happen and kudos to them, but it must come from the top.

I've been asked to speak in a lot of different forums about this and different companies will ask me this question. I always ask 'Where is your board on this? Where is your CEO? Where is your chairman? What did they say? What do you put in your annual report or communicate in your business town halls? Where is the acknowledgement of and importance of representation?' If it doesn't come from the top, it's not going to work. That is absolutely foundational.

The second thing is to create a safe space to allow that community to flourish, and make sure you have the right exec sponsor for those communities. These communities require someone, often an ally, that tends to be more senior to steer them and to include their voices in the broader work that's being done. If that connection doesn't happen you will continue to be a junior, grassroots kind of movement in the corner. Perhaps you can organize a few parties, some talks, but it doesn't really change the DNA of the company. Again, a connection to leadership is absolutely critical.

MARKETER IN FOCUS
Benazir Barlet-Batada, Senior Marketing Director at Mondelez International

Cadbury is a rare kind of brand that manages to feel local despite being part of a huge global company. Several of their adverts are commonly ranked as some of the most popular ever in the UK and yet despite that local feeling they're a truly global brand and part of a much wider corporation. In recent years they've deliberately worked to champion several aspects of diversity, especially with a focus on old age, but it was a Creme Egg advert that included a gay kiss that got a lot of people talking.

There was a lot of love for the advert, but also a few vocal people with strong opinions against it, both coming from a backdrop of prejudice but also even from within the LGBT+ community itself. Benazir is a senior marketing director in the UK team who has also been part of building equity for the brand globally as part of her more than a decade with the company. She shared a perspective on how they are trying to truly reflect modern Britain and what they learned from the noise that advert created.

Q: Why does representation matter to you?

A: It's super-important to me as a British Asian female. Growing up I didn't see anyone that looked like me in the media. I saw stereotypes but no one I really identified with or saw as aspirational. I was literally that young girl like everyone else watching *Friends*, watching *Baywatch*, eating crisps, eating chocolate, sat on the sofa worrying about my homework, thinking about would I ever get a boyfriend.

I also had a different world at the same time because I would also be wondering how much my aunties would laugh at me if I spoke bad Gujarati at home. You have the British culture and the Asian culture, and you get caught between two worlds, which is positive as well as difficult to navigate at times.

You've got many positives – the food, the music, the rich culture, but in terms of the British media you never really saw anyone that looked like you. I think therefore you always grew up wanting to look like a white girl because that was deemed more accessible or more desirable.

We talk about the fact you can't be what you can't see. I didn't have role models growing up and I still think I've done quite well as a marketing director, so I don't think it's as clear cut as that. At the same time, I see the role models today – I'm a super-fan of the Obamas, they've done such good work and that doesn't mean that they haven't had racism or struggles on their way. There are some fantastic Indian CEOs that are out there now too like Jayshree Ullal from Arista Networks or Arvind Krishna, the CEO of IBM, so there are great role models now.

I would have loved more when I was growing up, and I'd still love more representation in the British media to better reflect the true reality of modern Britain. When you walk around outside, I'd love to see more of that reflected on the screen. I'd love it for everyone to see people's uniqueness, to celebrate and embrace everyone as they are, so ultimately everyone feels accepted.

Once you start to see everyone on the screen you start to not judge people for how they look or the stereotypes you started off with. You start to not think about what people look like or worship or choose to love. You start to see the real people inside because that's what really matters and that's how progress is made.

Q: Can you think of any good examples of representation?

A: I've got a couple examples that come to mind. First, I think of Disney, not necessarily as a marketer but for the content they're making. I've just been super-impressed with all the images I've seen on LinkedIn and Facebook about the film *Encanto* and it prompted me to go watch it. Disney isn't perfect I know, but I do appreciate that they're trying to get better, I appreciate all these positive nudges upwards.

A lot of the older films have disclaimers on them saying this is no longer representative of today's modern society's views, and they are now trying to create film and content that put people of colour as the hero roles, and which show more diverse stories. I appreciate that and what I love about it is that the positive image it shows of brown and black people and their culture in the media can influence the perceptions and behaviours of black and brown children.

I've got two mixed race children and I really appreciate it and I think the more positive and more powerful the conversation, the bigger impact it can have on these communities. I think it's important for kids of colour to be able to see positive images of themselves and to help their self-esteem, their self-acceptance and their confidence. I didn't have that growing up, but I love the way that *Encanto* in particular goes further than just showing a couple of brown people or a couple of black people, it actually shows a difference in texture of hair. It's telling a story from their perspective rather than them just being colours.

I really appreciate brands that have tried to do things that others have shied away from. For example, typically when you see black or Asian families represented, they tend to be mixed race families, but Tesco's Love Stories campaign showed an Asian family with three Asian lads cooking together. Sainsbury's did a Christmas advert that featured an all-black family, and I've seen it from Ikea as well. In the real world there's more fully Asian families or black families than mixed race ones, so of course it's good to represent all kinds of families.

The Sainsbury's Christmas advert, 'Gravy Song', was also nice to have a dad and daughter talking. It was really sweet, it was really authentic, it was casual representation, and you could identify with it, but it got some bad backlash from a few people and that was a real shame. It's great, however, that they defended the advert and they simply said, yes, this is modern Britain.

Q: How are you approaching this at Cadbury?

A: Cadbury aims to be a fabric of the nation brand and to achieve that we need to represent the nation. We need to represent everybody and that means being diverse and fully inclusive in our advertising. It's on us as individuals, and on us as a company, to make sure that we pressure test ourselves and do that.

It's not right to miss out a group because then you're missing a whole consumer group and we really want to resonate with everybody. We are the biggest FMCG brand in Britain, we're a national icon and we truly want to be representative to everybody here.

One of the things we've done is team up with the charity Age UK. We've had a three-year partnership with them and our campaign with them was all about raising awareness of the 225,000 older people who often go a whole week without speaking to anybody. We tried to raise awareness of the plight of loneliness and encouraged the nation to donate their words.

We created a film called 'The Originals' where we changed our angle to highlight how amazing older people are and that if you take the time to talk to them you'll be amazed at what you can learn. It was celebrating their differences, celebrating how much wisdom and how much experience they have, and how much they can give to younger people.

We took it right through the line with PR, social media, into stores, onto our packs. We worked with Cadbury FC, our football partnership, and we teamed up with Manchester United to bring older consumers to a match and to meet some of the players. We believe it's the right thing to do, and we told that story right through our media and other channels.

Q: Tell us about the Creme Egg advert that got a lot of attention.

A: In 2021 we made an advert for Cadbury Creme Egg and it got a lot of headlines – both positive and negative – for including a same sex kiss. The advert was about celebrating our 'Golden Goobilee' and 50 years of the brand and when we set out to make it, we just aimed to show how people of all walks of life, ethnicity, shapes, sizes, abilities, sexuality, basically how everyone in Britain, loved Creme Eggs.

It was diverse as it was meant to represent modern Britain, and it's a 30 or 60 second advert and the gay kiss was just three seconds or so of that. None of us appreciated the attention and the impact it would have, especially around that kiss, because that's what the media really focused on. We didn't intend it to be sensationalist, we intended it just to be representational of modern Britain.

We set out to be diverse both in front and behind the lens and that was super-important to us. Fifty-four per cent of the crew identified as female, black, Asian or ethnic minority, including across traditionally male dominated roles. The director of photography had a young trainee as a mentee to drive diversity in the industry, and that was super-important to us.

We were really surprised by the public reaction and all the media attention around the gay kiss. If we look back at it, we've learned so much along the way. For example, we didn't anticipate the reaction to the ad so we had to immediately put safeguards in place for the couple, because as soon as we realized what was going on we needed to make sure they were fully supported, that they were media trained, and we needed to make sure we were ready to respond to the media with our perspective. We focused a lot on helping the couple to understand the impact that could have on their personal lives and how to deal with it.

We came out proudly defending the advert and really showing that we were an ally to the gay community, and whilst we were fast in reacting, we're conscious we didn't get it all right. We have been criticized by some members of the gay community that we sexualized a gay couple by showing them kissing. At the same time the debate was, well what's wrong with a gay couple kissing, and of course nothing's wrong with it.

We don't tolerate hate; we don't tolerate anti LGBT+ sentiments. Cadbury is not like that, none of us who work at Mondelez tolerate that. There are things to learn, of course, and on this point about sexualizing the couple perhaps we should have shown them doing something ordinary, maybe just eating dinner together – on topics like this there will always be many differences of opinion and I don't know if there is a right answer, but it's a fair challenge.

Q: How do you look at diversity from the perspective of a global brand?

A: Cadbury is consistently about acts of generosity but we do that differently with different groups in different parts of the world. What we do in the UK is not necessarily what we do in Australia or what we do in India, but we have this theme of generosity which is absolutely the right thing for the brand.

Cadbury isn't like Oreo, we don't have one global advert, we're not Coke. We don't do one advert from the head office that runs in every country. We're a fabric of the nation brand, so India do their own advertising, Australia do their own, the UK do their own. Sometimes we might link up themes but we tend to very closely represent the people of the country and represent the cultural issues going on in that country. I guess that's why it feels iconic and local in all those markets. If you speak to someone in any of those countries, they will tell you that Cadbury feels like a local brand.

We have the theme of generosity and that spirit of generosity is linked to the founder and back to the Cadbury family and what they truly believed. That resonates throughout the whole brand all over the world, but the activations and what we do in different countries is different. For example, in South Africa we've really focused on childhood literacy, in other countries we focused on other topics, like when we've worked with Age UK. Not every brand at Mondelez will take a stance, it really depends on the brand foundations, the purpose and having the credibility to challenge stereotypes over the years.

Don't just think about the creative. There's in front of the lens and behind the lens, but don't just think about the making of the ad, also think about the media channels where you put it. That's important. There are loads of media channels to engage with under-represented audiences and there's an opportunity there.

There's no one-size-fits-all approach across Mondelez even with our media channels, so in the US they actively engage and seek to be more active with the Hispanic communities. They dub adverts or make specific adverts in Spanish but in the UK we've discussed whether we should do that, for example, with the Asian community. We went and got some advice from the community and from media owners, and it would work for first generation Asians, but it's not relevant for second or third. Even a lot of the first generation often speak English.

The last things I want to say are the need for stakeholder buy in and the need to be consistent and credible. With Age UK we agreed upfront to a three-year partnership because we decided to be consistent. That means investment in time, investment in money and investment from our stakeholders.

You need to make sure that you don't come across as a one-hit wonder. You need to be doing the right thing for the public and the community, especially on a brand like ours. For Cadbury, speaking to the next generation in the next decade when we do this work, we need to make sure it's right, it's credible and it's impactful, so that it actually does move the brand.

Q: What's your advice for marketers looking to get started on this journey?

A: We're lucky that we have great partners. We work globally with the UN's Unstereotype Alliance to look out for and remove stereotypes, we work with the WFA, with Free the Work, who are fostering diversity behind the lens. Working with partners is key and then just giving it a go, start by talking with your agency, talking with media partners. Be clear on whether you're doing hygiene factors versus making a stand, and certainly not every brand has to make a stand.

16

Measuring success

We are all just starting on this journey towards more inclusive marketing and need to create a learning culture both within our own businesses and across the industry. You may not be able to get conclusive results from any single individual campaign, but you need to look holistically at how you are building a body of knowledge, effectiveness and insight across your work.

The simplest answer to how you measure the success of inclusive marketing is that it should be the same as any marketing – good marketing is ultimately something that builds your brand and eventually drives sales for your business, in either the short or long term. It is of course easier said than done to measure that in practice, and then trickier still to work out how much of a factor your increased inclusion may have been in driving those results.

There is a commercial upside to inclusive marketing that comes as a combination of growing into new, untapped audiences and the more distinctive impact and cut through your inclusive communications can have. Ideally you would have brand tracking set up around your brand. If so, you can try to work with your research partner to include a question that starts to track specific consumer perceptions around your brand's inclusion, or you can just correlate overall brand tracking with your increasing efforts.

Marketing's job ultimately is clearly to drive sales, which may come in short-term conversions or might be about longer-term brand building and eventual follow-up. Depending on your route to market, there are various methodologies you can use, such as econometric modelling, closed loop sales studies using store card data or of course direct to consumer sales tracking. Inclusive marketing can be very impactful in the short run, but unless it's being set up with a specific performance objective you should be cautious about assuming all the brand impact will be felt in sales immediately.

Overall effectiveness and business impact is clearly the top priority to measure, but it's also important to consider how you will measure the increased diversity and inclusion of your work alongside that, and potentially how you can track the improvements of the inputs into your process as well as the end result outputs.

Quantifying how truly inclusive your marketing is, is not an easy thing to do in itself, especially when some of that inclusion can be baked into thinking and actions behind the scenes, or part of less visible decisions such as your media plan. Undeniably, the most visibly measurable part of your inclusive marketing is the on-screen representation that ends up featuring in your various adverts and communications.

No single piece of advertising or communications can expect to be fully inclusive of all aspects of society, and it's likely to feel like quite a forced 'tick-box' effort if you try to make it. Over time and multiple executions, however, especially across multiple different consumer touch points and media channels, you should be able to get a sense of whether you are building inclusion more broadly in.

There are rudimentary ways you can start to try to capture this, such as building a manual tracking of key diversity characteristics and their presence in your adverts, evolving through to some attempt to classify whether such characters are given equal billing and importance. Ultimately, whether the representation is good and authentic is slightly subjective but there are resources that can help you try, such as the Unstereotype Alliance Metric or the Gender Equality Metric (sometimes called the GEM score and designed by the US Association of National Advertisers).

Both are effectively survey methodologies that could augment any existing post-campaign research you are running by asking respondents whether they believe diversity is well presented in the content. Both originate with a focus on gender and asking whether the portrayals of men and women are positive but can be expanded to ask about any relevant character trait you are considering or trying to include. It can, however, become unwieldy to ask about every possible aspect of inclusion, and potentially pointless for aspects that are not represented at all, whether positively or otherwise.

However you choose to start measuring it, over time you'll start to build up a sense of whether you are making positive improvements in the area of representation. In doing so you'll hopefully uncover some successes, but also likely some challenges where progress is still slow, but this just gives you an opportunity to explore barriers and capability gaps in more detail.

If you are responsible for a larger marketing organization and trying to really get into the weeds of this, it can be helpful to think of some metrics which track progress in the inclusion of some of the inputs into your marketing. If you are going to develop or recommend some form of training or guide in this space, it might, for instance, be helpful to measure and set targets on how many people have completed that, or read the *Inclusive Marketing* book if you choose to recommend it.

There are other literal inputs you might want to consider measuring, such as a supplier diversity programme that looks at the breadth of partners you are working with, a media diversity programme that looks at the paid media channels you are investing in, or of course wider D&I measurement of your own team and the teams you are working with on projects.

Where you are making progress and can capture the impact of a specific campaign or your overall approach, it's worth considering how you then create a case study to best tell this story. Showing the impact of your inclusive marketing can help create a positive feedback loop internally and open new opportunities, but it can also be an external opportunity to show industry leadership and help others to also adopt more progressive approaches. Consider how you could work with a local or global advertising association to find and share more best practice in this space.

Inclusive marketing thinking can get you to great and effective work, but it is not a magic bullet that guarantees marketing success. It's as important to learn from what isn't working or hasn't delivered value for your business as it is to capture and celebrate the successes. As inclusive marketers we might wish we could create dedicated campaigns that understand and represent countless different aspects of our consumers, but there are also practical realities about resources and scale that we need to understand, as well as exploring how diverse content created for a specific audience may work effectively well outside of it.

This book has guided you through a dozen stages of the creative process and provided some advice and guidance on each, but you may well have found that some are more critical or relevant to your business currently than others. That's totally understandable and ultimately you must start somewhere and focus your efforts to make a difference, consider even monitoring the roll out of your inclusive marketing process and tracking which stages of the process you've succeeded in positively influencing and where there is perhaps more work to still be done.

CHECKLIST

Measuring success

Key questions to ask yourself:

1 What was the commercial upside?

2 How are you tracking the impact on your brand?

3 Does your measurement approach represent diversity?

4 What is the diversity across the portfolio and creative output? Are you making progress in positive representation?

5 What capability gaps still exist?

6 Can you make a positive case study to inspire and engage internally or externally?

7 Have you truly understood and learnt from the actual response to your work, whether positive or negative?

MARKETER IN FOCUS

Zaid Al-Qassab, Chief Marketing Officer at Channel 4

The UK TV station Channel 4 is both a publisher broadcaster media owner and an advertiser in its own right. Quite uniquely, the charter on which it was founded specifically challenges it to be more diverse and representative of the population and that has been born out in much of the content that has been commissioned over the years, including the show *Queer as Folk*, mentioned a few times previously in the book. They've also done industry-wide research to track shifts in representation and inclusion across advertising.

With so much content, it can be hard to ensure every piece is inclusive, but their CMO Zaid Al-Qassab speaks to the importance of doing a broader audit of all the work together, and also how critical it is that marketers come prepared to challenge senior leaders on this topic. He's also been a public advocate of the importance of talking more about mental health issues and supporting those who find themselves facing them.

Q: Why does representation matter to you?

A: The way I talk about diversity is the facts, what people are there and where they are from. There are benefits to diversity if people can contribute fully, because diversity reflects the society and the consumers around us. That brings insight to a creative industry that needs insight, that needs to understand people. The diversity of people in the room brings thoughts that are more diverse, which is good to relate with your consumers, good for the creative process, and it stops groupthink.

I often think that the financial crisis in 2008 was the result of a whole load of similar bankers and accountants who had worked out clever ways of making money from subprime loans without ever thinking about the end user. It doesn't take you long to realize that if you give loans to people who have poor chances of paying them back, that one day that's going to go belly up. If you'd had a marketer in the room they should have noticed that straight away, they shouldn't remove themselves enough from the end user not to have to think about it.

Diversity is good but diversity is just the facts of who is there. For me, inclusion is the feelings of the people who are there. Do they feel that they can contribute, give of themselves, use their background in the discussions, share ideas that are part of their lived experience? Representation needs both because it's not enough just to see yourself if the story being told doesn't feel authentic and inclusive.

It's important to the media industry because we want to be able to represent the societies, the people, and the communities that we serve. Doing so is going to make us a more successful industry.

There's a solid business reason why it's important, but then personally I also have a perspective as a mixed-race person. Growing up, I experienced and know the harm of racism and I also know the positive value of diverse backgrounds and what that brings.

In more recent years, as someone who's a depressive I also know the harm from bias and assumptions about mental health, and because of that I feel passionate about educating people on the value of representation, inclusion and diversity.

Q: What can we do to ensure mental health is better supported in our industry?

A: I think it is still a taboo subject, although it's getting better. You're more likely to go into work and tell people you have had a cancer diagnosis than you are to tell them that you're a depressive or are suffering from anxiety. That's not a good thing, but I guess 20 or 30 years ago you wouldn't have mentioned the

'C' word either, so times do change. I'm optimistic about times changing and I think they're changing quite fast at the moment.

One of the barriers in our industry, which is usually a very open and communicative industry, is that marketers and creative people are meant to be the life and soul of the party. We're meant to be the 'ideas people' in the room, we're meant to be the people who are always high energy. That's the stereotype and with that stereotype and that expectation from other people it's quite hard to open up and say 'I suffer from depression' or 'I suffer from anxiety' because it doesn't play well into the image of why you want a marketer in the room.

I think our industry has been particularly poor at starting to talk about this and I'm hoping that we can now open that discussion up and get a little bit more comfortable with it.

Q: Can you think of any good and positive examples of representation?

A: Channel 4 has run the Diversity in Advertising Award each year for the past six years and invites brands to pitch for £1 million worth of media value by coming up with more diverse and inclusive advertising.

In 2017 Lloyds bank won and they did a piece of advertising that was about unseeable forms of disability, including mental health, which I thought was very powerful. Last year EA Sports won for a piece of work that was about Muslims in football leagues, and in previous years the award focused the industry to think about gender and LGBT+, among other areas of diversity. This year's winning campaign by Tena has just launched and it spotlights the stigma around menopause in its response to our challenge to advertisers to improve authenticity in age representation.

That's been a real boost to the industry, to be actively talking about and promoting those things, and I think during that time we've seen many brands realize themselves that there's something to be done in terms of diverse representation. Again I feel positive about the way things are going.

When there was a backlash against Sainsbury's featuring a black family in their Christmas advert, the whole industry really came out and said that wasn't right or justified, and in fact we are going to make sure we feature more diverse ethnicity in our ads, which has got to be a good thing.

We also do quite a big piece of research now every year, Mirror on the Industry, where we look at diversity in UK advertising and there is both a long way to go and things are getting better. There is progress and we ought to recognize that, but the progress we're making has not brought the diversity of advertising up to the representative national averages of ethnicity or disability, for example.

Any sensible marketer would realize that representing the people out there, who they're trying to sell their brand to, is a sensible thing to do if you want people to relate to it. Once you bring it to people's attention that there's a compelling business case, not just an ethical case, for being more representative you start to see that change.

Q: How can marketers work to drive more inclusive content?

A: There's an inbuilt advantage of working at Channel 4 because we were set up to represent the diversity of Britain and we're measured on that by OFCOM. They look at who makes our shows, where they're made in the country, how diverse the talent on them is, and who are the diverse viewers watching. It's the purpose of Channel 4 to create change through entertainment, that's what we talk about, that's why we're here.

I do think there are things that other brand owners can do that are simple as well. Whoever you are, it's not that hard to have a look at your own advertising and think about the diversity of it. When I was in my last role as CMO at BT we decided that we would just do an annual audit, to look across a whole range of pieces of advertising and ask ourselves has this been representative across the year.

There's a real advantage in that, because it takes out of the equation all the naysayers who say this is tokenism. You can't make an advert that has one black, one Asian, one gay and one lesbian in it – your ads would all be ridiculous. My answer to that is, you look across a range of advertising across a period and check that it is diverse. Don't do advertising by numbers, just make sure that you've featured people with all forms of diversity across the scope of all your campaigns. I recommend everyone does that – looks back at a period of advertising and judges it that way.

One caution is that in recent years we've seen an increase in advertising featuring people who are ethnically diverse but not much progress in terms of them being the lead character. You can look at your work dispassionately and judge it against the society we live in and the diversity of Britain or whichever countries you're advertising in around the world.

Q: Have you seen advertisers over-rely on mixed race families and tokenism?

A: The first thing to say is that the data from the research shows that there is still less ethnic diversity in most advertising than there should be, so I don't think I would criticize anyone who is deliberately trying to cast in a more diverse way.

There's a way to go and the backlash that we've started to get of 'why does every advert have to have a black person in today?' is not based on facts. Perhaps one advert in 20 has such inclusion and some people are saying it's in every advert. Personally, I'd praise anyone who's thinking about diverse casting in whatever way.

Anecdotally, you do see a lot of ads where there's a black woman and a white dad or vice versa with mixed race kids, but that's a lot better than where we were a few years ago. In some ways, maybe that's even more progressive, because mixed-race families have unfortunately historically been controversial.

Q: Practically, how have you worked to make your marketing more inclusive?

A: I'd like to pretend that it's easy, but it's not. The WFA guide and this book's approach to thinking about diversity in different parts of the advertising process are good places for brands to start. Marketers should have a look at what the advice is step by step.

This isn't something that you can really do in a tokenistic way. Channel 4 shows the Paralympics every four years and we approach it as the biggest campaign and biggest brief that we have. It's not just a little sideline where we get to show some disabled people – our last Paralympics campaign for Tokyo was about two years in the making.

We worked with disability charities like Scope and we worked with 20 different paralympians themselves to get the insight to make sure we did it right. We tried to work out how to be bold and cut through without causing offence, which is a difficult line to tread sometimes. We tried to make it impactful and to tell real stories, not stereotypical stories. It is a big piece of work and that piece of work we know changes societal attitudes. We have research that shows 85 per cent of people said it made them think differently about disability when they saw it. That's good progress but it's not easy progress.

In terms of ethnicity, Channel 4 started what we call our 'Black to Front' project which is about putting black talent in front of and behind the camera. Whilst talent on screen has improved quite a bit, in terms of black talent being behind the camera it hasn't caught up nearly as much.

This is a job for our whole industry, including production. It's not just a job of putting people on screen. We managed to get 60 advertisers involved and they all had to commit that they would make advertising that would have black talent as the lead talent. People will say that's tokenistic but sometimes you have to force things. Once it's in their blood, once you go through the process of thinking actively about casting, and once you see the business results of having more diverse advertising, that will compel people to do more.

Q: How do you cope with negative feedback and challenges?

A: It's inevitable in a creative process that people don't like everything you do. Whatever advertising and communication you do, it's more sensitive to have those discussions when it's about diversity. You must stick to your guns. If you have used genuine insight, genuinely worked with people from those communities, and done it in good faith, then whilst it might not be perfect it's a lot better than doing it without thinking.

We always get criticism of our Channel 4 advertising because it is always diverse, and it always winds someone up. We're prepared to face that down and say you don't have to like it but we're not going to stop doing it.

There are plenty of studies or meta-analyses done by the big consultants to show the value of diversity. In particular, a piece of work from some years ago by McKinsey where they looked at the diversity of different boards of companies and their relative success on the stock market. They found that more diverse companies tend to have better results.

The logic is easy to understand – you've got a bunch of people in the room who have different points of view, different backgrounds, and they will better understand all the consumers out there and better come up with various ideas. I don't think it is rocket science, it is just human nature – you avoid groupthink and narrow ideas by having a diverse room.

There are lots of studies that have looked at that relationship to business results, and I know you summarized some at the start of the book. Anyone who faces challenges, I always tell them the first thing they should do is take that argument to their board. Don't just argue through the lens of something being ethically or morally right, take an argument that is a business argument to people who are business people. Don't be ashamed that that's what you're doing because if that's what convinces them then that's fine.

Sometimes as marketers we get stereotyped as being the colouring in department and just the fun creative ones. Whenever you're talking to the CEO, the board, or other senior stakeholders, you've got to come armed with numbers and language they understand and they can buy into.

The success of what we do is dependent on being able to talk the language of everyone else in the company and everyone else in the boardroom. You need to convince finance directors that you're spending money wisely, and the only way to do that is to speak their language and show the effect it has on the business.

It does become a self-fulfilling prophecy because if you're good at that then the finance director will want to give the marketing department more money to do good work, to do effective work. At the end of the day, we should be their favourite department – marketing is what grows your business, what builds your brands and ultimately what brings the money in. Finance departments should love marketing, and often they do.

When I'm having a beer with a finance director who doesn't get it and we're having a light-hearted debate about how much money we waste on marketing, I always challenge them – it's really easy to add up how much money you've got, which is your job, but it's really hard to make that amount of money go up, which is my job.

PART SIX

Conclusion

How to drive change

17

Case study: Driving change at GSK/Haleon

The marketing process is a complex one, with inclusion considerations at every stage and that can feel overwhelming. Whilst the best advice is often just to start small and start somewhere, this chapter is a deep dive into the case of one company and how they tried to drive this change within their business.

I worked at GSK Consumer Healthcare, now known as Haleon, as part of their global media team. I led their paid advertising approach and much of their digital transformation across the Europe, Middle East and Africa region. That's a fantastically diverse area with vastly different cultures and colleagues and it was a pleasure to have a team that reflected this and naturally brought a diversity of thought into our discussions.

If you are not familiar with GSK as a company, you are quite likely to know some of the brands they produce, which span the scientifically driven consumer healthcare space. They're a global leader in pain relief, with brands such as Advil, Voltaren and Panadol. They specialize in oral health through Sensodyne, Polydent and Parodontax (Corsodyl). They have a strong portfolio in respiratory, including Theraflu (Beechams), Otrivin and Flonase. Finally they work in the space of vitamins, minerals and digestive health thanks to Centrum, Eno and Tums. They also happen to make Chapstick.

During my time there, I also started to vocally speak out about the opportunity for us to drive more inclusion through our marketing, and in due course I was asked by our CMO Tamara Rogers to lead a global initiative to drive exactly that. It wasn't perfect, as nothing in a global and complex company ever can be, but we succeeded in driving substantial change both at a macro level and through specific projects we chose to lean in on.

Whether aspects of this approach are right for you will depend a lot on the size and maturity of your own business, but hopefully you can learn something from the journey we went on, just as I have learnt a lot from hearing about the experiences of other companies.

The #RepresentationMatters project at GSK

When you think about driving inclusive marketing across an entire global, multi-brand business, then it isn't just about influencing one brief, one campaign or one process, it's about shifting systems and mindsets on a much bigger level.

In GSK the challenge was not in winning over senior management, indeed the impetus to drive the inclusive marketing agenda really came straight from our CEO Brian McNamara. He sat on the company's internal LGBT+ council and the question came up as part of our Stonewall Equality Index work as to what we could do with our marketing to champion and support the community. He and Tamara took this as an opportunity to push inclusivity across all diversities and the 'Representation Matters' project was born.

Separately to this, GSK was introducing a new overall marketing mentality about bringing more humanity into our work and a mission to 'deliver better everyday healthcare with humanity'. Inclusion is really the result of truly wanting to understand and respond to the nuanced humanity of our consumers and so the project was a natural fit – it's about being totally consumer obsessed.

Our goal was to deliver more inclusive advertising – to train and empower our marketing teams around the opportunity of positive representation, to help our partners understand it is an expectation, and ultimately to ensure it pulls through into briefings and marketing processes. We believed that at all stages of the marketing process, including but not limited to the communications we create, there is an opportunity to better represent audiences. We knew our brands must go on a journey from not considering diverse audiences to fairly representing them, or even purposefully driving action for change.

This project touched many different parts of the organization, and to ensure strong alignment and impact we created a core working group with representatives of several different global marketing and capability teams.

We called this group the 'coalition of the willing' because it really self-selected as those willing to go a little bit outside their day jobs to challenge the business and drive this change. We met at least monthly to share the progress we were seeing from different markets and teams, and to drive key aspects of our central agenda.

We laid out a three-year plan, which was to start by sparking the change and driving the initial conversation and awareness that this was a business priority. Year 2 was a focus on scaled education and tangible action, whilst our ambition for year 3 was to show real courage and external leadership. Within this, our strategy was to focus on three areas:

1 *Our people:* Inspire them on the opportunity with senior leadership, internal recognition, and external inspiration. Empower them and remove fear so that everyone felt a responsibility for driving the change and the ability to take immediate steps. Ultimately to build capability and practical knowledge through training and workshops so that people know what to do.

2 *Our brands:* Work with key brands and campaigns to create lighthouse examples of best practice that others could follow and learn from. Ensure that inclusion considerations were embedded in our global and local brand processes and ways of working, including amongst core brand teams but also across media, insights, design and other functions.

3 *Our community:* Build a core community to drive and advocate for the project, but then really look externally to understand the community we can be part of and the wider influence we can have. This included partnering with our procurement team's supplier diversity programme, developing some specific D&R focused external partnerships, and committing to external industry engagement such as leading the WFA Task Force.

The initiative launched virtually during the Covid lockdown and to really drive home its importance and get local market engagement we ran three regional webinars. Each was hosted by the President of that region, with a panel of senior stakeholders sharing why this topic mattered to them. We also brought in inspiring external speakers who could talk from their own experiences of why this mattered, what good looks like and how they've driven this in their own business. As with this book, we spent quite a lot of the sessions unpacking the personal motivations and stories that bring to life the power of representation.

We knew we needed to encourage and empower our teams, who at times felt nervous about pushing in this direction, so as well as the senior leadership endorsement we rolled out a new series of workshops called '#IAmRemarkable'. It's an initiative our partners at Google had developed and which we adapted. It focuses on encouraging and inspiring women and diverse colleagues to bring their full selves to the office and really be willing to speak up. It was open to anyone in the marketing organization who wanted to take it and saw the emergence of a positive community as those who had taken the session went on to become trainers and lead future sessions themselves.

The most crucial part of the initial project was the roll-out of a simple best practice playbook and a short e-learning module that every marketer in the business was required to take. Using an early version of the thinking in this book, we trained the teams on the key stages of the creative process and the opportunities for inclusion or possibility of exclusion if we were not conscious of our own biases and assumptions. Over the course of the year over 1,000 marketers and related colleagues took the training, which ended with a pledge that they would individually look to apply these considerations in their day jobs. This new capability was hosted on a simple intranet site on which we also curated external best practice, case studies and all the video content from the launch events.

The overall project also saw us identify several key opportunities to push our capability and understanding and to prove our new ways of working. Supported by money from our sustainability team we were able to centrally fund activations that we used to demonstrate best practice across the key phases of the marketing process.

Stage one: Inclusive briefing and strategy

An area we were particularly keen to explore further was around insights and data. We had brands keen to talk to and represent specific communities, but whose standard consumer research didn't provide them with a detailed view on how the attitudes or expectations of these communities might differ. We wanted to understand whether there were distinct needs, new business opportunities and cultural nuances that we might have been missing or that we could actively lean into.

The whole consumer insights industry is on a journey in this space, and certainly doing more to ensure that research draws from more representational samples. It's an inevitable challenge, however, that if you're trying to simplify your understanding of your target audience down into something manageable, you are going to have to look at 'average' notions of your audience and lose a lot of the distinctiveness that makes people human and unique. Whilst that's still a part of marketing, we wanted to explore layering on a much deeper and deliberately diverse level of understanding around different cultures.

We chose to partner with a company called DECA Media Consultancy – they are built on the back of a network of diverse media publications but have flipped that from being a paid media opportunity into using those communities to pull insight and cultural understanding. Perhaps more so than with more mainstream publications, these diverse journalists are finely tuned to the specific cultural heartbeat of their communities, and of course to an extent their writing also defines that.

The brand we chose to partner with for this project was Centrum, a vitamin brand that was doing some wider repositioning work at the time and wanted to understand the business and communication opportunities that existed within several communities. As a global brand they took a multi-market approach and focused on the UK, Germany, Italy and Saudi Arabia – the latter certainly being something of a contrast to the others. In each, the DECA team helped identify some of the biggest and most relevant communities for us to explore. In the UK for instance that included British Asians and the LGBT+ community, whilst in Germany we included a focus on the large Turkish immigrant population.

Analysis started with a big data approach using keyword scraping across the network of diverse publishers but moved into more hands-on reading and interpretation of key stories and context. Where we were able to identify potential trends or areas for further exploration, we moved into more bespoke research first through surveys and then into specific focus groups that key publications helped us curate.

The result was a hugely detailed report that unpacked surprisingly nuanced attitudes towards proactive healthcare, vitamins and general well-being. It's notable that there is a huge amount that unites people from very different backgrounds and experiences and plenty of territory you can play in where you can be relevant to everyone, but also opportunities to really cut through when you understand specific distinctions.

It was, for instance, interesting to understand how important the topic of more natural based health products was within the British Asian community, not least because it's a culture in which there are more established natural remedies of their own. From a media planning perspective, it was interesting to learn that the Turkish population in Germany, perhaps unsurprisingly, heavily consumed content from Turkey and was more likely to be seeing adverts there than in local channels.

The brand team have used this to inform some of their broader strategy, several specific campaigns and executions and a specific partnership that is referenced later in this case study.

Stage two: Inclusive planning

The training we rolled out included some Unstereotype Alliance resources exploring what good marketing inclusion looks like, but we knew to truly get to it we had to have diverse perspectives inputting into the work. Ensuring that we had that inclusive input across our work was a big focus area for us that we were looking to solve both in the short and the long term.

GSK as a business has long had internal diversity and inclusion targets and makes real tangible efforts to build an inclusive and welcoming culture. I can honestly say it was one of the most diverse places I have ever worked, but that unfortunately still leaves a gap away from true statistical representation of the wider population. To ensure we made the most of the internal representation we did have we started working with our ERGs to involve them and explore processes whereby they could provide occasional feedback, input or even audits of our marketing output.

We also looked at how we could bring in additional perspectives through the partners that we worked with and made it clear that this was an expectation even of our established agencies. With Publicis Groupe, our global media partner, we began working on a joint D&I agenda and even took a seat on their internal diversity council. We identified a number of diversity focused partners who could help us on this journey, which included DECA and their parent company Brand Advance, but also the consultants Creative Equals, volunteer organizations such as Outvertising and Bloom, and media partners such as Gay Times. Bringing in these perspectives at different stages of our creative development and testing process helped us rapidly build confidence and best practice.

Looking longer term, we wanted to ensure we as a business were having a positive impact on the future of diversity and inclusion across the whole marketing industry. Rather than try to start something completely new, we looked to external partners whose work we could support and amplify. One small example of that was sponsoring the mentoring scheme that Bloom, a UK group for women working in marketing, launched.

A bigger initiative was partnering and supporting the Brixton Finishing School, an organization that provides a wide range of advertising-specific training and development designed to attract and enable people from more diverse backgrounds, especially from different socio-economic backgrounds, to get into the industry.

We chose to sponsor the course jointly with Publicis as part of our joint D&I agenda and indeed to offer a placement to someone off the course which was split between time working at the agency and working on the client side to get the full exposure. We helped them develop a new 'media week' syllabus to talk more about the media side of the industry and recorded a broader introduction to marketing with fellow-sponsors KFC. The course has seen hundreds of people come through it and make their way into the industry, and we hope it's part of creating a much more inclusive environment for all.

Stage three: Inclusive production

Although there were wider initiatives within the business relating to supplier diversity and how we thought about our production, this was another opportunity for us to work on a specific project and build out a case study that could educate and challenge our other colleagues. In this instance it became a multi-year partnership between the UK publisher Gay Times and our Sensodyne and Voltarol brands.

Gay Times is a magazine and online publisher and certainly not a traditional creative agency or production house, but working with its editorial team presented an opportunity to truly get under the skin of the LGBT+ community and explore different ways of reaching them. We explored two distinct approaches which covered the spectrum between casual representation and inclusion through to more deliberate campaigning and storytelling.

With Sensodyne, as Tamara discussed in her interview, the team looked to recreate a long-running campaign that shows people reacting in pain to particularly hot or cold foods. It wasn't telling a specific LGBT+ related story but we worked with the Gay Times team to cast an intersectional range of people from across the community to take part in the ads, and also worked with them on ensuring that as many people involved behind the camera were from the community as well. It was important for us to create a positive and inclusive production environment where the people we were working with felt able to be themselves.

For Voltarol we explored a different route and partnered with the charity Pride Sports to help them provide resources and assistance for LGBT+ inclusive sports clubs who were having to adapt to the varying Covid restrictions. We worked with them and Gay Times to then identify several athletes from across those clubs who were willing to tell authentic stories of how important getting out and being part of a sports community had been for them over these difficult years. Voltarol is a brand that helps tackle pain and really celebrates the 'joy of movement' and so was able to associate itself with these positive stories whilst to an extent taking a back seat to the individuals involved.

Localization is an interesting topic that came up a few times as we rolled the overall project out. The Gay Times work was only intended for the UK but as word spread other markets did become interested in it and we learnt that there were greater opportunities for such content to travel than we had realized. Whilst relevant aspects of inclusion do vary around the world, LGBT+ content is notable as an area where sadly there can be quite strict legal or cultural barriers to sharing it.

The #RepresentationMatters project, like this book, was more about telling people the right questions to be asking at different stages in the process rather than giving them all the answers, and as such it did translate and land in a range of culturally diverse areas. Whilst the US and UK were early leaders in the space, it was actually in our Middle East and Africa regions where the local leadership got most excited about the initiative and did the most work in terms of localizing the approach, rolling out market-by-market deep dives and really building it into their strategies. We were perhaps guilty of our own stereotypes and prejudices in assuming other markets might pick it up faster.

Stage four: Inclusive launches

Working with the Gay Times team helped us shape and produce this content as well as to get input and advice as we looked to test it. We ultimately launched it by amplifying it not only across their network but also much more broadly to a wider mass audience, where the Sensodyne work actually outperformed the previous executions we had created in the series.

As the project had begun with a challenge from our LGBT+ Council it was key to us that we kept our ERGs updated and engaged throughout and indeed made a strong effort to present the launch at a number of such forums as well as sharing widely on our intranet. We presented these cases extensively across the business, had them nominated for both internal and external awards, and created a strong appetite from other teams to be the next great case study for inclusion.

We measured these specific campaigns largely using pre- and post-campaign surveys, but also by ensuring they were included in some of our wider marketing performance modelling. More broadly across the business, we started looking at the overall inclusion across our full portfolio of creative and how we could set benchmarks to improve that. We adopted the 'Unstereotype Alliance Metric' which is a set of questions you can build into your consumer testing to explore how gender, or other diverse characteristics, are presented within your communication. Our CMO built both an improvement in our overall output and 100 per cent completion of our e-learning module into her objectives for the year, which is always a good way of making sure things get done.

It was also key for us that we were pushing for this change outside of our business and across the wider industry. It was because of that that we volunteered to co-lead the WFA's Diversity Task Force and shared the training materials that we had produced as part of that. They became a core foundation of the open-source Unconscious Bias guide which the WFA went on to launch, and indeed the underpinnings of the framework explored in this book.

Coming back to the Centrum research project, we also explored a specific and unique partnership with the LGBT+ volunteer organization Outvertising. As part of their 2021 Awards, we launched an open brief in which we shared some of the relevant insights and data we had found through our own research and a creative challenge to help come up with a simple inclusive campaign for the brand. The winning entry was produced as a final piece of content and launched across social media channels at the start of 2022. As sponsors of the awards themselves we ran a panel in which the judges unpacked some of what they'd learnt from judging the different entries and seeing how different creatives were building new inclusive marketing muscles by working on the brief.

Coming into its third year, we made a conscious decision to scale down the centrally driven elements of the project, not because inclusion was any less important but on the contrary because we'd succeeded in building it into every brand and market's priorities and now wanted to support them as they continued to explore what this looks like in practice.

We saw some fabulous examples of this starting to happen and the benefits of being a truly global company. Our UK Voltarol team, for instance, saw an advert they loved from our South African team which showed a black couple adopting a new child and thought it was a great bit of creative that they could also use in their market, without needing to recast or reshoot it as perhaps some marketers would have done in the past.

There's still a long way to go and many of the brands are still working out what their purpose is and which communities it makes sense for them to specifically look to engage, but it was a successful example of persuading a business that representation truly matters and shifting the structures and processes until you can start delivering that.

18

Partnering to help drive change

As part of the core framework in this book, we highlighted the importance of agency and team selection, and the broader topic of internal D&I which that relates to. For brands looking to become more inclusive, partners are a huge opportunity to accelerate that and to leap ahead by learning from their experience. There are far too many great partners now in this space to begin to talk about them all, and of course different partners working in different countries around the world, but we highlight here some of the kinds of partners you might want to look out for.

Supplier diversity approaches

As well as partners specifically dedicated to inclusive marketing, there is an opportunity across your entire business supply chain, and certainly within marketing, to ensure you are working with a more intersectional selection of suppliers. Formal initiatives to increase the diversity of the companies you work with are sometimes called 'supplier diversity' schemes and led by procurement teams.

There are different ways of measuring and defining this, but typically you will look at the ownership of the companies you work with and set meaningful targets to increase the number of minority owned and operated businesses. It may also be relevant to push those businesses around the suppliers that they in turn work with, to understand how much of your budget is going to diverse businesses right down the chain. It starts by undertaking an audit of your current situation so you can set a benchmark and look to continually improve.

No doubt there will still be many good reasons to continue working with larger organizations, with public or less diverse ownership. Here you can still hold them accountable around the diversity they have in their leadership and the inclusion initiatives they have within the business. Consider blending the use of more traditional partners with smaller diverse organizations that can provide specific expertise, products or services.

Other advertisers and associations

You are not alone in going on this journey; many other brands are trying to drive the same inclusive marketing agenda. Some will be ahead of you, some may be behind you, but this is an area where most are willing to collaborate and share best practice.

There are formal examples of this happening that you can plug into, most notably through global or national marketing associations. The WFA's Diversity Task Force fed into the content of this book, and they have publicly curated a range of resources, guides and references on their website (www.wfanet.org). National associations like the Incorporated Society of British Advertisers (ISBA, www.isba.org.uk) in the UK and the Association of National Advertisers (ANA, www.ana.net) in the US have active diversity forums and opportunities for marketers to share best practice amongst themselves.

Consider joining one of these or reaching out to them, or to other marketers you know, and ask them to share best practice or case studies. If you're truly passionate about this topic and want to drive change not just in your business but across the whole industry, then ask about ways for you to volunteer or be involved in their groups. Some may require your company to be a member of the association to take part, but there are voluntary groups that do not.

If you're trying to inspire and motivate your business to drive this change then running an event with outside speakers from other respected marketing companies can be a great way of showing what is possible. Many such speakers may be willing to talk about this subject for free, but it is always best practice to offer a speaker fee or charitable donation where possible, especially as such speakers are in increasing demand.

In the UK ISBA have partnered with the Advertising Association and IPA on an initiative called 'All In'. Similar to the WFA, they have curated a range of available resources and they also ran a detailed census of the advertising industry to get a better understanding of the barriers and challenges different groups face. The action plan developed on the back of that is featured on their website alongside a range of resources that you may find helpful.

The Unstereotype Alliance is an initiative convened by UN Women in partnership with a number of global brands and creative agencies that works to improve gender portrayals in advertising. They have produced helpful resources and measurement approaches, some available publicly, and others for companies that sign up as members.

Industry volunteering groups

This will vary a lot depending on where you happen to live and work as a marketer but across the globe there are a healthy range of volunteer groups that have been set up by passionate individuals keen to make a bigger change in the industry. Typically, they will focus on a specific area such as women, LGBT+ or racial considerations, and will try to both create a positive and supportive community and provide training or agitation across the industry. Hundreds of these such groups now exist but a few I have personally been involved with in the UK include:

- *Outvertising* (www.outvertising.org)
  A group that creates a positive community within the advertising industry for LGBT+ professionals as well as works to increase the amount of representation that group receives within the marketing that companies produce. They run mentor schemes, events, awards, a range of training initiatives, and regular socials for people to get to know one another.

- *The Conscious Advertising Network* (www.consciousadnetwork.com)
  Advocates specifically in the adtech and media space around subjects including hate speech, misinformation and climate change denial. They work with a range of NGOs and have an ongoing partnership with the United Nations to help advertisers understand the influence their media budgets have on content and how they can safely control that.

- *WACL* (www.wacl.info) *and Bloom* (www.bloomnetwork.uk)
  Examples of two networks specifically supporting and empowering women working within the advertising and marketing sector. Both organize a range of events, training sessions and mentoring, as well as building more informal communities and networking. Bloom runs a great form of 'reverse mentoring', which pairs men up with women in the industry to better understand some of the different challenges they face.

- *Brixton Finishing School* (www.brixtonfinishingschool.org) *and Media For All* (www.mediaforall.org.uk)

  These organizations are all about recruiting, developing and supporting the next generation of more diverse talent into the industry. They're great destinations to point possible future marketers to, but they're also really rewarding organizations to volunteer for, or for your company to partner with. By providing training, shadowing, internships and other support we can help people from very different backgrounds get a start in the industry, and find brilliant new employees for our teams.

- *DICE* (www.getdice.co.uk)

  A number of people who fed into this book came back to the notion of 'you cannot be what you cannot see' in terms of representation in the advertising content we're making, but this is true of our industry and its events too. Diversity and Inclusion at Conferences and Events (DICE) campaigns to see better inclusion in presenters and panellists at key events, and offers accreditation for those able to meet their inclusion standards. Hopefully, as we attract more diverse talent into our industry, they'll also be more likely to see people who represent them on our stages, winning our awards and leading our teams.

Publishers and media owners

As discussed in the 'Paid media' section, there are big opportunities to partner with diversity focused media owners who specialize in serving their specific communities. Not only can these be great ways of reaching such communities, but the editorial team will often have, or be able to develop, rich insights as to how that community will connect with your brand or think about your category.

Rather than just thinking about them at the end of the process as a way of getting your content out there, you can build longer-term partnerships to really tap into their nuanced cultural understanding. Work with them to develop and test content and campaign ideas long before they're ready to be pushed out live across their channels. Learn from their own editorial and your activation as to what works best, and keep evolving over time.

Building a longer-term partnership can help you build up a really authentic connection with that audience, avoid allegations that you are just jumping on a bandwagon and get much more value out of the relationship. As diversity focused media owners are often quite small, you'll reduce the requirements for them to always be pitching for new work and can be sure that every penny you spend with them really counts and helps fund inclusive voices.

If you work with a media agency, they should be able to help identify and engage a range of such titles, or consider whether your ERGs might be able to advise on relevant titles. There are thousands of titles globally for every imaginable aspect of inclusion, and even though many of their audiences will be small they can be highly influential, and content you create together can be amplified through advertising to much broader targets.

In the UK the LGBT+ community, for instance, is well served by big titles such as *Gay Times*, *Attitude Pink News* and *Diva Magazine*, but there are also a wide range of smaller niche titles that cater to different subcultures. You can find more positive voices relevant to very mainstream audiences as well, for instance Freeda Media, which was set up to provide a more positive and empowering media network for women. In very ethnically diverse areas, you'll often find that traditional local media does a good job of representing and responding to different communities, and there are a wide range of great publications that exist relating to people's ethnicity, religion or other intersectionality.

Today you can also find digital solutions such as ad tech, private market-places or diversity networks (e.g. Brand Advance) that enable you to advertise programmatically across a large number of diversity focused media owners at the same time. Whilst you'll lose some of the close partner-ship, insights and content opportunities that come from a direct relationship, this can be a great way of building scale across smaller titles or amplifying a campaign across key demographics.

Remember that influencers are also a powerful opportunity to work directly with diverse voices, to get their feedback and perspective on things, and for your advertising to fund their continued work and storytelling.

Marketing diversity focused companies and consultancies

There are also some brilliant companies now out there, totally dedicated to helping marketers on the journey towards inclusive marketing. DECA Media Consultancy helps brands with insights and strategy by learning from a wide range of inclusive media publications and authors. The Diversity Standards Collective taps into an inclusive network of consultants to help you test, explore, and develop ideas. Creative Equals is a broad inclusion consultancy that offers unconscious bias training similar to the approach in this book as well as wider transformation projects, and a series of public initiatives to tackle issues in the industry. The Unmistakables helps organizations build inclusive cultures, structures and behaviours, which ultimately lead to more diverse outputs.

The list could go on much longer, but the point is that there are some wonderful organizations out there if you start looking and asking around. What you will need will depend a lot on your own maturity and journey but having a partner to help guide you is invaluable, however advanced you are. Even as we make improvements to the diversity of the people in our teams, we will never truly be able to represent every possible perspective in the room, but organizations like these can help you step out of your bubble and really challenge yourself to see things from different perspectives.

If you don't know where to start, then go back through some of the interviews in this book and see if any of the organizations there have inspired you. Attend or even just look at the agenda for diversity related marketing events in your area to see the companies and individuals that are out there. Begin by reaching out and speaking to one of them and I am sure they'll be able to help you find other suitable partners to support you.

MARKETER IN FOCUS
Sion Walton-Guest, Co-Founder at The Globetrotter Guys

Alongside more traditional media opportunities, the influencer space has emerged as a new route for marketers to reach consumers. It's an unregulated space that you should approach with caution, but if you find the right partners it can be a great way not only of driving scale but also creating authentic content. That's particularly important with inclusive marketing in mind because working with a diverse range of content creators can help you reach new audiences and in doing so also directly fund and support those voices.

Sion Walton-Guest is one half of The Globetrotter Guys, a couple who took two years off from their day jobs to travel the world and found themselves starting a blog and social media content series. They've carved out a niche for themselves in representing the unique opportunities and challenges that face the LGBT+ traveller and have worked with a range of brands looking to authentically speak to their audience.

Q: Who or what are The Globetrotter Guys?

A: 'The Globetrotter Guys' refers to myself and my husband and in January 2018 we quit our day jobs and went on a one-way plane ticket around the world. At that time we also started to see the emergence of a lot of travel blogs so we learnt how to create a website, how to use our social media channels to reach our audience, a bit of amateur photography, and decided to set up a travel blog ourselves.

We were constantly on the road for two years, which really helped us grow quickly and people started to take an interest in where we were travelling and what we're doing. It became something a bit more substantial than I expected, which is a great thing.

We have continued to grow and develop from there and now part of what we do is share travel guides to different destinations through the eyes of ourselves as a gay couple. We appreciate we cannot represent everybody though so we do also make sure to interview other people from different countries to get their take, not just as somebody different to ourselves, but as a local, because the tourist versus local perspectives can be very different.

Q: Why does representation matter to you?

A: Representation in marketing matters to me because it takes a lot of the guess work out. What I mean by that is, and I can take travel as the easy example, when I'm looking at a destination or somewhere to travel to as an LGBT+ traveller, I have a massive list of things to consider before I go. Is it going to be legal? Am I going to be safe? Am I going to be comfortable? Can I be myself? Do we need to book a twin room? All these extra things that others don't have to think about.

When it comes to representation if I see a travel destination campaign and they are very inclusive, and I can see myself represented, then that starts to take away some of that guess work that I have to do and makes me immediately have an affinity with going to that destination.

The same can be said for any campaign or any brand. I will naturally start to feel an affinity with it and it'll help me make decisions about where I want to spend my money. I think if a brand has good representation and inclusion in their marketing campaigns, then it tells me a lot about its values, and that's something that's quite important. I don't think people should underestimate the impact of seeing yourself represented properly.

Q: Can you think of any good examples of inclusive marketing and representation?

A: One of the best examples I can give for travel is Visit Stockholm. We were invited on a press trip with them, and they take inclusion very seriously there, it's so ingrained in all their activities that it's not an add on or an extra. They've got whole sections of their website dedicated for LGBT+ travellers to tell them what's on offer for them.

When they were running that press trip, they took influencers and bloggers from the entire spectrum of the LGBT+ community. Not just the typical white, gay, male couple that I know we fall into. There's so much more to the spectrum that needs to be represented and they did a really good job of doing that, and they continue to do so each year.

With them as an example, they have representation across all the activities from website and materials to videos and social media. It's not just a one-off clip, it's more holistic and it's more embedded. I had no idea what to expect from Stockholm, but we fell in love with it, even if it was freezing.

Q: How can marketers use influencers to talk to diverse communities more authentically?

A: It's hard to speak for the entire influencer industry, and there is no regulation, but let's assume that we're talking about working with good influencers that have an authentic audience and are doing it for the right reasons. We are accidental influencers; we started the blog as a hobby, and it just happened.

If I am going to work with a brand, I'm going to do my due diligence on them, but equally they need to do the due diligence on us. They need to do more than just have a glance at an influencer's profile, and the high-level numbers. I feel it's important to get to know the influencer and their audience – know what their values are and make sure they align with the campaign or with the brand.

That's going to be a critical starting point for it to be effective because if you're trying to sell or promote something that doesn't align with what you really believe, people are going to see straight through it. If a brand approaches an influencer and that influencer isn't asking them some hard questions then as a marketer I would be sceptical about whether they're doing it for the right reasons, or just doing it for the money. Having meaningful conversations, building that relationship, and understanding the reasons for doing it on both sides, other than just ticking a box, is a very important starting point.

Then I think it's useful for the brand not to be overly prescriptive with exactly what they want. You need to appreciate that if you're working with an influencer then they know their audience, they know their content, and they know what resonates best. I think consumers take things on board better when they are delivered conversationally, and typically the relationship an influencer has with their audience is more conversational, casual and informal. When the messaging feels like it's coming from an acquaintance you take it a little more seriously, but that's only possible if that relationship's there to start with.

I am always looking for substance from brands and they should want substance back from me. An example of that would be Barefoot Wine. They have got a very longstanding history of working the LGBT+ community. Right back since 1989 – you can track what they've done. When we were first approached, I went to their website and found all this information about them, and then I absolutely wanted to work with them because I can stand behind that and I want to tell my audience about it.

There have been times where we've seen a proposal, but we've decided it was not for us because it wouldn't reflect well on us. I like to ask the brand why they are doing this campaign and what are they looking to achieve. I want to make sure it's not just a box-ticking exercise and that they are doing it for the right reasons. It's good to understand if this is a one-off thing or is it building up to something, to know what other things they are planning on doing. Has their company seen and understood the need to take positive action for the right reasons? That can be hard to figure out but it's a valid question.

Q: Do you receive negative comments on your content? How should brands deal with that?

A: We consider ourselves quite lucky with the comments that we receive. With one or two exceptions for the past four years, we've been very lucky. One exception was a video we recently posted about a gay cruise with all these guys dancing with each other and there were a lot of really stigmatizing comments about HIV and Aids. The way we approached it, and would suggest others approach it, is not rising to it. Being calm, collected, rational, factual and helpful. So rather than getting into an argument about HIV I shared links to Stonewall or resources like that and encouraged people to go read that and become more educated.

Even if they probably won't take the advice, visibly putting the help out there and responding to it rather than just leaving it felt right. As a consumer I think if I saw a brand letting hateful things go and not responding to them then that looks bad as well. It could even be a simple statement to say thanks for your comment, but these are our values that we stick by.

That said, whilst I want to reason with people half the time, remember on many platforms that you can delete comments on a thread. On certain platforms such as Tik Tok you can have your settings so if people use certain words in their comments they simply won't appear. I'm sure you can think of plenty of derogatory words towards communities that you could have filtered out before they even appear. There are a lot of pre-emptive things that you can do as well as responsive things when such comments do appear.

Some brands that have received backlash have back-tracked or distanced themselves and that's awful. The implication there is that they didn't really believe in what they were doing to start with. It makes you think that it's just performative and they are not doing it for the right reasons. It's a much higher reputational risk long term to pull a campaign, especially as the backlash that you get probably isn't from the customers that you want.

19

The future of inclusion

If you came to this book hoping for an easy answer and a simple guaranteed way of making your marketing more inclusive, then I apologize if you're still looking for it. Inclusive marketing is about being more empathetic and asking yourself more questions and as a result this book is filled with more questions than answers, and in some of the perspectives shared you may even have found slightly competing opinions on how to succeed and what 'good' looks like.

That's perfectly alright because, just like the consumers we serve, marketers ourselves are unique, individual and have different opinions on things. You can find people who strongly believe all representation and inclusion comes from a positive place, and others who see a lot of it as shameless commercial cash-ins. Similarly, some people feel strongly that all positive representation matters and is a step in the right direction, whilst others push back on shallow efforts to look good without meaningful change and social action to support them. Some would point to examples where well-meaning efforts by brands have actually caused unhelpful backlash or pressures which have made things worse for those they are trying to represent and would have great caution about encouraging more 'support'.

Personally, I strongly believe all marketing can be inclusive, casually representative and play a role in breaking down stereotypes and opening new aspirations. I see that some marketing can go further than that to champion causes or even drive meaningful societal change but that is the exception rather than the rule and depends hugely on your brand positioning and category.

We are at a notable moment in history where we've truly started to realize and address much of the lack of inclusion, diversity and fairness in our society but of course have a long way to go. It's an important first step that we are thinking about and trying to solve this, and longer term we'll hopefully have an industry that is naturally more inclusive and doesn't need to be pushed so hard to think in these ways.

Many of the labels that we apply to diversity are in themselves limiting inclusion. After all, whilst I am a gay man I am much more than that, and whilst I am similar to some gay men and members of the LGBT+ community I am also very different to others. We are intersectional and naturally have different aspects of our humanity which matter to us, and in true inclusion we'll start to worry less about the buckets and more just about the overall authentic output.

There's also a convergence of wider sustainability topics, with important conversations around the environment and overall social impact of our businesses coming together with the topic of diversity. Many businesses are also starting to understand the role they play in an overall supply chain and the powerful influence they can have over their suppliers, or even those they supply to, as we try to improve on these topics together.

We'll start to close this book as we've been doing throughout, by hearing a couple of interesting and thought-provoking perspectives, both on what good inclusion looks like and potentially on where we go next.

MARKETER IN FOCUS
Gabriella Hall, Marketing Director/D&I Consultant

Every marketer in this book has shared some of their favourite examples of where representation is starting to be delivered well, but there is also a sense that we are still in the initial stages and much of it can be quite tokenistic. For a slightly different view I spoke to Gabriella (Ella) Hall who sees that we are going through an awkward phase in history and still need to get out the other side, and how from her own perspective some well-meaning intentions to represent can have the opposite impact.

Ella has had an extensive career leading and directing marketing campaigns originally within the media industry itself and more recently in a range of, fitness, financial services and education companies. She provides some of her consultancy through the Diversity Standards Collective, a company dedicated to helping marketers get more inclusive perspectives and research.

Q: Why does representation matter to you?

A: Only in the last couple of years have we really seen a change in representation in advertising – by this I mean that I believe that we as a population have diversified but marketing hasn't really caught up yet. Eighty per cent of the ads I see, even though some of them are better represented, are still about the nuclear family. At the same time the number of single people in the UK has grown by 8 per cent in the past 10 years and 15 per cent of families are lone parents, so the traditional 'Oxo family' is less the norm. Even if there are two parents and two children there is increasing diversity in the gender and identity of these family members that are no longer just Mum, Dad and Jack and Jill.

By 2036 one in four of us will be over 65, and having seen my parents age vs my grandparents, who at 65 seemed old, I can say I have seen the change in my lifetime. Sixty-five no longer means sweet tea and cigarettes in old people's homes. My mother at 74 still plays golf and drives around Spain in a 4x4. Are we representing this ageing population well? I would say no.

I think what we see from Marketing/advertising does have an impact on us, you and I know this as, even as marketing folk, we are still subject to the subliminal impact of a good ad, or the pillars of a good brand – even though we may not even notice it. I still only really trust brands with a good broadcast presence, despite buying millions of pounds of digital media each year. So as part of the fabric of our lives I think ads have a responsibility to represent the UK as it is now. Or it can lead to people feeling that they somehow failed socially if they are not meeting that norm or are somehow 'outside' the norm.

Representation matters as people can identify with what may be seen as 'difference' only if they know what different really looks like. TV/radio/social/outdoor have mass reach opportunities and tell daily life stories, and are well placed to change the dial on representation.

Q: Can you think of some good examples of representation in advertising or media?

A: It is quite difficult to think of any advertising that gets it right because I often feel that much of today's work is in that early stage of wanting to try to fill a gap quickly and therefore it can sometimes look tokenistic, despite good intentions. Having said that, the new Virgin Atlantic Campaign is obviously wonderful – but they do have the advantage of having a more diverse brand image to start with. I think for many brands inclusion, especially dealing with gender and identity, is new and not always easy to navigate. There are fewer lived experience people working in the sector.

We could learn, I think, from broadcast media content, especially within platforms like Netflix, shows like *The Great* and *Harlots* where they have just been naturally diverse work well – for me anyway. I am a history buff, and the under-represented history is seldom told. For example, a historical perspective of people of colour living and working in London in the 1760s, that was a fact. Having molly-houses (gay brothels as they were at the time), that was a fact. Having trans houses (these people sadly could not physically transition but people who identified as being in the wrong physical body). These are all things that were going on way before we all had this conversation, and these shows have done their research and created compelling and interesting characters that we identify with. This, I think, breaks down borders as these shows are saying, these are human stories, these people had lives and cares and needs too and things like gender identity issues are not new.

I think the fact that content creators are participating in the change in representation is great. They have just cast great actors regardless of the traditional stereotypes and it is wonderful to see differentiation, to see people in shows that traditionally would not have gotten those jobs. I have always thought that marketing and advertising has not caught up with that yet, we're still stuck in our three or thirty seconds of glory and trying to make it work right now.

On the positive side, the intention to be inclusive really is there. Agencies and some media owners are really embracing change and diversity in their employees and their thinking – which is fantastic.

Q: What do you think it would take to get to really good marketing work?

A: I am a massive advocate of reading and understanding other periods of change, like the French Revolution. Maybe not the answer you were expecting! If you have not read about the French Revolution, then read about what that change was because there are some similarities with where we are today. You go from one complete extreme to another and within that quick period between 1789 and 1795, where you see massive upheaval, you also see a society that is trying to cater to the needs of people on a large scale that have previously not had a voice. Of course this leads to many tiers and factions but also people are saying things because they do not want to go to the guillotine and eventually everyone becomes apathetic and the old system returns.

I think in many ways that is like where we are today. People who have had to be silent (for example, trans people, people who identify differently, etc.) want to be heard and seen, but at the same time people who have not experienced these issues (the majority) don't necessarily know why they should agree with a level of representation. To some degree it does not make any difference to their day-to-day life, for example if you are a mum of three kids and you have got to get them to school, suddenly you are supposed to be aware of all these things and consider why someone is upset about something else. There are a lot of demands on people and the pace of change is intense. What I am saying here is that for long term positive representation, ongoing strategy is critical.

So how can marketing help with this? I think that the starting point of this is good solid representation at source. As the traditions of the nuclear/traditional society relax marketing certainly has a place in representing a wider, richer society but that representation is not likely to have real roots and resonance if the original brief did not have the input of people who understand the nuance of life from an unfamiliar perspective. I do not think there is enough diversity at the root. My work with Diversity Standards Collective has introduced me to some forward-thinking agency groups and clients but these are more the exception to the rule still. Better hiring policy and warmer more inclusive workspaces are key.

If you believe that all business has accepted trans/gender identity politics, then just drop in to any LinkedIn conversation and you will see that people are still being savaged for being who they are by intelligent people who wear business suits and shop at Waitrose. I believe in free speech, but I think the majority of what I hear and see is fearful bile, it reminds me of the first gay kiss on *EastEnders* – I guess all change starts somewhere.

What will happen is that society and in turn marketing will mature over time and eventually being trans, being gay, being whatever will not be the issue but now we are in the beginning of a change. I think we will eventually move into systems of true merit.

I am very much in the liberal zone of believing that none of this should matter. In the future we will never have to talk about it because the fact that I am trans and you are however you identify is not a thing. Per my previous point though, until people are there because they want to be there, and because they are naturally there, it will always be an awkward/new proposition.

Q: Do you agree that whilst representation matters, marketers really must listen to communities to better understand what form that representation should take?

A: I think just putting trans, gay, bi, lesbian, queer + people into a box and saying you are talking to a community is lazy. These are human individuals. We are lumped into an LGBT+ box because we do not fit the social norm of whatever else is out there. Also it means that we are saying somehow we are always different to the expected norm and surely that is not right. Is there a straight 'community'?

But to contradict myself! Yes! In the short term, while marketing is trying to catch up and hopefully make more long-term meaningful changes in hiring and challenging the established 'norms' we do need spokespeople for under-represented 'communities'. The only risk here is one or two people representing hundreds of thousands of people at differing stages of life.

There is a risk also of creating stereotypes or alienation if marketers become too single minded. The trans issues are currently lumped into one in the media (anyone under that banner regardless of where they are in their journey, starting thinking, identifying, neutral, fluid, or fully transitioned for years and living in their corrected identity in legal and social terms) and news media/Twitter is awash with hatred that previously was not so present. This was highlighted with the conversion ban issues in the UK.

There is a fine line and many nuances that need to be considered so as not to cause more harm than good, despite good intentions. I think that is where talking to people with experience is important. Some people want to be trans, some want to transition and move on, some don't have a preference or intent. Putting things under one banner for simplicity is like saying all people that live in the Cotswolds wear wax jackets – it's not true and will leave people feeling unrepresented, and by the way I live in the Cotswolds!

I would like to say also that, hopefully, we are all going to get old and from what I have seen this is a group of people who are still invisible in modern marketing. People who are living longer and who still shop, eat and go to the gym never seem to be represented and yet despite all the good social change this issue just takes a back seat. Are we actually communicating with these folks in marketing? If we look to great research and design innovation centres such as The Helen Hamlyn Centre at the Royal College of Art we can see that the designers are looking to the future, designing age inclusive workspaces – why is marketing not thinking this way? I guess because your average account director, creative director, marketing director is likely to be 45, not 65 or 75 – but why should they not be?

So, representation from community does matter, yes, but if we want people to understand and identify with this difference the way this is done is important. I think seeing more representation in its true form, people living lives first and being 'different' second, can be supported in marketing. I recently did a working session with Lucky Generals, and I was really enthused by their passion to understand, but also their diverse teams and the subtle ways that brought 'difference' to the fore.

Q: What is your advice for marketers trying to get this right and to get out of these boxes?

A: It is about having the insight to know where it is appropriate and where it is not. If you look at, say, health and fitness, then yes it is relevant for all and there are commercial opportunities that can be championed at the same time as showing solidarity for all types of human being regardless, but I also think we need to cater for core markets, or brands will start to feel disingenuous!

I also agree that ads have a need to meet a commercial demand and so should also ensure they keep their core customer base. That is just good business! It is about the appropriate use of the community, but there is not enough insight really to support that yet. It was only last year that there was a UK census of gender in its true form, and it is going to take a while for that data to filter up through other providers so media planners are often left with inadequate insight pools.

As you know, Jerry, I am a media geek really, so if it helps, one of the ways I approach these challenges is to think about my format. Alongside broadcast media, things like broadcast PR are invaluable for brands getting spokespeople into news outlets and kick starting the conversation. I did some work with the charity Just Like Us via Broadcast Revolution. The CEO Dominic Arnall and I were on *ITV News* talking about trans kids in schools and the support needs they may have to feel included. It may not look or feel like an ad, but it's a bit of very well-placed paid content and it certainly has a place for any brand that wants to enter into a conversation – this just takes a bit more thinking.

When I was at the Open University, we did a series called the Open Diaries which was dialogue between a tutor and a student, and it was showing how people really do change through education. One of the students happened to be a female to male trans man and they wanted to talk about that as part of their story and it fitted. It was well received because it was a natural part of the dialogue, and it was about how that person is brave, interesting, and exciting.

That is the kind of representation that is important to me as a marketer, but that then brings me back to the secondary point here which is a challenge of whether advertising is really the right vehicle here alone and without broader context. In many ways the real vehicle is broadcast content where you can tell a big story – I really like the move by Mediacom and some of the big agencies to look at broadcast content and pulling media and creative solutions back together again and also to develop media owner partnerships. This gives the opportunity to tell broader stories and have brands become part of that story.... This person has also gone through trial and trouble, this person has felt loss, this person is a human being.

Real storytelling is powerful for any brand, and I think broadcast and marketing marrying together is where it is really going to happen because you start to develop people, places and scenarios that consumers really identify with.

Q: What is your biggest tip for people trying to avoid some of the mistakes you mention?

A: I think, have conversations in the mirror. If you stand there and say a thing that does not seem right when it comes out of your mouth, then perhaps think again.

Then talk to other people – for instance there is the Diversity Standards Collective where you can consult on these areas with diverse people before you go to market. There are good research panels that can help you before you blunder and do anything embarrassing!

Finally, look to your teams, are you representing the UK in 2022 in all areas? If not how can you build toward that for the long term?

MARKETER IN FOCUS
Ali Hanan, CEO and Founder at Creative Equals

Ali Hanan was a creative director, and one of the very few female ones at the time, until in 2016 she founded the organization Creative Equals, with the specific mission of bringing more diversity and inclusion into the marketing industry. As well as a range of schemes to achieve that, her organization trains and challenges marketers similarly on the unconscious bias that exists across the creative process and how to avoid it in our work.

Few people have such broad experience of both the opportunities and challenges of bringing more inclusion into our industry and I spoke to her broadly about what she's learnt and where the future of inclusion needs to be heading.

Q: Why does representation matter to you?

A: It starts right back in my early career. I joined Ogilvy back in 1999 and by 2003 only 3 per cent of the world's creative directors were women. In one of the years I was there, a Chief Creative Officer, Neil French said – and he was sacked for it – that the reason why women don't make it to the top in advertising is because they all 'wimp out and suckle something'.

The challenge is that even over the last 20 years, while the amount of female creative directors has risen, it has only gone from 3 per cent to 26 per cent in 2022. We have a philosophy and ethos at Creative Equals that 'who makes the work, shapes the work'. So, of course, if you don't have representation at the creative table, teams write their own bias into the work, including stereotypes, tropes and privileges that shape unauthentic, non-representative work.

In 2015 I was sitting at a creative agency and a young female member of the team came to me and said: 'Oh, you're Ali and you're actually a woman!' They went on to say they had assumed 'Ali' was a guy. I asked them why they would assume that: 'Well,' they said, 'we've been to 15 different agencies, and you are the first female creative director we've met.' At that moment, I decided I am going to start a challenger brand for the sector to do better on inclusion. If you start looking at that 26 per cent intersectionality, only 1 per cent come from a black, Asian or multi-ethnic background. At the current count, there are only two female, Muslim creative directors in the UK that I am aware of.

Q: Can you think of any really great examples of representation and inclusive marketing or media that personally impacted you?

A: Back in 2006, it was 'Evolution', Dove's first Campaign for Real Beauty, where the directors took a woman's face and showed exactly what happened in the edit suite. They showed the Photoshop elongation of her neck, how they transformed the model's eyes, face structure and eradicated her skin flaws. Millions of women around the world went, 'Oh right, that's what happens!' We had been given this absolutely unobtainable vision of what beauty looks like and, of course, no one can replicate this perfection – it's fake. It was a collective eye-opening moment. The campaign evolved into different executions, one with 'real' curvy bodies, but all wearing simple white pants. Of course, it feels outdated now, but, at the time, it felt revolutionary.

One recent campaign I love is by a lingerie company, UnderArgument. They cast their models using 'blind' casting, based solely on the power of their stories, so there's no bias. It's all about the stories they tell and that's how they get to feature. I think it's powerful to see this flip with casting based on the authentic stories of people's lives, rather than their 'look'.

Q: Thinking about the marketing process and how we build inclusive marketing and representation right from the brief at the beginning to the output at the end, how do we make sure that happens?

A: The challenge with any process is that you've got multiple stakeholders along this system, who all have their own privilege and bias. You can unpack the start of the system and write a brilliant brief, but then as you progress through it, as the work goes into production, for example, even right at the end when it goes into post-production, you can swap out a voiceover that isn't inclusive (in the UK this is often done on class), lighten skin tones or have whole people edited out of an advert because they 'don't fit'. To change this, you need to educate everybody along the whole 'system' on what to look out for in terms of inclusion.

How do you start? The first thing is to write an inclusive brief and to think about the bedrock of that brief. Are we even gaining diverse consumer insights as part of our insight gathering? Going back to the heart of the business problem, what is it you are solving and 'who' – which audience – can solve this for you? Where are your blind spots to unlock potential growth? Older customers, for example? As you brief it to your creative agencies, who is the team working on the brief? What time frames have they been given to prepare their concepts and storyboards (note: bias comes into quick decision making)? Does that give creatives time to check in with different communities for bias?

You've also got to think about how we're going to measure the work when it comes out, so consider how it goes to market, what media buy you're investing in, and equally how you're measuring ROI on your diverse audiences. Who are the audiences you are (or aren't) talking to, and how do you actually gain audience insight and social media feedback on creative work? How do you use that loop to go back to drive the insights on subsequent briefs?

The brief is the bedrock of all creative work, but this is not accessible in itself, written out as copy on an A4 template. If we want diverse teams to work on our briefs, how do we further consider what they might need? How do we inspire visual thinkers? Or dyslexics? What's the audio clip to go with the brief to inspire people who are visually impaired? In its current state, the brief 'template' itself is not fit for inclusion.

Q: Looking at the big picture, where do you see inclusive marketing going next?

A: We need to begin thinking about long-term system change and some of the global macro movements that will impact us all. With all the conversations around sustainability and climate change, you can't talk about either of those two aspects without talking about diversity, equity and inclusion. At the moment there's a real tension between these priorities, because every company has a huge sustainability agenda. If we were truly championing sustainability, we would design our products with 'total universalism' in mind. Rather than producing hundreds of shapes and sizes of products we would look for the universal 'design for all' – that's a progressive sustainability agenda.

With post-pandemic recovery, there are impacts across all diversity and inclusion pillars. One of the biggest challenges is retaining working mothers who have been adversely affected by the pandemic, as well other marginalized communities. We've massive global cultural shifts on the horizon. For example, 24 per cent of the globe is Muslim; one in six of us are going to be over the age of 65 by 2030. We need to think about our blind spots when it comes to representation in terms of focusing on this growing older market and faith representation.

We need to reframe DEI in the world of 2023 into corporate social justice, because you cannot have sustainability programmes without really thinking about the marginalized groups that your brand can impact. CSJ is the bedrock of the 'S' in ESG.

Conclusion

A personal perspective on marketing 'purpose'?

We've made it most of the way through this book on inclusive marketing without really talking about the concept of purpose-based marketing. We did introduce a concept of a scale of inclusion that stretches from exclusion and stereotyping, through to positive inclusion, and beyond that to potential active purpose and campaigning. Not every brand is likely to ever get to that final point, and certainly not every advert needs to be a campaign for social justice, but it's a fair question to discuss whether any of them should.

A quiet debate about the role and value of 'brand purpose' has rumbled on in the marketing industry for many years, and like many of our debates it's often hard to find a balanced middle ground. I polled my Twitter followers, a marketing science/strategy-heavy audience, and 51 per cent of them said that no, brand purpose does not ultimately help brands grow bigger and faster. In fact, only 26 per cent were confident that it did.

I'm very loosely defining 'brand purpose' here as the need for marketers to find something bigger and more meaningful for their brands to stand for – social justice, environmental changes, or really anything other than what you buy them to do. The question then is whether this has some tangible impact on your brands' performance, and if so whether that's driven because consumers truly base purchase decisions on it, or something else. The cynical might argue that purpose is a way to help guilty marketers, who hate the idea that their whole job is just making money, sleep at night. The more optimistic might point to changing consumer expectations and requirements to stay relevant in this space if you want to compete with others who are more progressive.

Purpose can appear in grand gestures, in epic five-minute mood films, and fully integrated campaigns which say more about a charity or a cause than the brand itself. Lightweight purpose can also appear in much more throwaway moments like posting a black square on Instagram or celebrating Pride month with a tweet. The best brand purposes provide a North Star to all the marketing that the brand creates beneath them – in most cases quite an emotional and rich storytelling North Star. My personal hypothesis is that purpose perhaps works more as an emotionally strong, unifying creative guide than because consumers are truly basing their decisions on the social justice position of a brand's Twitter account.

At the end of an entire book advocating for the role brands play in portraying positive diversity and representation in their advertising, you might be surprised to hear that I am relatively neutral on the bigger picture of purpose. I don't for a minute doubt that brands can have an impact on society, and I strongly encourage us all to make that a good one. Some purpose initiatives most certainly do, though I'm sure many do not. I think there are wonderful steps brands can take to tear down stereotypes and I am all for brands working away on their purposes, partnering with charities and making the world a better place. I think brands showing support to their consumers around Pride, or Black Lives Matter can be a great thing, especially if it's backed up by internal policies and wider action. I just think we might want to be realistic on why some of that works.

One thing I have found confusing in my career is the mental gymnastics and disassociation that can go together for some people, or whole businesses, in this space. Organizations can be hugely clued up about the realities of marketing science, the need for new customers and penetration, the scathing disinterest and 'disloyalty' (or repertoire loyalty) of consumers and yet swayed by a good Simon Sinek quote. On the one hand, many of us recognize that we need to build strategies that slowly build basic mental and physical availability, and that even having people think about your brand at all in a purchase situation is a huge success. On the other hand, we sometimes also believe in 'the power of why' and the notion that consumers are making their decisions based on an in-depth analysis of the very purpose and business practices of your business.

Nearly everything we know about consumers tells us they really don't care – as much as anything, brands exist to stop consumers having to think about what they buy, not to encourage them to spend more time researching it. I've long been inspired by Martin Weigel's 'How (Not) To Fail' presentation which hails apathy as the greatest and most wonderful creative obstacle marketers face. Our biggest challenge is not communicating and convincing fans of our product to buy more but getting people who couldn't care less to notice us at all. It's hard for me then to also imagine a parallel world in which consumers spend hours researching every company and brand they buy to understand exactly what they stand for.

To my mind, purpose is a powerful tool to cut through apathy, not because people really care, but precisely because they actually don't.

Say you're trying to sell some washing powder. There's only so much you can say about your latest active ingredient or smell before all but the most dedicated launderers have tuned out. Take a step back and associate your product with cleaning up the world, tackling environmental issues, or fundamentally empowering kids to play because 'dirt is good' and suddenly you have a lot more to talk about. Rich emotional territory that will make great advertising, connected ecosystems and build emotional connections and fame. Now, is the average consumer actually aware of or impacted by your charitable partnership or environmental commitments? Quite possibly not.

Yet creative and emotional advertising is scientifically proven to outperform and your purpose opens a door to a whole world of just that. In fairness you can also get called out for this behaviour and jumping on social and cultural trends, if you don't back it by action and pull it through your brand – it's better to fully invest in purpose-driven marketing and then make some adverts celebrating that, than to pretend you care about causes in your communications whilst there is no tangible impact on your business approach.

It's fair to say that the best purposes, as well as being a good creative North Star, are also not an over-stretch. Now, many relatively mundane products can play a higher order role in our lives – I personally see no issue for instance in believing that chocolate can trigger momentary joy, bring people together or do other lovely things because many times in my life I've seen chocolate do just that. I'd have more hesitation if you told me your chocolate bar's brand purpose was solving global hunger, or campaigning solely for racial equality, unless you happen to have an incredible and authentic back story in that space.

Some would argue that there is scientific evidence that purpose works (and to be clear I'm not really arguing that it doesn't). Unilever is often hailed as the proof point here and they really do some wonderful things as a company and with their brands, for which I truly commend them. They report regularly that their brands with purpose outperform their other brands, which does indeed seem like evidence. That said, it's also true that they develop fleshed out purposes for their biggest and most important brands. They also then choose to invest far more in those brands across all touch points, and of course those purposes no doubt play a handy role in elevating the emotion and impact of the content created along the way. In many ways, I have no doubt that purpose is helping their business and helping their brands grow, but I have some questions around whether that's because of any sort of conscious consumer awareness or interest in that purpose, or something more passive and broadly emotional.

Dove hugely elevated itself from a slightly generic brand (albeit a quality one) to a vastly more defined and successful one by embracing its Real Beauty purpose. In such a human and emotional sector, and with a purpose that fundamentally made them appeal to a broader range of their target audience, the purpose they have adopted is a clever piece of marketing strategy and a wonderful creative North Star. Yet even there I wonder how many of their customers would honestly answer that they were buying it specifically for the higher purpose it stands for, versus generally having built up a strong affinity for it over the years due to great communications. I've long been a fan of Ben and Jerry's but managed to consume their products for years before hearing, in a marketing conference, about their devotion to purpose and causes, although they have become more vocal about this in their communications in recent years.

Generously, perhaps even a majority of consumers these days pays some attention to ethics and purpose-related topics at some point. Many of them may even choose specific brands or products because of these factors. If you ask consumers about this, they tend to say it's a good thing and probably would influence their purchase decision.

There's less evidence that anything but a tiny handful, however, is applying that as a filter across the majority of things they buy. Picture a supermarket with 100 people in it – how many of those are actively evaluating the ethics and purpose of every product they put into their trolley? The answer of course is zero, because if you truly based your shopping choices on this, you wouldn't be in a supermarket at all but in a shop with a focus on eco products and refillable packaging. None of which is to say that the shoppers in that store haven't in some way been influenced by purpose, in the same mysterious ways that all advertising influences us, builds association and creates mental availability.

The world is, however, much more transparent than it used to be. People are much more aware of social issues, and bad news travels much faster than it used to. On some topics of environmental impact, or negative public scandal, expectations can move fast, and you can find yourself easily caught out. What might at one point seem like a 'woke' niche can rapidly become an established norm and looking globally you can already see markets like the Nordics where consumer expectations for environmental impact are having tangible business impact. I think it's fair to assume that some key sustainability attributes, especially your environmental footprint, will move rapidly to being an expected condition of business in many categories (and certainly in premium ones) but no one will think you are purposeful and wonderful for it, they will just think you're doing the basics well.

There are likely to be some step change moments along the way. Something like the introduction of 'carbon labels' to notify consumers of carbon footprints could very rapidly make this at least a consideration in purchase for a far greater audience – after all, whilst consumers probably aren't researching your ethics they may well be willing to look at a traffic light summary of them. By this stage, though, we're not really talking about higher purpose but the cost of doing business.

Now one of the 'it depends' factors of the value of purpose is that if you approach it in a very blunt and slapped-on way it certainly can backfire – if you profess your support of Black Lives Matter whilst paying your black employees less, or champion Pride whilst not appropriately providing for trans needs then don't be surprised if you are called out. This starts to explain why purpose might work better as a true business North Star impacting your total approach than just as a tacked-on gimmick in an ad campaign, even if most of your consumers remain blissfully unaware.

Marketers should also perhaps be aware, though, that changing consumer perceptions are just as likely to come from your personal data strategy as they are your environmental or social impact. The Conscious Advertising Network has challenged brands that purposeful activity can be hugely undermined if your advertising is accidentally funding hate speech, disinformation and climate change denial – regrettably much of it still is. We need to do more in the 'brandy safety' space and evolve it from being about avoiding negative headlines for our brands and into truly consciously investing in a quality internet that provides safety for our consumers.

Will a consumer really care or notice if you don't support Pride or Black History Month? Probably not, though there are a fair few who will broadly look positively on you if you do. The reality is that brands can be involved in terrible scandals about faking emissions results or sourcing products through modern slavery one month, and this will still often be largely forgotten by the next. It's also worth noting that truly caring about such ethical matters will likely remain a preserve of the richer, middle classes for some time. Many consumers simply don't have the money power to choose, but that doesn't mean we cannot help make their purchases pain free.

There have been some stand-out examples of purposeful inclusion and storytelling to champion minority voices and perspectives and deliberately break down barriers. I think it's fantastic that marketers are using their scale and impact to do this, and fully believe that benefits diverse consumers and the business bottom line. Yet a lot of the best work in the representation space is far more casual than that – positive casting and inclusion, unstereotyping, different perspectives and voices. The advert doesn't have to be about diversity to tackle and embrace it.

The whole industry should move along the spectrum from regrettable exclusion of minority groups, past awkward tokenism and stereotyping, to a place of positive representation and inclusion where the faces seen and the stories told in our adverts truly reflect the world around us. You don't need to be charitable to do this; you just need to be a marketer doing their job and engaging with broad audiences and modern society. Now, some brands will choose to go much further into the purposeful representation space, and good on them. If nothing else, it will give them a lot more to talk about and most likely some powerful and emotional stories to tell that resonate widely.

All that said, companies do still have options of being totally ruthless corporate machines or willing to use some part of their influence to make the world a better, or at least not worse, place. That might be their communications, their supply chain, their policies or indeed how they choose to spend or donate their money. Investing in good causes can engage colleagues, generate PR, help drive emotional brand campaigns and lots of other things. CSR is a reality of modern business, and having worked at a charity before I've seen the direct and brilliant impact that it can have on all sides.

In conclusion

Writing this book and speaking to dozens of people as part of that has been a great experience for me, and I do hope that reading some of their words and the advice that has come out of them has been enriching and challenging for you too. A lot of it seems obvious, and as the imposter syndrome has crept in I've started to wonder whether this book is needed at all, but sometimes it's helpful to have a lot of obvious things collected for you and put down in one place.

It seems clear that being truly inclusive and representative is part of our job as marketers, and that the empathy needed to unlock that is a crucial skill we all need to continue developing. Marketing is a complex process and, especially in larger companies, a huge machine with many moving parts. There's no simple shortcut to getting to better and more inclusive marketing but a whole range of questions and challenges we need to ask ourselves at every stage, only some of which are captured in this book.

By the time you're reading this book new challenges, opportunities and thinking will have emerged but most of the questions contained within will remain useful. The same can be said for wherever in the world you are practising your marketing, and whilst cultural nuances and what diversity means will vary greatly the steps you can take to capture and reflect it should hold relatively true.

There are different perspectives on what good inclusive marketing looks like, but I think a consensus is that we're going through a slightly awkward 'teenage' phase. We're all trying to get this right, and even more broadly working as a society to hopefully become more tolerant, understanding and inclusive of different people. True inclusion comes when all these different labels for diversity start not to mean anything and where our adverts can casually reflect that society without anyone thinking twice about it.

We may be quite a long way from that utopia. Cultural change has taken decades in the past, and for every step that disadvantaged groups take forwards there often seem to be one or more steps backwards in other spaces. There is no guarantee that society will continue to become more open and accepting, and indeed there are many examples of new restrictive rules and attitudes that are pushing attitudes backwards. As Ella highlighted in her interview, the UK media has become a uniquely hostile place for trans people, and their lives are considerably worse than they were just a few years ago.

The move to define all progressive and inclusive thinking negatively as 'woke' and part of a radical agenda is another example of how certain aspects of society are looking to push back on inclusion and acceptance. They feel it challenges their status quo or can be a scapegoat for wider issues we see around us today. I believe in a world where we can build things that are better for everyone and not have to tear others down to achieve that.

Marketers are merely the wallpaper in the background for much of this change, and however great the advertising you make is, it's unlikely to fundamentally alter the direction of society. That said, as we've heard throughout this book, representation really does matter. As a cumulative effect, the advertising we produce and the media it funds can open a world of opportunities to people or leave them feeling isolated and second class.

There's a fabulous opportunity to lean into more inclusive advertising and in doing so not only do something good for society but also do something great for your business, and even for your own career. I hope this book helps you on that journey, and the fact that you've taken the time to read at least some of it is a very clear indicator that you care and are going to make a difference wherever you work.

I do worry that with a book like this, in diversity forums and in the articles that get written on this topic, we are often preaching to the converted. Your secret mission, should you choose to accept it, is to persuade someone who really doesn't care about inclusive marketing, or thinks it's a complete waste of time, to read some of this book now too.

My biggest hope is that in 10 years' time we've managed to build this thinking into our industry, we've attracted and developed new and varied talent, and we simply don't need to write or buy books like this anymore. Until that point, thank you so much for taking the time to read it and I do hope you've taken onboard some practical advice along the way that will improve your own marketing. I'm sure there are many more tips and questions we haven't covered in this book and I look forward to hearing them and building them into future editions.

20

Checklist appendix

Key questions to ask yourself

For each of the 12 stages of the marketing process outlined in the book the chapter ends with a checklist of key questions to ask yourselves – these were developed jointly with feedback from across the WFA Diversity Task Force and are compiled here into one overall checklist for your records.

Stage one: Inclusive briefing and strategy

Business and brand strategy

1 Who is your audience? Who is excluded? Are they a potential business opportunity?
2 Does your audience reflect the emerging consumer base for the category?
3 Is there a deliberate diversity and sustainability opportunity for your brand?
4 What's the next credible but authentic step forward your brand can take?
5 Is your business willing to stand up for what's right and truly reflect your consumers?
6 Are senior stakeholders bought in?

Strategic insights and data

1 Is there any bias in research used to gather insight?
2 Does the data capture representative perspectives or just broad generalizations?

3 How are consumer 'pen portraits' or mood boards depicted/visualized?

4 Have you managed to capture nuance and avoid generalization?

5 What are the perceptions of your brand within representative targets?

6 What do you know about the cultural tensions and audience in each active market?

7 Are stereotyping concerns tested with the affected group?

8 Have you engaged experts who can help advise on how specific audiences might positively or negatively interpret your intentions?

Marketing and creative briefs

1 Does your brief make it clear that representation is key?

2 Does it bring clear stimulus/inspiration?

3 Is the target/audience definition a stereotype? Could it be more progressive?

4 Who is excluded? Are they a potential business opportunity?

5 Have you considered different perspectives to help you with the direction of the brief?

6 What are the inclusive expressions of your brand's emotional benefit?

Stage two: Inclusive planning

Partner and team selection

1 Do you have a procurement diversity approach and a supply chain of diverse partners?

2 Have you asked partners for evidence of representation across their overall output?

3 Could a minority owned, or focused, partner augment the work of your Agency of Record?

4 Are you working together with your agency on this journey? Is there more you could be doing to support them to become more representative and diverse?

5 Which organizations could you partner with to encourage future diversity within the industry?

Creative development and product design

1 How are you applying the Unstereotype Alliance's 3Ps?

2 Do the characters come across as empowered, in control of their lives?

3 Have you considered beauty as a dimension of personality rather than just physical appearance and attraction? Is there a stereotypical interpretation of beauty? Tall, thin and fair for women, tall, macho and strong for men?

4 Where could diversity help originate powerful storytelling?

5 How diverse is the creative team and their inputs? Do they understand how different communities like to be represented?

6 How will diversity be reflected in different ad formats/lengths?

7 Have you considered how you can make your products and experiences inclusive, as well as your advertising?

Consumer testing

1 Does pre-testing include a check of bias or stereotyping?

2 Are stereotyping issues researched amongst the affected group, as well as with experts who understand how those groups are likely to react?

3 What influence could the storyboard have? Does this prompt any areas of concern or opportunity?

4 Have you leveraged input from your own businesses's ERG groups or diversity council?

5 Have you created a safe space for frank and honest critique of the creative and interpretations?

Stage three: Inclusive production

Production

1 What is the casting brief? Have you allowed enough time for an inclusive casting process? Could an under-represented group play a greater role?

2 Have you considered whether props or wardrobe choices reinforce stereotypes?

3 What is the diversity of the full production crew?

4 Is the shoot an open, inclusive and unbiased environment, with safe spaces and accessible facilities (e.g. wheelchair access or gender-neutral bathrooms)?

5 Will there be a triple-bid tender including female/other under-represented directors?

Post-production

1 Is there diversity in the post-production team?

2 What is the casting for any voiceovers? Are you avoiding stereotypes?

3 Have you considered colloquial nuances of accents?

4 Are there opportunities to make assets more accessible (e.g. closed captions, audio descriptions)?

5 Have you ensured the approval processes account for bias?

6 Have you double-checked that the final edit delivers on your diversity ambition (in all cut-downs)?

Localization

1 Are there any local cultural nuances that could make your content inappropriate?

2 For the adaptation of existing asset, does the casting truly reflect local diversity?

3 If replacing diverse casting, are you changing it to be more representative, or the opposite?

4 What data can you access to support a more progressive agenda?

5 If you are using an older copy, is the content still appropriate?

6 Has the global or local context changed?

Stage four: Inclusive launches

Media and 360 activation

1 Are your media plans safe from funding inflammatory content, hate speech or disinformation?

2 Are there any channels that would be inappropriate to be present on?

3 Could your marketing mix, data usage or brand safety settings exclude certain groups?

4 Have you considered actively including or partnering with diversity focused media partners or influencers? Could you even create new content together?

5 Are there unexpected touch points relevant to new groups?

Launch and consumer response

1 What is the monitoring/response plan for any feedback on representation? Are your social media teams briefed?

2 Are you prepared for how to respond to any hateful comments you receive?

3 Are you ready to respond if the communities you are trying to positively represent raise questions?

4 Have you prepared responses to best/worst possible outcomes?

5 What are your internal launch plans? Have you engaged your ERGs?

Measuring success

1 What was the commercial upside?

2 How are you tracking the impact on your brand?

3 Does your measurement approach represent diversity?

4 What is the diversity across the portfolio and creative output? Are you making progress in positive representation?

5 What capability gaps still exist?

6 Can you make a positive case study to inspire and engage internally or externally?

7 Have you truly understood and learnt from the actual response to your work, whether positive or negative?

INDEX